MORNING LIGHT

A BOOK OF MEDITATIONS TO BEGIN YOUR DAY

Amy E. Dean

HAZELDEN®

Hazelden
Center City, Minnesota 55012
hazelden.org

Library of Congress Cataloging-in-Publication Data

Dean, Amy E. (Amy Elizabeth), 1953–
    Morning light : a book of meditations to begin your day /
Amy E. Dean. — 1st ed.
        p.   cm.
    Includes index.
    ISBN 978-1-61649-108-6 (softcover)
    1. Affirmations.   2. Attitude (Psychology)
3. Alcoholics—Rehabilitation.   4. Drug addicts—
Rehabilitation.   I. Title.
    BF697.5.S47D425 2011
    158.1'28—dc23

                                                    2011024084

Editor's note
Alcoholics Anonymous, AA, and the Big Book are registered trade-
marks of Alcoholics Anonymous World Services, Inc.

Cover and interior design by David Spohn
Typesetting by BookMobile Design and Publishing Services

MORNING LIGHT

Dear Reader:

I dedicate this book to you. I wish you success in all aspects of your recovery. May the spirit of the program transform your life in wonderful ways today, and in the years that lie ahead.

This book is dedicated to

_____.

(insert your name here)

INTRODUCTION

Those who are in Twelve Step programs need to be able to deal effectively with their recovery from addiction and, at the same time, with making changes that will bring them closer to their desired quality of life. Self-help books are just one of many powerful tools that can be used in facilitating the changes you want and need to make.

I am honored that Hazelden has welcomed this new offering. *Morning Light* is designed to be a perfect companion to my first meditation book, *Night Light*. I welcome all of my new readers as well as those who were first introduced to me through *Night Light*.

Each meditation contained herein is designed to focus on a particular topic, issue, or feeling you may experience as you begin your day. In each month you will also be able to focus on one of the Twelve Steps of the program. On the first day of each month a prayer is offered to accompany a Step; on the last day, a reflection is provided for that Step. In addition, on the fifteenth of each month you will find a reflection on an Aesop fable, with a moral that relates directly to the gifts of recovery. I hope you enjoy these elements and find them helpful to your recovery.

And, as always, I welcome your thoughts, comments, and feedback. Please visit my website at www.amydeanwriter.com.

—Amy E. Dean

JANUARY

We admitted we were powerless over alcohol—that our lives had become unmanageable.

—Step One

A prayer is a humble and heartfelt communication with a power greater than yourself. A prayer can admit a weakness, communicate a need, or convey praise and gratitude. Prayers can unburden your heart, give you strength and courage, and deepen your faith and trust in a Higher Power. Use the following prayer as you work on your understanding and acceptance of Step One.

Step One Prayer

Higher Power, I am powerless over my addiction. Addiction has controlled my life and made it unmanageable. It has had a terrible impact on my life and many others.

I am ready to let go of old patterns. I am ready to release toxicity from every facet of my life. I am open to receiving and using the tools of the program so I can take greater control of my life. Although I have felt unwilling to change in the past, I feel empowered today. I will no longer deny I have an addiction. Higher Power, I am an addict.

I ask for your help today with my addiction. I trust in your power and believe that, through your guidance, you will lead me into a true lightness of living—free at last from my addiction. Higher Power, thank you for listening.

Just cause you got the monkey off your back doesn't mean the circus has left town.

—*George Carlin*

A new year holds promise and provides a "second chance." A new year also can be a time when you see all that you have yet to accomplish and question your ability to face those challenges. You may think it was hard enough to admit you needed to stop your addictive behaviors and even harder to stay focused on recovery. To know that a new year heralds the continued need to stay on the same path can seem daunting.

Make this year different. Resolve to look *within* you, at what you can and need to do for yourself, and to look *outside* you, at what you can do for others. While self-awareness is key to your recovery, remember that recovery is both a hand reaching out and a hand being grasped.

Recovery does not happen in isolation. One of the strengths of the program is interdependence and fellowship. Attending to your needs as well as to the needs of others can provide you with renewed energy to recover from your past, commitment to stay focused on the present, and the ability to foresee a future that holds hope and promise.

I will awaken each day to a new beginning—not just for myself, but also for others.

If your mental attitude is right, if you face life the right way, if the right spirit is in you, if you put yourself in tune, everything you do . . . will give you a real sense of pleasure.
—*Orison Swett Marden*

Start your day with poise and serenity. If your alarm doesn't go off, you can remain calm. If a traffic jam slows your commute, you can be at peace. If a friend cancels on you, you can be forgiving.

You can do all these things when you decide "I will not allow anything to disturb my mental balance or throw my mind out of its serenity." Facing life with inner strength means not allowing people, places, or things to destroy your harmony with the world. Facing life with peace of mind means you are in charge of your destiny and your recovery. Facing life with understanding and forgiveness means you have built a strong relationship with a Higher Power. Then you can view disruptions to your well-being and purpose as trifling, small incidents that are short-lived.

Today you can choose to be defeated by life's little insensibilities, conflicts, and disappointments, or successfully handle whatever comes your way without disruption to your inner peace.

My achievements today will reflect my attitude. I will choose to face life with a serene spirit and calm poise.

You cannot weave truth in a loom of lies.
—*Suzette Haden Elgin*

Before you admitted you were powerless, you may have created a false reality that enabled you to see yourself as you wanted to be and validated the lies you fabricated. The worse your addiction became, the more lies you may have told and the more you repressed the truth—until eventually the lies became the truth.

Honesty is not simply the absence of lying, but the commitment to truthfulness. The program teaches you the difference between being honest and being rigorously honest. Admitting you are powerless over your addiction is being honest.

But rigorous honesty means living each day with total awareness of what is true and what is untrue, and speaking always to the truth, no matter how painful. As you go to meetings, be inspired by the honesty of others. As you work with your sponsor, learn how to view your past actions and behaviors with an objective eye. As you read and reflect upon the teachings of the Big Book, gain a greater understanding about the importance of honesty with yourself and others. As you follow the Steps, seek total honesty with yourself. As you connect with your Higher Power, learn how honesty can lead to forgiveness.

Today I will be honest with myself and with others.

We should think seriously before we slam doors, before we burn bridges, before we saw off the limb on which we find ourselves sitting.

—*Richard L. Evans*

Sometimes you may feel as if you are at war with yourself and others. Conflict is created by the simple fact that you made the decision to no longer engage in your addiction. So it is not unusual to resent those who seem to have it all together. Such feelings can build into self-directed anger or anger toward others.

Acting upon your anger rarely leads to any good. You may say things that cause others to distance themselves from you, or make poor decisions that take considerable effort to undo. You may lash out at yourself in ways that disrupt your sense of serenity and put your recovery at risk.

What matters most is not the situation you are presented with, but the way you handle it. Rather than lash out in anger, ask, "What can I do to create greater harmony within myself?" You can achieve greater peace and serenity by talking through your anger with a trusted friend, sharing your feelings at a meeting, and using prayer and meditation to calm yourself.

"When one door closes, another opens." Today I will see everything as a positive opportunity for learning and growth.

Morning.
New day.
Joy of birth.

—Deng Ming-Dao

Just as there is an air of mystery to night, with sunrise comes the joy of possibilities. What lies ahead?

Too many people start the day with little appreciation for the amazing miracle of a new dawn. They rarely live in the present moment. Like them, you may start a new day overloaded with commitments or plagued by the same old feelings of doubt or insecurity. You may begin the day haunted by ghosts of the past or phantoms of the future.

A Chinese parable tells the story of a wise man who challenges villagers to move a mountain together—a task that requires everyone to move a small amount of dirt and pebbles each day. Even after many hours of labor, he says, the task will be so grand that it will take generations of villagers to accomplish.

Rather than refuse to work or devise ways to speed up the project, the villagers choose to move the mountain. In performing the task, time means nothing to them, nor does reaching the goal. Rather, it is the task itself, and the ability to focus on that task, that is most important.

I offer a prayer giving thanks for the opportunity to experience a brand-new day. I ask for the strength to fully live in each moment.

You have been under attack from the enemy, he has tried to steal your money, your marriage, your home, your children, your job, your peace, your joy, your love and today we declare "no more" and today we declare that we are on the road to recovery.

—Doug Dickerson

The road of recovery offers some smoothly paved surfaces, but often it has obstacles such as potholes and downed limbs. It is a bumpy, unpredictable path that can challenge your commitment and drain you physically, emotionally, and spiritually. At times you may feel your strength so depleted that you want to give up. And you may come across those who sense your near-defeat and tempt you to travel an easier route.

You have been down that road before! A road filled with those who wanted your companionship because you were as sick and wounded as they were. Those who said you did not have a problem.

Beware of those who will try to distract you. Know that there will be times when you move forward and times when you experience setbacks. The path that offers the greatest challenge is often the one leading you in the right direction.

The road to recovery will offer challenges to my strength. Today I accept these challenges and know that the more I work the program, the better I will become.

Health—what my friends are always drinking to before they fall down.

—Phyllis Diller

You may question your resolve or need to stay sober when nearly every day new research credits moderate drinking with living longer and other positive outcomes, such as reducing or preventing diabetes, rheumatism, bone fractures and osteoporosis, and poor cognition and memory.

But what such studies often fail to mention are the negative effects of drinking, such as obesity, high blood pressure, and mental impairment. While it may be tempting to use such studies as an excuse to drink, you know your behaviors do not reflect those of a moderate drinker. Your recovery depends upon steadfast devotion to improving your overall health and quality of life while remaining committed to your sobriety.

Sound health requires daily attention to your spirit, mind, and body. A healthy body requires good nutrition and engaging in a daily exercise program. A healthy mind depends upon a good night's sleep and exercising your mental capacities through learning and enjoyable activities. A healthy spirit needs a relationship with a Higher Power built and strengthened through prayer, faith, and trust.

Today I will focus on abstinence and maintaining a healthy lifestyle.

I don't know what your destiny will be, but one thing I know: the only ones among you who will be really happy are those who will have sought and found how to serve.
—Albert Schweitzer

At times you may feel there is no vision to run eagerly toward, no joy to give a sense of purpose, and no desires to fulfill your day-to-day existence.

Centuries ago, sages would give of their knowledge and skills, without any thought of personal benefit or financial gain. The message of compassion and selflessness they were teaching was far greater than any riches or personal gain. Their satisfaction came from the knowledge of how their actions gave hope to others.

Each time you reach out to another person, you send forth a tiny ripple of hope that grows more powerful with each person it touches. In doing so, you become more capable of seeing that you are not the only one who may be unhappy or suffering. In fact, you may see that your current difficulties pale in comparison to what others are experiencing. Your gift of hope to others is also a gift to yourself.

Today I choose to be of use. I will offer help to those who are feeling overwhelmed so they see they are not alone in their struggles.

The greatest healing therapy is friendship and love.
—Hubert Humphrey

In the past, the people you called friends may have been those with whom you drank or drugged. Their excessive caregiving may have directly or indirectly encouraged you to keep drinking or using. They may have lied for you, made excuses for you, or did everything they could to protect you from the consequences of your actions and behaviors. However well-meaning such actions were, you understand now that these friends were not helping you.

The program teaches that unhealthy friendships are with those who continue to drink or drug, those who are codependent or enablers, and those who do not want you to change. By continuing to associate with such people, you run the risk of relapse.

The program uses the slogan "Stick with the winners" to promote the role healthy friendships can play in maintaining abstinence. The winners are those who can and will offer the highest level of support in recovery. Begin today by thinking about each of these special people and how your life is better because of them. Take time to reach out to the friends you have made in the program.

Healthy friendships are like angels sent from my Higher Power. Today I will remember that I need to cherish these friendships always, for they are blessings in my life.

I find no force as devastating as the force of "can't." Within its meaning lie the roots of powerlessness. Within its vulgar four letters lies the destruction of lives; lives not lived.
—Anonymous

Some very simple words can weaken your strength and resolve, impose limitations on your actions and behaviors, and keep you stuck in the same place. For example, saying "I can't do that" prevents you from even trying. Declaring "I should quit smoking" or "I shouldn't get so angry" are positive goals, but such phrases do not often motivate you to act. Using the words *always* and *never*—"I am always going to fall short" or "I never will become a better person"—only perpetuates negative feelings of self-worth.

To overcome these limitations, change your vocabulary. Substitute *can* for *can't.* Replace *always* and *never* with *sometimes* or *occasionally.* Use *will* rather than *should* or *ought to.* You will be amazed at the power such a simple change can make. Using more positive words can help you remove obstacles you have placed in your way and develop strengths you never knew existed.

Today I will ask a friend to point out when I use words that show my limitations and not my strengths. I will change what I say so both my words and my actions convey a can-do attitude.

I can feel guilty about the past, apprehensive about the future, but only in the present can I act.
—Abraham Maslow

Worry prevents you from living in the present and causes you to fret about what has already happened or what might happen. Too much worrying can exaggerate situations and drain you of the energy you need in the present.

To cure worry, learn to distinguish between facts and fantasies. For example, you may be worried your sponsor will end your interactions because of a disagreement you had. Ask yourself, "Is that a fact?" The answer will help you figure out whether your worry is based on fact or fiction. Then consider actions you can take. Ask, "What can I do about this right now?" Rather than worry your sponsor will walk away from you, talk to your sponsor so you can resolve any differences. Develop similar plans of action for other worries so you can stop looking backward or peering fearfully ahead.

It has been said, "Yesterday's a cancelled check, tomorrow's a promissory note, but today is cash. Spend it wisely." Seek out those things that you can change and let go of your worries about that which you cannot control.

I have the power to make my worries gigantic or to shrink them. Today I will take action to live fully in the present moment.

Happy families are all alike; every unhappy family is un-happy in its own way.

—*Leo Tolstoy*

You may not only be an alcoholic or addict, but also an adult child of an alcoholic. Because of the dysfunction in your childhood home, the focus was not on your growth out of childhood but on the problems of your parents. You were usually taught to assume adult responsibilities well in advance of adulthood. As a result, you may be overwhelmed by feelings of confusion, fear, and insecurity. While you are living in an adult's body, you have the unanswered emotions of a child.

There are many resources available, including Al-Anon as well as Adult Children. Both self-help groups follow the Twelve Steps of AA, dealing openly and honestly about how the drinking or chemical dependencies of others affected you. These groups teach your five basic rights: to be free from the past, to learn a new way of life, to express feelings, to develop self-esteem, and to ask for help.

Adult Children groups offer you a new way of life. Your feelings can be validated by hearing what others have to share, and you can learn how to express your feelings in a safe environment.

Today I will begin or continue to attend meetings that help me to recover from the negative effects of my childhood.

I think we fall in love with people who have something to teach us. And sometimes that is a hard lesson and sometimes it's a safe and loving lesson.

—Mary Bradish

Love can make you feel strong and sure, confident in the knowledge that someone has "got your back." Other times it can make you feel weak and vulnerable, particularly when you need to give openly and honestly. Unhealthy relationships involve disharmony, mistrust, and a lack of understanding and support. Partners in a healthy relationship understand and support each other's needs and seek harmony in their shared companionship.

Love, like life, has its ups and downs. Things get out of balance, causing anxiety or indecision. Ask yourself, "What do I need to learn from what I'm feeling right now?" You may discover you are not the cause of the upset or your feelings are not based on your current relationship, but on the threads of past relationships that unraveled.

Even though love's emotional expression can change from time to time, the existence of love will not. Love is a constant, no matter what form it takes in your life.

Today I will understand and accept the form love takes not only during the easy times, but also when times are hard. I will seek out serenity and be open to whatever lessons I am being taught.

The Horse and the Mule

Traveling together, a horse sported a fine coat and a magnificent saddle with ornate decorations, while a mule was burdened with a heavy load. Its coat was matted and filled with burrs.

"Oh how I wish I could be as beautiful and graceful as you are," the mule told the horse. "I wish, too, that I was as unburdened and carefree."

A few days later, a great war broke out and the horse went into battle, while the mule carried supplies. During a skirmish, the horse was gravely wounded and lay dying upon the ground when the mule came upon him. It was then that the mule realized, that in being himself, he had fulfilled his purpose and been kept safe.

The moral of the story: *Be secure in who you are.*

You may look at others and what they have, and wish you had the same characteristics or were in the same place as they. Ultimately, how you feel about who you are determines your level of self-esteem. Even though there are things you want to change about yourself, these things make up who you are today. No matter what your defects or imperfections, accept who you are in the present moment.

Today I will appreciate who I am and what I have.

Surely this must be an ancient proverb: If the situation is killing you, get the hell out.

—Hugh Prather

Imagine you have embarked on a mountain hike. Although it is a winter day, the conditions are right for your climb. But as the hours pass, it begins to snow and the temperature drops sharply. You can barely see the path before you and have a hard time maintaining your footing. In addition, your clothing is soaked, you are starting to shiver, and your hands and feet are growing numb. What do you do?

Before you joined the program, you may have believed that your addiction was under control. No matter how bad things became, you may have told yourself or others, "I can stop any time I want."

But now you are more aware of how addiction took away your ability to make good choices. You can choose prayer and meditation to let go of fear and resentment. You can go to meetings and draw strength from others. You can follow the Twelve Steps in all that you do. You always have the choice to turn your life over to a Higher Power, rather than stay on a dangerous path.

In all circumstances, I will remember that I have the choice to follow a path that keeps me safe and free.

The best six doctors anywhere
And no one can deny it
Are sunshine, water, rest, and air
Exercise and diet.

—*Adapted from a nursery rhyme*

Exercise can lift a sour mood, soothe anxiety, sharpen mental concentration, ease insomnia, and build confidence. When you combine exercise with healthy eating, maintaining a consistent sleep/rest schedule, and spending time outdoors, you will feel better and stronger.

Starting today, resolve to embark on a daily exercise routine. Set aside a specific time of day when you are apt to feel more motivated and energized. Join a health club, walk or jog in your neighborhood, attend a fitness or yoga class, join a recreational sport league, or participate with an exercise video in your living room. Vary your activities to make your exercise routine more challenging and motivating, or engage in the same types of activities to measure your improvement over time.

Begin by exercising at least twenty minutes a day, three days a week. If you miss a day, just pick up where you left off. Keep a journal of your progress to provide a visual record for continued inspiration.

It has been said that "Action may not always bring happiness, but there is no happiness without action." I will use exercise to improve my physical, emotional, and spiritual well-being.

We must learn to accept ... life and to accept ourselves,
not blindly and not with conceit, but with a shrug and a
smile.

—Harvey Mindess

A Taoist story tells of an old farmer whose livelihood depended upon his one horse. One morning the farmer woke to discover the horse had run away. When his neighbors learned of his misfortune, they asked him what he would do. The farmer said, "I will wait." The next morning, the farmer heard a great commotion and saw that his horse had returned with two wild horses.

A few days later, the farmer's son was training the wild horses to work on the farm when he was bucked off and broke his leg. Neighbors asked the farmer what he would do without his son's help, and he replied, "I will wait." Shortly afterwards, war broke out and the army needed men. But the son could not go off to war because of his broken leg.

Sometimes life throws you a curve ball and things do not go as you planned. More often than not, things will resolve over time. View everything that comes your way—the good as well as the challenging—with acceptance of whatever you are given.

Today I will adopt a wait-and-see attitude with everything that
comes my way.

Tell me, did you write the song "I'll Never Smile Again"?
—Cary Grant to Deborah Kerr in
An Affair to Remember

Some people spend their lives searching for happiness. Others set guidelines to help determine when happiness is achieved. Yet searching for happiness can be elusive, defining it impossible, and setting guidelines conditional. The pursuit of happiness can be one of endless struggle, competition, frustration, and disappointment.

Rather than look outwardly for happiness, think about what makes you happy, no matter what you have in life, what your circumstances are, or how you are feeling. Maybe the song of birds brings you happiness. Perhaps your children or your pets make you happy. Maybe having coffee with a friend or engaging in a hobby makes you happy.

True happiness is not a feeling; it comes from within. It is the ability to keep an open heart and mind so you can let in those things that help you feel joy. It is the belief that good things can happen and difficult times will not last forever. It is the understanding that simple things— the smell of a fresh-baked cookie, the feel of snowflakes falling against your face, a hug, a beautiful sunrise—can bring happiness, if you are willing to let them in.

Today I will think about those people, places, and things that inspire happiness within me.

The ideal day never comes. Today is ideal for him who makes it so.

—*Horatio Dresser*

The best thing about the future is that it comes one day at a time. Focusing on your day-to-day life with this philosophy in mind helps keep your mind from wandering ahead to tomorrow, or lagging behind to yesterday. Your mind stays in the present, when you can do the most good for yourself and for others.

In the present moment, you can only do things one step at a time. Someone who has been overweight and embarks on a diet sheds pounds one at a time. An author writes a book one word, and one page, at a time. A chef prepares an elegant meal one dish at a time. Someone who is in recovery does not shed the effects of addiction in an instant, but gets better one minute, one hour, and one day at a time.

Be mindful of the old saying that a journey of a thousand miles starts with a single step. Fully experience each moment that lies ahead today by choosing to take small steps and to savor each precious moment.

Whenever I feel like I am getting ahead of myself, I will use the slogans "One day at a time" and "Live for today" to keep my mind focused on the present.

. . . the tortoise is good at nurturing energy, so it can survive a century without food.

—*Chinese proverb*

The ancient Chinese taught that it was wise to emulate the tortoise because it knew when to withdraw into itself to remain safe and restore its energy. Like the tortoise, you can choose to withdraw from energy drains. Getting caught up in other people's problems, spending time with negative people, or finding yourself in situations that are far too dramatic can disrupt your serenity. You may think you can help resolve a problem or shift someone's negative outlook to a more positive one, yet get caught up in a whirlpool of drama or negativity.

Many of the people you will meet will be wonderful sources of positive energy, inspiration, hope, and serenity. Others will be Gloomy Guses, Angry Andys, and Negative Nancys. Some meetings you attend may be dominated by people who spend more time complaining than by working the program.

Whenever you find yourself around negative people or situations, take a step back. Cultivating a sense of inner peace will help you keep your focus on staying clean and sober.

Today I will cultivate a sense of inner peace. I will choose to be around people who inspire me and will attend meetings that keep my focus on my recovery.

The most difficult part of attaining perfection is finding something to do for an encore.

—*Author unknown*

Living life striving for perfection can be as difficult as making a piece of furniture without any wood, nails, or tools. Whenever you set impossible-to-reach goals, create expectations that you will make no mistakes—ever—or constantly demand that you be the very best in all you do, what you may find is that you rarely achieve such things. From time to time you may, but the odds are not in your favor. No one, really, is perfect.

Demanding perfection of yourself, while noble, more often than not results in defeat or shortfalls. In fact, often your quests for perfection will lead to mistakes, errors in judgment, or things done in haste.

Mistakes are a fact of life. But rather than view them as annoyances that reveal your weaknesses or prevent you from achieving perfection, consider them to be important communicators. Mistakes are valuable guideposts to destinations along your path of recovery and growth. They provide important cautions and help you refocus your concentration. So, there is a value to falling short in your quest for perfection. Mistakes and missteps are what you learn from. Without them, you would not learn how to persevere.

Today I will accept that perfection is illusive. Instead, I need to strive to be the best person I can be.

The problem with alcohol, tobacco, marijuana, cocaine, and other dangerous substances is that they betray our trust. One consumes them to feel good, and they secretly work to destroy one's body.

—Rev. Samuel A. Trumbore

Trust is a leap of faith, and in the past such leaps may have led to great falls, trouble, and long periods of self-doubt.

To open your mind and heart in trust, use the Steps of the program. Step Two (Came to believe that a Power greater than ourselves could restore us to sanity) encourages you to be open and welcoming to a Higher Power, and to trust that you are being taken care of by a powerful, caring presence. Step Three (Made a decision to turn our will and our lives over to the care of God *as we understood Him*) shows that you trust this presence is there for you. Step Five (Admitted to God, to ourselves, and to another human being the exact nature of our wrongs) provides you with the strength to be honest with your Higher Power, yourself, and others. And Step Seven (Humbly asked Him to remove our shortcomings) is your trust in action.

I will follow the Steps and let them guide me through difficulties and triumphs, and teach me to trust that my Higher Power is always there for me.

How does one kill fear, I wonder? How do you shoot a spectre through the heart, slash off its spectral head, take it by its spectral throat?

—*Joseph Conrad*

You squander time and energy when you fret about bad things that could happen or when you imagine countless scenarios in which you are rejected, you fail, or your health is in jeopardy. You waste golden opportunities when you ask "What if . . . ?" rather than "Why not . . . ?"

When you dwell in a state of thinking something will go wrong, you become immobilized by fear. You can become so timid in your actions that you never develop self-assuredness that will help you ride out the storms of life.

Imagine you are a little boat sitting in the harbor about to set sail. There are boats much bigger, which could capsize you. Storms could toss you against rocks. But, then again, maybe these things will not happen.

Today imagine you have the opportunity to set sail out of your protective harbor. What lies ahead is unknown. View the uncertainty as an adventure. Take full advantage of each moment today. Get out of your comfort zone and discover what you can do.

Although I have no idea what may happen from minute to minute, today I will believe that everything happens for the best.

And remember, we all stumble, every one of us. That's why it's a comfort to go hand in hand.
                                    —*Emily Kimbrough*

Coping with the challenges of recovery depends not only upon your inner resources, but also upon your relationships with the people in your life. The more people available to you who can offer help and guidance, the healthier you are likely to be. Being a member of a self-help group provides you with a wonderful fellowship of like-minded individuals. These are people who understand what you are feeling. You can call upon them when you are craving a drink or drug. They can help you make it through each day, free from your habit.

Take time today to assess who you can contact when you are in crisis. Maybe you have not had the time to ask a fellow member to be your sponsor. Or perhaps you are new to the program and shy about reaching out to others.

Create a Help List of members' telephone numbers and e-mail addresses you can use during a time of difficulty. If there is no one for you to call or e-mail, then reach out today at a meeting and ask for contact information.

Today I will create a Help List of people who can be there for me. Through their support, I will know that I am not alone.

I know no subject more elevating, more amazing, more ready to the poetical enthusiasm, the philosophical reflection, and the moral sentiment than the works of nature. Where can we meet such variety, such beauty, such magnificence?

—*James Thomson*

There is the story of a religious teacher who spent hours preparing his daily sermons, seeking to impart the greatest wisdom and the most stirring observations. Parishioners often commented on how wonderful and inspiring his talks were.

He was about to deliver another of his sermons when a little bird came and alit on a nearby window sill. It began to sing away with a full heart and all those present listened. Then, as suddenly as it had arrived, the bird flew away. The preacher thought for a moment. He scanned the pages of his sermon, then looked out at the parishioners and announced, "The sermon for this morning is over."

While many things can be worked hard for, some things simply exist—and exist well. Appreciating nature and being able to connect with it in some way increases your ability to appreciate the blessings in your life and the beauty that surrounds you each day.

Today I will notice the natural beauty around me. I will marvel at the beautiful songs of the birds, the crispness in the air, and the sight of bare trees against a winter sky.

Hurry up and learn patience.

—Wes Smith

When he was in his mid-80s, cellist Pablo Casals would play his instrument for more than five hours each day. Someone once asked him why, at his age and with his expertise, he still worked so hard. "Because," he replied, "I have a notion that I am making some progress."

No matter your age, you may feel that you have accomplished little in life. You may reflect upon the years when you drank or drugged and feel deep regret over all the time you let slip by.

Be patient as you learn and grow in recovery. Do what you can, when you can. Try not to rush ahead too fast, nor look behind too long. When you feel you are progressing more slowly than you would like, trust that you *are* making progress. Each step you take leads you closer to where you would like to be. Each goal you set makes your dreams and desires that much more attainable. Live as Casals did—no matter your age or where you are in life, know that there is still time left for you to learn and achieve so much more.

Today I will not regret the time that I have lost. Instead, I will trust that I am exactly where I need to be—at this moment in time.

Alcoholism isn't a spectator sport. Eventually the whole family gets to play.

—Joyce Rebeta-Burditt

Alcoholism is a disease that affects everyone. Just as germs can be spread, so too can the effects of alcoholism spread to others. When you were using, here are some of the qualities you may have shown to your children and partner:

- You are autocratic and inflexible, and you discourage growth in others.
- You do not give quality time to others, and you focus on self.
- You do not show or express feelings.
- You are incapable of caring and nurturing others.

Being in recovery provides you with the opportunity to develop and strengthen new qualities that you can show to your children and partner. Starting today, you can:

- Listen to your partner and children, and be flexible.
- Set aside quality time to spend with your partner and children.
- Share your feelings and encourage them to do the same.
- Discuss areas that may be difficult to talk about.

Today I will see myself as part of a family "team." I will be open and honest, giving, forgiving, and loving.

We run heedlessly into the abyss after putting something in front of us to stop us seeing it.

—*Blaise Pascal*

Although recovery places you firmly in the present, the work you oftentimes need to do requires you to look at your behaviors and actions of the past. These memories are hard to accept as being part of your history, and for many years you may have successfully repressed them.

To move forward, you first need to accept that you are your past. To deny your past is to deny yourself; the life you lived up to this point comprises who you are today. So, you cannot fully grow or change without reflecting upon the past with honesty. You may think, "Why should I remember the horrible things I said or did when I was using? No good can come of it. There is nothing I can do about such things now."

But there are many things you can do. You can use the Steps to finally put those bad memories behind you. You can tell your story at meetings, share your past history with your sponsor, admit to your Higher Power your transgressions, and make a searching and fearless moral inventory. Such honest reflections will lead you to bring about positive change.

Today I will look at my past with honesty and share this past with others.

Nothing evades our attention so persistently as that which is taken for granted. . . . Obvious facts tend to remain invisible.

—*Gustav Ichheiser*

Desperate to feel better, a heavy drinker decided to pray to God. She began by admitting she was not certain that she believed in a Higher Being. "But," she said, "I am willing to try." In her prayer, she acknowledged her drinking was out of control. She prayed for a long time, ending with a single word: *please.*

That night she was back at the bar. The next morning she prayed again, asking God, "Why didn't you help me stop drinking? I asked for your help." Again she found herself back at the bar. As she stumbled home, she began to cry and shouted to the sky, "I just don't understand! Are you not listening? I keep asking for your help to stop drinking. What is it that I have to do to get your help?"

At that moment she heard a voice. "Have you admitted that you're an alcoholic?" the voice asked. "Have you gone to a meeting? Have you done anything to change, besides asking me how to do what you should be doing yourself?"

Today I will use prayer to understand the purpose my Higher Power has for me, and to gain greater understanding of those things I need to do for myself.

Most of us are about as eager to be changed as we were to be born, and go through our changes in a similar state of shock.

—*James Baldwin*

Addiction places you into a form of slavery that keeps you from being free to live up to your fullest potential. That is why the First Step in recovery (We admitted we were powerless over alcohol—that our lives had become unmanageable) is so important.

The First Step places a mirror in front of you and asks that you open your eyes to the dangers and ravages of addiction. You need to see what alcoholism has done to your body, your mind, and your spirit. By opening your eyes, you can clearly see what you have destroyed in yourself and in others. You can see when you escaped from responsibilities, love, and purpose.

But just as this mirror reflects the negative effects of your addiction, so too does it show your positive aspects. It reveals that you are brave and courageous; not everyone can admit powerlessness nor strive toward making positive change. The mirror reflects a person, like any other—someone who has strengths and weaknesses, passions and hopes, dreams and desires.

Looking in the mirror is something I need to do every day. Today I remember to always be honest with myself and with others.

FEBRUARY

Came to believe that a Power greater than ourselves could restore us to sanity.

—*Step Two*

A prayer is a humble and heartfelt communication with a power greater than yourself. A prayer can admit a weakness, communicate a need, or convey praise and gratitude. Prayers can unburden your heart, give you strength and courage, and deepen your faith and trust in a Higher Power. Use the following prayer as you work on your understanding and acceptance of Step Two.

Step Two Prayer

Higher Power, I believe in your power to restore me to sanity. I know everything you do is for my greatest good and the highest good of those around me. I am committed to living a life free from addiction. I am committed to release from the struggle, fear, and hopelessness I felt in the past. I am ready to let go of the insanity of using and to replace it with the sanity of sobriety.

I ask for your help so I can do these things with strength and purpose. I ask for your guidance so I may open my heart to love and forgiveness. I ask for your help so I may live each day true to a mission of sobriety, and to reflect this mission in my every word and action. Higher Power, thank you for listening to my prayer.

Problems, unfortunately, can be addicting. Like it or not, we take a certain amount of pride in the very problems that distress us.

—*Eloise Ristad*

Imagine you have been asked to stand in a frigidly cold room. Chances are you would take one step into the room and then run right out. Now imagine you are placed in a room that offers a comfortable temperature. You are told that the temperature will gradually drop until it reaches subfreezing. You stay in the room, and may even remain long after you begin shivering or even after the room becomes unbearable.

The difference between the two examples is that in one you are given no chance to adjust. The same is true for living with pain and suffering. For as long as you believe that your problems are infinite and any solutions elusive or nonexistent, you may become increasingly anesthetized to the difficulties in your life. You may feel far more comfortable holding onto feelings of doom, disappointment, and confusion than striving to find ways to decrease or eliminate your problems.

Recovery gives you a choice: stay in a life in which you face constant problems, or surrender to a life in which you actively explore different ways of thinking and acting.

I free myself from pain by seeking solutions to any problems I may face.

The biggest lesson I've learned . . . was that if you have all the fresh water you want to drink and all the food you want to eat, you ought never to complain about anything.
—Eddie Rickenbacker

When the airplane he was piloting was shot down during World War II, Eddie Rickenbacker spent nearly twenty-one days floating in a life raft in the ocean. He was hungry, thirsty, and uncomfortable. He lived from day to day, having no idea whether he would survive. After he was rescued, he focused on the very basics in life and lived each day grateful for a second chance.

Are you content, or are you looking for something bigger and better? Are you grateful for challenges, which strengthen your commitment, or are you trying to find an easier path?

It has been said that money can buy a bed but not a good night's sleep, books but not intelligence, a house but not a home, and amusement but not happiness. You can attain a deeper level of happiness and satisfaction in life by following this simple tenet: *Keep it simple.* Use this phrase to maintain focus whenever you find you have lost sight of the simple blessings you have been given.

Today I will be satisfied with what I have and what I have been given.

You never move forward if you stay in the same place.
—Meghan McCain

Making the decision to be clean and sober marks your willingness to embark on a new way of living. It is a time of joyous deliverance from your past. With deliverance comes a gradual release from unhappiness and unhealthiness, bitterness and regret, and fear and anxiety. Through the support and tools of the program, you are breaking free from your habits and old ways of doing things. You are changing for the better!

While recovery represents a huge and positive change in your life, the forward progress you make will not always consist of giant steps or even grand "a-ha" moments. For the most part, you may find recovery to be repetitive and predictable. Even though you are deeply committed to your sobriety, you may find that there will be times when your new beginning feels rather unexciting.

At such times, it is important to remember that in order to get to this new place, you had to crawl out from a very dark hole. That, in and of itself, is truly amazing. Try not to forget that being clean and sober each day is a glorious achievement, and one that is necessary to progress forward.

I will remember that what I bring to each day and what I receive are what matter the most.

The basis of optimism is sheer terror.

—*Oscar Wilde*

The optimist sees the lightbulb as a device that provides valuable illumination. The pessimist sees the lightbulb as impermanent and undependable—something that will go out at the most inopportune time. The difference between having an optimistic, positive attitude and a pessimistic, negative one is simple: optimism allows you to see the opportunity in any difficulty, while pessimism encourages you to see the difficulty in every opportunity. The optimist can adjust responses to any situation; the pessimist cannot.

Do you see challenges as opportunities to experience something new and exciting, or do you see such things only in terms of their poor timing, the time and energy they will take to fix, or the cost?

Recovery teaches that it is how you view any given situation—with an optimistic, positive attitude or a defeatist, negative one—that determines whether you move forward with ease, or if you will resort to a familiar pattern of ineffective behavior. By becoming more aware of the habitual, and oftentimes negative, ways in which you view situations, you can learn to adjust your outlook. You can discover that responses that enable you to see the possibilities can bring about change for the better.

Today I will develop awareness of how I respond to situations so I can learn to be more optimistic.

Rather than viewing a brief relapse back to inactivity as a failure, treat it as a challenge and try to get back on track as soon as possible.

—*Jimmy Connors*

Remaining clean and sober, especially in the early days of your recovery, can be challenging. You may even question whether you really do have a problem. But even "old timers" in the program know how easy it is to get into trouble. "Sobriety," it has been said in meetings, "is the leading cause of relapse."

Most relapses happen with a gradual shift in attitude, feelings, and behaviors. If you start to notice that your general outlook is becoming more negative than positive, if your emotions and feelings are difficult to control, or if you skip meetings or avoid your sponsor, these are warning signs that your sobriety may be in jeopardy.

Whenever you feel stressed or vulnerable, you may need extra help. Just as you might take more vitamins when you feel a cold or flu coming on, so too can you increase your relapse prevention dosage. Reach out to your sponsor and those in the program, attend more meetings, meditate and pray, and avoid situations and people who could trigger a relapse.

Today I will not take my sobriety for granted. I will give thanks for everything and everyone who will help me maintain my sobriety for another day.

*All growth is a leap in the dark, a spontaneous unpre-
meditated act without benefit of experience.*
—Henry Miller

From time to time you may move through the day with
little energy or interest, as if on automatic pilot—taking
the same route to work, eating the same meals, attending the same meetings, or spending time with the same
people. You may ask, "Where am I going in my life?" But
a more productive question is, "Where am I *growing* in
my life?"

Although familiar routines provide comfort, they can
prevent you from experiencing new challenges, excitement, and opportunities for change and growth. Doing
something new or different every once in a while can
help you break out of the rut of your daily grind and give
you something new to think or talk about.

Today, strive to experience something new and different in your life. Take a new route to work. Stop at a
different coffee shop. Strike up a conversation with someone you do not know at a meeting. Accept an invitation
to dinner. Such experiences can spark a new interest in
your life and stimulate you into a new way of thinking,
feeling, and acting.

*The goal of doing something new is awareness, not anxiety.
Today I will be open to new experiences and view them as a
source of challenge, novelty, and excitement.*

Appearances aside, we need no advice but approval.
—Coco Chanel

Decisions based on people-pleasing take the focus from your wants and needs and place it on the wants and needs of others. You may feel that you are protecting yourself from criticism and disapproval by acting and verbalizing in ways you feel will earn acceptance and approval. But the time you spend focused on pleasing others is less time spent on yourself, and you may become out of touch with who you are and what you want and need.

Your recovery depends upon your ability to understand and act upon what is right for you. This does not mean that you have to be selfish, self-centered, or uncaring about others, nor does it mean that every decision you make has to be based solely upon what you want. It simply means that you need to take care of yourself first so your commitment to your recovery remains strong.

If you are unsure of your wants and needs, simply change the word *should* to *want* whenever you need to make a choice. So instead of thinking, *I should go to a meeting tonight,* you can think, *I want to go to a meeting tonight.*

Today I will keep my focus on what I want and need to become a stronger person. I will make choices that support my recovery.

Making mental connections is our most crucial learning tool . . . to see patterns, relationships, context.
— Marilyn Ferguson

One day, on the famous "bullet train" from Kyoto to Tokyo, passengers rushed to one side of the train just in time to see thick clouds suddenly part, revealing the beauty of Mount Fuji. They exclaimed with excitement and took pictures until, just as suddenly, the clouds once again hid the mountain.

The incident affected the rest of the journey. People who had been strangers started talking to one another, more aware of all around them. Those who had been sleeping awakened and watched the scenery pass by as the train sped to its destination.

Those passengers shared a common connection that brought them unity. The same is true in your recovery. You are an essential part of every meeting you attend. The story you bring to others is a story with which they are familiar. The thoughts and feelings you have resonate with them. Every time you share thoughts and feelings, you become empowered. It is through this connection that you can come to realize that you are an important part of the world.

Today I will be aware of the simple truth that I belong. I trust that I am part of everything and everyone around me.

*If you're feeling miserable, force yourself to smile broadly,
holding your goofy grin at least ten seconds. When you
relax your face, you'll actually feel happier.*
                                                    —Sandra Stier

It has been said that humor may be hazardous to your
illness. Research shows that those who are seriously ill
can use humor and laughter to help turn the tide of their
illness. Yet when you are in pain, depressed, or stressed,
the last thing you may want to do is smile.

A smile can open up a positive flow of energy, while
laughter can provide a positive balance to negative feelings. They can be as beneficial to your body as aerobic exercise and as helpful to your mind as a peaceful
meditation.

When you laugh at your problems and see humor in
challenging situations, you open yourself to greater capabilities for handling whatever comes your way. A smile
or a laugh can take you away from your problems and
troubles—if only for a few moments—and provide you
with the ability to see things with different eyes and a
fresh perspective. You may discover that something you
were obsessing about is really quite inconsequential, and
something that caused you great upset is really not as terrible as you thought.

*Today I will remember that it is okay to laugh through my tears
and smile through my sadness.*

It seems to me that there are two great enemies of peace—fear and selfishness.

—*Katherine Paterson*

Imagine you are going on a vacation. A friend has offered to help you pack your bags, take you out to lunch, and then drive you to the airport.

You lay out the clothes and toiletries you will take, and your friend starts to pack them but not in your usual way. So you tell your friend how the items should be packed. Later your friend takes you to a restaurant. But it isn't one you like, so you tell your friend to take you to the place where you want to eat. As your friend drives you to the airport, you notice it is not the route you would have taken, so you tell your friend the route to take. When you arrive at the airport, is it any wonder that your friend is more than happy to toss your bags out of the car and leave you on the curb?

When things do not go the way you want or planned, let go. Reach out to your Higher Power for the serenity you need.

When I humbly reach out to my Higher Power, I give up my need to control. Today I trust that my Higher Power will always hear and answer my prayers.

There are no victims, only volunteers.

—Anonymous

Are you a volunteer for pain and negativity? If you are uncomfortable talking to a constant complainer, do you make yourself accessible, or do you avoid that person? If someone asks you to do something that makes you uncomfortable, such as attending a party where you know there will be drinking or using, do you say yes or no? If someone tells you a tale of woe, do you try to match the story with your own heartbreak? If someone asks, "How are you?" do you put on a sad-sack face and share all the things in your life that make you feel unhappy?

When you volunteer for pain and negativity, you continually place yourself in situations that perpetuate them. So rather than stay in an uncomfortable situation, leave. Excuse yourself from conversations or activities with those whose words or actions bring you down. Strive to respond positively, rather than negatively, to others. Seek out people who are centered and optimistic and who have inspiring things to say. Seek out the positive in all that you do, and you will find that you no longer want or need to be a volunteer for negativity!

Today I will choose to participate in helpful, positive, and uplifting experiences. Such things can provide more comfort and joy in my life.

God gave us life. What are we willing to give him in return?
—*Oral Lee Brown*

Think of those people who only call when they need something, rarely if ever give a gift, say they are too busy to offer assistance, or focus solely on themselves in conversations. You would consider such people to be selfish, and you might, over time, distance yourself from them.

Now think about your relationship with your Higher Power. How frequently do you connect with your Higher Power? Do you pray only when you need something? Do you think and speak only of yourself in your prayers?

Just as there is a balance of give and take between two people in a healthy relationship, so should there be a healthy give and take between you and your Higher Power. Ask what assistance your Higher Power needs so that this loving presence can be felt by those around you. Open your heart and fill it with love and compassion, even for those you may not like. And set aside time to assist others who are less fortunate, so that they may understand that God considers the needs of all.

Today I offer assistance to my Higher Power. In my prayers, I will ask of what service I can be so that my usefulness on earth can benefit those around me.

We do not love people because they are beautiful, but because they seem beautiful to us because we love them.
—*Russian proverb*

How would you write the words "I love you" to someone you love, using twenty-five words or less and without using the words "I love you"?

Intimate relationships can have a profound influence in your life. They can take you outside yourself, encouraging you to think about and give to others. They can make the less enjoyable aspects of life more enjoyable by providing companionship, communication, and support. They can bring you shared experiences, joy, and laughter. They can offer romance and passion. They can provide stability and security. They can strengthen and deepen love, both self-love and love for another person.

Perhaps the love you feel today is different from love you were shown in the past. The healthier you become, the more you will understand that love has a far deeper meaning than sex. Love is based on courtesy and kindness, openness and honesty, and acceptance and trust. Love is having a generous heart, a willingness to forgive mistakes, and a desire to see and fully accept who another person is.

Today I will write an "I love you" essay to someone I love. I will focus on the good qualities of that person and communicate how wonderful our love feels.

The Wolf and the Crane

A wolf had been eating when a bone became stuck in his throat. Soon, the pain became excruciating. He rushed to a pond, thinking water would loosen the bone. But he could not swallow. Frantic, he looked around and saw a crane watching him. "I would give anything," he rasped, "if you would remove this bone from my throat. Your neck is long and your beak is strong. Please help me."

The crane agreed. It lowered its neck and put its long beak into the wolf's throat, removing the bone. "I would now like the reward you promised," said the crane.

But the wolf growled. "It is enough that you have placed your head into my strong jaws, and I have spared your life. Be gone with you, or you will be my next dinner."

The moral of the story: *An enemy's promises were made to be broken.*

While making a fearless moral inventory, you may remember when you mistreated others, pushed them aside when they tried to keep you safe, or made promises you did not keep. Your promise today—to live a clean and sober life—can help you to make amends to them.

Today I will make a list of those who helped me and were always there for me and make amends to them.

The only way to keep your health is to eat what you don't want, drink what you don't like, and do what you'd druther not.

—Mark Twain

While abstinence is an addict's best choice to better health, it does not magically take away the harmful, and sometimes lasting, physical effects of addiction.

No matter what stage of recovery you are in, it is important to get a medical checkup each year. Be honest with your doctor about your past lifestyle so you can receive appropriate attention and treatment. Make it your daily effort to strictly adhere to your physician's advice.

There are other things you can do to build and maintain better health. In times of stress, take a mental time-out by using prayer and meditation to calm your mind and relax your body. Get plenty of rest through a good night's sleep. If you have insomnia or sleep apnea, use meditation techniques to ease your way into sleep or seek treatment from a clinic that specializes in such issues. Each day, eat with good nutrition in mind, even when pressed for time. Finally, incorporate some form of physical exercise into your daily routine—preferably outdoors—so you can circulate fresh air through your lungs and body.

Today I will live by this affirmation: My body is a temple. I will keep the spirits outside.

I wish I knew what people mean when they say they find "emptiness" in this wonderful adventure of living. . . . I'm afraid I'm an incorrigible life-lover and life-wonderer and adventurer.

—*Edith Wharton*

Being in a recovery program does not mean that you cannot live life to the fullest. Sometimes the greatest achievements, the most beneficial changes, the strongest relationships, and the most learning can take place when you are clean and sober.

In your years of use and abuse, you most likely passively watched wonder, passion, and your sense of adventure disappear. You believed that drinks or drugs would make your life an amazing experience.

Recovery empowers you to try new things, participate in new adventures, or try a different way of acting. You have the chance to step out of old roles you once played and become more solidly positioned in the sheer enjoyment of all that life has to offer. So, today, resolve to include more adventures in your life! Climb a mountain or train for a road race or triathlon. Give back to others by volunteering at a soup kitchen or devoting your time to a worthwhile cause. Explore a career change or learn more about a particular subject. Hone a talent or polish a craft. Pick something you want to do, and then do it!

I am a life-lover, life-wonderer, and life-adventurer.

*I only went out for a walk, and finally concluded to stay
out till sundown, for going out, I found, was really going in.*
                                                    —John Muir

When your mind, body, and spirit are troubled, going out
into nature can help you work through some of the difficulties in your life and reconnect with yourself in meaningful ways. Sometimes all you really need to feel better
on the inside is to hear the sounds of the great outdoors
and breathe in the fresh air.

The best way to begin to connect with nature is to
take a slow, meditative walk around your neighborhood.
Notice how different the month of February looks from
the month of July. Feel the ground beneath your feet.
Breathe in deeply and savor the air. Hear the sound your
feet make as they connect with the ground. Hear the
birds.

Then turn and retrace your steps, watching for things
you overlooked the first time. Think or say out loud, "I
am one with the sun. I am one with the trees. I am one
with the wind. I am one with the birds. I am one with the
universe. Because of all these things, I am one with myself
and my Higher Power."

*Today I will connect with nature so I can deepen my spiritual-
ity and strengthen my connection to myself.*

From what we get, we can make a living; what we give, however, makes a life.

—*Arthur Ashe*

Did you ever consider that you can effect positive change in others? Because you are in a program of recovery, you have firsthand knowledge about the dangers and downfalls of drugs and alcohol. Because you admitted you were powerless over your addiction, you have an enlightening experience to share with those still trapped in lives focused on drinking and drugging. Your story can be inspirational and eye-opening to others.

You have much to contribute to your community, charities, churches, and to others in recovery. Volunteer work—whether at your favorite meetings, in local organizations, or in more far-reaching causes—can strengthen your recovery as it provides hope and help to others.

Start by volunteering to make coffee at a meeting or clean up afterward. As you grow and strengthen in recovery, volunteer to speak at a local high school on the topic of recovery, deliver lunches and dinners to those who are homebound, or read stories to children at your local library. When you see yourself as a valuable resource with much to contribute for the good of others, you may be pleasantly surprised at the energy, compassion, and expertise you have to give.

Today I am ready to extend a helping hand to others.

People are like stained-glass windows. They glow and
sparkle when the sun is shining on them. But, if the sun
goes down, their true beauty is revealed only if they have
a light from within.

—Anonymous

A Native American ceremony used for spiritual renewal
in the winter months, when darkness comes early, encouraged the return of the sun through connection with
the Great Spirit.

At night, to the steady beat of drums, the tribe would
gather in a circle around a fire. One at a time, members
would sing, chat, or speak of a wish for the future, a desire for the present, or a memory from the past. Each
member would toss into the fire an object created for the
ceremony.

The voices of the tribe would join in as the object
burned and the speaker prayed, asking what needed to
be done to make a dream come true, what new strengths
could be developed to let go of a past memory, and what
could be done in the present to reach a desire. When all
members had taken a turn in the ceremony, the tribe
would unite in a dance to the beat of the drums.

I trust that there is a light within me. Today I will pray to my
Higher Power to release the darkness and replenish this light.

Scientists announced that they have located the gene for alcoholism. Scientists say they found it at a party, talking way too loudly.

—Conan O'Brien

It has been said, "The true spirit of conversation consists in building on another man's observation, not overturning it." In fact, the word *dialogue* means talking between two sides. A dialogue includes an exchange of thoughts, opinions, and feelings. It means expressing yourself but also hearing what others have to say. It means opening your mind and absorbing the words of others.

Thinking only of your pleasure, considering only your own needs, and talking over the conversations of others are not components of good communication. Freedom of speech does not give you the license to say anything you want whenever you want, just because you feel like it. Communication with others requires responsible use.

One of the most important tools in recovery is listening—not just to others, but also to your Higher Power. It means opening both your ears and your heart to understand what others are going through. It means listening with attentiveness rather than framing what you are going to say. It means letting someone speak fully, without interruption. And it means communicating through prayer—but then listening to the guidance of your Higher Power.

Today I will think and listen before I speak.

The regularity of a habit is generally in proportion to its absurdity.

—Marcel Proust

Before you entered a program of recovery, how did you measure your progress in letting go of bad habits? Did you tell yourself, "I only had one drink instead of the whole bottle," or "I only bought five scratch tickets this week," or "I only used once last month." Such statements represent false progress. No matter how such justifications may have made you feel better, you were still actively engaged in your habit.

Progress is measured by what constitutes true success. If true success is to never drink again, then having one drink is not successful. If true success is to quit gambling, then buying even one lottery ticket is not successful. If true success is to get clean, then using is not successful.

The motivation to achieve progress begins within you. Without your buy-in from the start, you cannot move forward. Each day you do not drink, or gamble, or use is a step toward success. Even if you experience false progress from time to time, each day presents you with the opportunity to strengthen—or re-strengthen—your resolve and commitment to being clean and sober.

Today I will be committed to my progress in breaking bad habits and in taking the steps I need in my recovery.

We are not unlike a particularly hardy crustacean. . . .
With each passage from one stage of human growth to the
next we, too, must shed a protective structure.
                                                    —*Gail Sheehy*

In his book *First You Have to Row a Little Boat,* author
Richard Bode reflects on his passion for boating. Looking
back from the vantage point of adulthood, he discovers
that a little boat from his childhood provided him not
only with great experience in learning how to navigate
the ocean, but also in learning how to move through life.
"God gave the wind," he writes. "I didn't pick the wind;
that was imposed by a power far greater than myself. But
I had to sail the wind . . . until it led me at last to a shel-
tered cove."

There are silent currents that flow in and out of each
day that may send you in directions you had not intended or anticipated. Resolve to stay calm if things do
not go the way you planned or hoped for. Resolve to be
one with your Higher Power and to use the strength you
receive to navigate any disruptions.

I will choose to face life today with a serene spirit and calm
poise. I will not fight the winds of change, but instead sail them
with ease into safe harbors.

What poison is to food, self-pity is to life.
—*Oliver C. Wilson*

Sometimes life presents you with a difficult loss, a great disappointment, or a seemingly insurmountable challenge. Life is filled with a great many unknowns—both wonderful surprises as well as unexpected disasters.

Self-pity is, essentially, an attitude of ingratitude. Self-pity looks at what you cannot do, what you do not or cannot have, what you have lost, and what you cannot change. Self-pity is absorbed and selfish, for self-pity says, "Look at me. I feel awful. My life is a mess. I will never get better." On and on self-pity goes, starting out as a trickling stream and gradually swelling into a raging flood.

A positive attitude is the dreaded and hated enemy of self-pity. A positive attitude focuses on what you can do, what you do and can have, what you have gained, and what you can change. A positive attitude displays care for yourself and others. A positive attitude seeks and sees progress. A positive attitude motivates and encourages. A positive attitude is the perfect companion to living a physically, mentally, and spiritually fulfilling life. Today, you have a choice: feel pity or embrace positivity.

Starting now, I will get off my pity pot and live life with both a positive attitude and an attitude of gratitude.

I have always delighted at the prospect of a new day, a fresh try, one more start . . .

—Joseph Priestley

Just as you begin your day washing yesterday's residue from your body, so too is it vitally important to begin each new day with a similar cleansing of your mind and spirit. That is because your mind and spirit can become warehouses for stored up fears, doubts, insecurities, anger, stress, and pain.

The beginning of the day presents an ideal time to engage in physical, mental, and spiritual cleansing so you can start anew, cleansed, and centered. In the same amount of time as it takes to shower, you can connect with your Higher Power and use the tools of the recovery program to strengthen your spirit.

Each morning set aside time to engage in stillness, quiet reflection, meditation, and prayer. Imagine the life you wish to experience and summon the strength of your convictions to make what you have imagined come true. Ask your Higher Power to bless the image you have created and to give you the power to hold onto that image throughout the day. Through regular cleansing of your mind and spirit, you can approach each day filled with energy, poise, and confidence.

I begin the day connecting with my Higher Power. My Higher Power will help cleanse my soul and free my spirit.

It is impressive to see a person who has been battered by life in many ways . . . still striving to find the path to a more fulfilling existence, moved by the wisdom in knowing, "I am more than my problems."

—Nathaniel Branden

Naturalist Henry David Thoreau left behind the comforts of home to live in the woods and fulfill his basic needs in a Spartan-like existence. He explained, "I wanted to live deliberately, to front only the essential facts of life, and to see if I could not learn what it had to teach, and not, when I came to die, discover that I had not lived."

Thoreau's desire to experience life more fully has, for decades, provided a power of example to many. Each person in recovery—including you—is a power of example. Each is a role model for those who stumble into the program, for those who lose their way, and for those who struggle each day with courage and hope. Each has a story that started in tragedy and is continuing in triumph.

When you see yourself as a role model, you can view your progress. You can understand how your story can be inspirational to a newcomer.

I will serve as a source of inspiration to others. I will freely give of myself and my experiences to those in need.

You stay young as long as you can learn, acquire new habits and suffer contradiction.
— *Baroness Marie von Ebner-Eschenbach*

Recovery can begin at any age. Your new way of living begins the moment you admit you have a problem and you make a commitment to a program of recovery.

Age presents no barriers to growth, unless you let it. An Irish proverb says, "Twenty years a child; twenty years running wild; twenty years a mature man—and after that, praying." While growing older can take a physical toll on the body, age will not impact your determination. While growing older can impact your mental capabilities, age will not impact your ability to learn new things. While growing older can weaken your beliefs, age will not impact your ability to strengthen your spirituality.

The tools of recovery are as effective for the young as they are for those who are older. The Steps are accessible and can be climbed through perseverance and dedication. Your Higher Power listens as intently to the prayers of a child as to those of an adult. Your Higher Power provides guidance and is always there for you.

Today I will understand that recovery is a gift that provides me with new awareness and new potential. Recovery keeps me young in heart and hopeful for a better future.

In walking, just walk. In sitting, just sit. Above all, don't wobble.

—*Zen Spiritualist Yunmen Wenyan*

How many times have you come to the realization that your life is out of control and that you need to make a change? Maybe you have come to this point not once, but several times. You may have made promises to yourself that you can and will begin a new way of living. But when morning comes, you may find that it is easier to talk yourself out of your resolution than to take the first step to making a change.

Striving to go it alone is one way to ensure failure. You can be your own worst enemy whenever you think that you alone can resolve all of your difficulties and challenges. Without trust and faith in a power greater than yourself, you can easily talk yourself out of making any change—no matter how big or small.

Today presents you with an opportunity to believe that a Higher Power can help restore sanity to your life. You have the choice to stick with old, familiar habits—the ones that haven't served you well—or to cease going it alone and asking for spiritual help.

Today I accept that a power greater than myself can restore sanity in my life.

Let us accept truth, even when it surprises us and alters our views.

—*George Sand*

Adding an extra day to the calendar year—February 29—serves a significant purpose. Because it takes the earth roughly 365 and a quarter times to turn on its axis and complete a full year's orbit around the sun, a day is added to the calendar every four years.

Out of this need to synch time with the earth sprung folklore. It was once thought that babies born on this day would be sickly and hard to rear. People believed the extra day would disrupt nature and that crops planted during a leap year would grow the wrong way. Women were granted the privilege to propose marriage on this day provided, one convention dictated, that she was wearing a red petticoat.

A similar blurring of fact and fiction occurs whenever you embellish the truth or deliberately lie to create a different reality. The more adept you are at seeing things as you would like them to be, the more truth they can attain in your own mind. Recovery not only teaches truthfulness, but also requires it. The more you work the program, the less comfortable you will feel with dishonesty and the more comfortable you will become with telling the truth.

With truth comes greater understanding. I will speak only the truth.

MARCH

Made a decision to turn our will and our lives over to the care of God as we understood Him.

—*Step Three*

A prayer is a humble and heartfelt communication with a power greater than yourself. A prayer can admit a weakness, communicate a need, or convey praise and gratitude. Prayers can unburden your heart, give you strength and courage, and deepen your faith and trust in a Higher Power. Use the following prayer as you work on your understanding and acceptance of Step Three.

Step Three Prayer

Higher Power, for so long you have been unknown to me. I have kept myself separate from you. Now I understand that I have never been alone. Even in times of great trouble and darkness, you have always been with me. Today I accept that thy will—and not my will—will guide me. I trust that you will provide me with direction, illuminate my path, and lessen my burdens so that I may do your will.

With a bowed head and an open heart, I ask that you show me how to live. I ask that you free me from the bondage of my past. I ask that you provide me with guidance in all of my actions. Higher Power, I accept you. I trust in you. I turn over my life to you.

Dawn is a shimmering of the horizon.
Dusk is a settling of the sky.

—*Tao*

Sunrise and sunset represent the measure of a day. When the sun rises and daylight comes, the moon sets; when the sun sets and darkness comes, the moon rises. Without such alteration, a day would not have a beginning nor an end.

So too are there cycles in your life: endings as well as beginnings. You may view the loss of a loved one as an ending. But you can also consider that your life after such a loss can be a beginning. Similarly, you may view the loss of your habit as an ending. But you can also consider that your life without the habit can be a beginning.

One way to ease the pain of loss is to write about it. Putting your feelings into words may make it easier to let go and transition into a new frame of mind or new way of doing things. You can compose a letter to a past habit you have let go, a departed loved one, or anything you have lost. Write those things you always wanted to say, but did not. Write about regret over conflicts left unresolved. Let your words flow freely.

Even though I may grieve today over a loss, expressing my feelings will help me work through this grief.

Failure after long perseverance is much grander than never to have a striving good enough to be called a failure.
—*George Eliot*

When Thomas Edison and his assistants finished their long labors over an improved prototype of the first electric light bulb, Edison gave the bulb to a young helper. But the nervous boy dropped the fragile bulb. Again, Edison and his assistants produced a prototype. Edison once more handed it to the boy. This time, he carried it safely to another room. In that simple gesture, Edison changed the boy's feelings of self-worth from failure and incompetence to success and self-confidence. How often do you pay attention to your accomplishments? More often than not you pay them little heed. Instead, you focus on past difficulties, false starts, and failures.

Samuel Beckett once said, "Ever tried. Ever failed. No matter. Try again. Fail again. Fail better." When you learn to pay scant attention to your failures, it means you have ceased to fear them.

Starting today, accept that mistakes and failures are inevitable. But they are also valuable teachers that provide lessons to help you change. By learning from your mistakes, you are more capable of moving forward.

I can rise each time I fall and learn something in the process. I will focus on my achievements and successes rather than failures so I can become more confident.

There is perhaps no more effective way to relieve psychic pain than to be in constant contact with another human being who understands what you are going through and can communicate such understanding to you.
—Frederic Flach

One of the greatest benefits in recovery is the support of others. Without this support there would be no circle of fellowship.

This inclusive fellowship touches everyone, and you are an integral part. Just as there will be times when you need comfort, support, and someone to talk to, there will also be times when someone needs your comfort, support, and a listening ear.

How can you offer support? Listen to the challenges others say they are facing. Draw from your experience to let them know they are not alone. Recognize the strengths others cannot see in themselves by pointing out and validating their progress. Offer a lighthearted outlook and assure others that ups and downs are a part of the recovery process. Set aside any desire to pass judgment about the actions of others. Refrain from giving advice, even when you feel you know the answers. Serve as a resource of positive energy. And offer guidance based upon the Twelve Steps and the lessons you have learned in your recovery.

Today I remember that recovery is a fellowship of supportive people.

Many of us spend our whole lives running from feeling with the mistaken belief that you cannot bear the pain. But you have already borne the pain; what you have not done is feel all you are beyond the pain.
                                                    —*Saint Bartholomew*

Chuang Tzu told a story about a man who was so afraid of his shadow and his footsteps that he ran away from them. But the more he ran, the louder the footsteps sounded and the more swiftly his shadow followed. Falling into a panic, he ran until he dropped dead from exhaustion. What the man never came to realize is that if he had only stopped running, the things he feared would have stopped chasing him. His wild imaginings would have been put to rest.

You may believe that when you run away from your feelings, you are more capable of avoiding them or making them disappear. But the truth is the more you avoid your feelings, the greater and longer your pain will be.

Once you stop running and face your feelings, the process of release begins, bringing relief from the pain, anxiety, and fear. In letting your feelings in, you are letting them go.

Today I will express my feelings of sadness, grief, anger, and joy. I will feel them, express them, and release them.

Time is a dressmaker specializing in alterations.
—*Faith Baldwin*

Think of the time-related devices you possess. You probably own at least one wrist watch. You have calendars in your office and home. Your car, your cell phone, and your computer display the time. All of these devices have value. They help keep your day organized, provide you with vital reminders of appointments and commitments, and generally keep you focused throughout the day.

Recovery provides a measurement of time that has similar value in your life: one day at a time. This twenty-four-hour plan utilizes a calendar with just a single day on it with only one to-do item: stay clean and sober.

While your goal is to never drink or drug again, to say that you will give up drinking or drugging forever presents a daunting stretch of time. Too, it provides you with little opportunity to measure your progress. But if, instead, you use the twenty-four-hour plan—if you say, "Just for today, I will not drink or drug"—you have a greater chance of success. You will be more focused on your goal and more capable of effectively measuring your progress at the end of the day.

Just for today, I will not drink or drug. I will use the twenty-four-hour plan to provide me with the framework for this achievement.

Those who have one foot in the canoe and one foot in the boat are going to fall into the river.
—*Tuscarora tribe saying*

In the past, how many times did you tell yourself, "This drink is going to be my last"? Or perhaps you said that, after one last cigarette, you would stop smoking; after one last hit, you would stop drugging; after one last scratch ticket, you would stop gambling; after one last piece of cake, you would stop overeating.

Engaging in the last of anything does not stop your craving, nor does it steel your will to walk away from it. When you make a promise to yourself, it must be one that is made with your full commitment—otherwise, it cannot be considered as a binding agreement. It is like speaking a truth with your hands hidden behind your back and your fingers crossed.

Renew your commitment—or make a full commitment—to the program. Say, "I will become fully involved" rather than, "I will have one last . . ." The program offers tools, support, and guidance that will help you make promises you are sure to keep.

Today I will be fully engaged in the actions I need to take and the support I will receive from others who understand what I am going through.

The difference between transformation by accident and transformation by a system is like the difference between lightning and a lamp. Both give illumination, but one is dangerous and unreliable, while the other is relatively safe, directed, available.

—Marilyn Ferguson

In the past, the *idea* of recovery may have frightened you or intrigued you. With no awareness of the components of recovery, you could only make assumptions. But now that you are in the program, you know that the *doing* of recovery requires conscious decisions to change. Very few people wake up in the morning thinking, "I want to do something so different and foreign to me that it will require every ounce of my focus, energy, and strength."

Doing requires the four Ps: preparation, patience, planning, and perseverance. Through dedicated attention to each of these things, progress can be made. Unlike lightning-bolt changes—those things that happen so suddenly that there is no time for preparation—changes brought about from your actions can provide you with the greatest sense of pride and accomplishment.

Doing the changes you are making today will light the path ahead of you so you can take each step of the journey with the confidence you need to take action.

Today I dedicate myself to making slow, gradual progress. I will be patient but dedicated in all of my actions.

It's this simple—if I never try anything, I never learn anything—if I never take a risk, I stay where I am.
—Hugh Prather

In the movie *Cast Away*, Tom Hanks plays a man who is marooned on an island after a plane crash. As the days turn into weeks, then into months, and finally into years, he loses hope that he will ever be rescued. But then the tide brings him a piece of metal and he forms an idea. If he could build a raft, using the metal as a sail, he could perhaps escape the island and return to civilization.

His plan works. He yearns to resume life where he left off, but everything has changed. Filled with despair, he visits a friend who asks how he was able to survive on the island. He thinks for a moment and then answers, "I knew, somehow, that I had to stay alive . . . I had to keep breathing . . . so that's what I did."

Recovery requires you to trust even when you feel there is no reason to hope. To embark on a new path requires you to try new ways of acting, behaving, and living. Unless you try, you will never know if you can succeed.

Today the risks I take will give me wings. With these wings, I can experience a new way of living.

A compromise is an arrangement whereby someone who can't get exactly what he wants makes sure nobody else gets exactly what they want.

—*Barbara Florio Graham*

Because recovery can seem like it is one struggle after another, you may feel as if you are constantly battling "enemies." You may not take the time to ask yourself, "Are these enemies real or imagined?" Instead, you may strive to safeguard yourself against what you think are personal attacks by others, attempts to control you, or deliberate actions designed to set up roadblocks in your recovery. In doing so, you may withdraw from interacting with those who have the most experience or your best interests at heart.

When you are at a heightened level of defensiveness or feel vulnerable, you can easily misinterpret words and actions and blow things out of proportion. Then, your battle with another becomes real.

To foster a less volatile and more cooperative spirit, first bring your emotions under control. When you feel defensive, take a moment to ask, "Am I overreacting?" Listen more closely to the words of others. You may find what you thought was criticism is really someone reaching out to you in kindness and support.

Today I will remove my battle armor and really listen to others. I will be respectful of them and keep my emotions in check.

Imagine how little good music there would be if, for example, a conductor refused to play Beethoven's Fifth Symphony on the ground that his audience may have heard it before.

—A.P. Herbert

From time to time you may feel bored with the meetings you attend. You may hear the same stories and slogans. You may interact with the same people. So you may come to the decision that since you are not drinking or using, you have your addiction under control and no longer need to attend meetings.

Rather than step away from meetings, consider ways to give meetings greater meaning. Perhaps you are bored with the stories people tell because you are only half-listening. Strive to listen more closely. Maybe you are tired of the same slogans because you have not fully appreciated their meaning. Choose a slogan and break it down, word by word, so you understand its purpose in your recovery. Maybe your disinterest in others is due to your lack of effort in getting to know them better. Engage with them so you can learn more about who they are.

Approach your next meeting with a renewed effort and change your way of thinking. A greater perspective will be your reward.

Today I will truly listen to the stories of others and seek new meaning in the experiences they are sharing with me.

There is no royal road to anything. One thing at a time,
all things in succession. That which grows fast withers as
rapidly; that which grows slowly endures.
                              —Josiah Gilbert Holland

In early spring, ripe tomatoes are found in grocery stores.
Garden shops have hundreds of flowers in bloom. Such
things have been grown in hot houses with controlled
temperatures and highly enriched soil.

A tomato that has slowly ripened outdoors in the natural sun and soil is far tastier than one that has been ripened in a factory. The exquisite beauty of flowers is more
breathtaking when the result of a normal cycle of growth.

It has often been said that there is no elevator to recovery; you must take the Steps. There is no "twelve and
done" process that signals completion. Working through
the Steps is something that requires more than one visit
to ensure recovery. Even though our world moves at a fast
pace—with e-mail, drive-through windows, on-demand
movies, and more—your recovery needs to grow and
flourish over time. Staying clean and sober is more than
just a matter of putting away the bottle and the drugs. It
requires daily tending, constant care, and patience.

Today I will slow down my desires and try not to push things
too quickly. With care and attentiveness, I will create an
enduring recovery.

Expecting the world to treat you fairly because you are a good person is a little like expecting the bull not to attack you because you are a vegetarian.

—Dennis Wholey

Some of life's lessons are hard. Just because you are honest with others does not mean they will be honest with you. Just because you hold the door for someone or let someone go ahead of you in traffic does not mean another will do those same things for you. Just because you make time for a person in need does not mean you will be given similar attention. And just because you have stopped using does not mean your family or a loved one will stop criticizing you.

Expecting others to acknowledge the hard work you are doing in recovery and provide you with praise or support—particularly from those you have harmed in the past—is like waiting at an airport for a cruise ship to arrive.

Expectations are unmet desires. Rather than be surprised or disappointed when others do not behave or respond to you in the same way you have treated them, let go of the desire or expectation.

If I feel good about myself, praise and recognition from others is not necessary. If I treat others well and attend to those things I need, I can feel good about myself.

There are always two voices sounding in our ears—the voice of fear and the voice of confidence. One is the clamor of the senses, the other is the whispering of the higher self.
—*Charles B. Newcomb*

During one Sunday service, a religious leader asked his congregation to pray for something that would make each of their lives better. Then he asked them to share what they had prayed for.

One woman had just lost her job and had no health benefits nor income. She said she had prayed for a new job. A man was concerned about his wife's serious illness and had prayed for her recovery. A mother shared a prayer for her adult son to give up drinking and become a better father to his children.

One member's prayer was unique. She had asked for the ability to let go of any fears, doubts, or insecurities she might have and to trust that no matter what happened to her, it was the right thing. Having trust that your life is under the care of the divine oversight of something greater than yourself can free you from worry and assure you that all is well.

I still my fears through prayer. Each day, I pray for the wisdom to be able to live in each moment and to handle whatever comes my way.

The Fox and the Stork

One evening the fox invited his friend the stork to dinner. For a joke the fox prepared soup and served it in a shallow dish. The fox could easily lap up the soup. But the stork, with its long bill, went hungry. The fox gave the stork a sly grin and said, "I am so sorry. It seems as if the soup is not to your liking."

"There is no need to apologize," the stork replied. "I would like to repay your hospitality and invite you to dinner tomorrow night."

The next evening, the stork served the fox a meal in a long-necked jar with a narrow mouth. The stork could easily reach into the jar and eat, but the fox could not and went hungry. "I will not apologize for the dinner," the stork said, "because one bad turn deserves another." After that, the fox and the stork were no longer friends.

The moral of the story: *Revenge may be sweet, but the damage it does cannot be repaired.*

No matter how wronged you may feel by the words or actions of another, remember that revenge, retaliation, and harboring resentment serve no useful purpose.

I will let go of past resentments and consider no one to be my enemy.

Holding onto anger is like grasping a hot coal with the intent of throwing it at someone else—you are the one who gets burned.

—*Buddha*

Anger is, in its essence, a protective response to a perceived hurt. The key word is *perceived*. More often than not, there is no need to protect yourself. But that does not mean your anger should be ignored. When you have a hard time going with the flow, you can say or do hurtful things. When you feel sensitive and others offer advice, you may push them away. When you are at a heightened level of stress or worry, anything that happens or is said to you can be like a match lit to your short fuse. All these things create a life of chaos—both for yourself and for others.

Deal with your anger by talking about what makes you feel angry. Be aware of what can spark anger, and practice a mental countdown during such times. Take a deep breath and count backwards from ten. When you do this, you can replace anger with calmness and focus.

Until you acknowledge there is a price you pay from the fallout caused by your anger, you will not seek ways to effectively change your behavior.

Today I will use a mental countdown whenever I feel angry.

A painful time in our life is what I call a "healing crisis." We are letting go of something old and opening to something new.

—Shakti Gawain

Healing is a combination of three components: letting go of something that has a negative impact on you, believing in yourself, and appreciating the gift of time, to get better—in mind, body, and spirit.

When a cut is healing, pulling the scab off inflicts more hurt. Simply put, healing begins when you leave the cut alone. The same is true of healing yourself. You cannot get better when you stay in difficult situations or associate with unhealthy people. Healing begins when you can let go of the negative people, places, and things in your life so you can free yourself from pain.

Healing also requires time and patience. Focus on each moment by taking care in what you say, what you think, and what you do.

Just as healing is a matter of time, so too is it a matter of opportunity. One of the greatest healing therapies is your connection to yourself. Healing takes place when you open your heart in love and acceptance of who you are becoming through the process of healing.

Healing is the journey I will take today. The destination for this journey will be to know myself better and to love myself more.

There was a period in high school when you had to figure out who you were. You'd think, "Well, I'm not fitting in with this group or that group." And then you'd start to examine your own inventory and wonder, "Is there anything I can do that is going to make me desirable?"
— David Letterman

When you were young, you may have done things to fit in that were not reflections of who you were, but of how you thought others wanted you to be.

While those days may be well in the past, it is not unusual to still feel inferior or not good enough. Today, with no addictions to use as a comforting crutch, you may be at a loss for how to handle workplace interactions or social situations.

There is one place where you need not worry about fitting in. You are a member of a program that treats all equally. There is no need to feel inferior or to strive to change just to please others. Even when you are uncomfortable or at a loss for words, take heart in the knowledge that you will always belong.

I will not worry about what others think of me. I believe that who I am becoming is who I need to be. I take comfort in the sense of belonging the program gives me.

I am an idealist. I don't know where I'm going, but I'm on my way.

—Carl Sandburg

To paraphrase the Big Book, when you focus on what is bad in a day, you may view your day as a bad one. But when you focus on what is good in a day, you can view your day as a good one. It is all in how you look at things and how you will interpret what you have been given: good or bad.

The program teaches that in order to be clean and sober, you need to conquer negativity and negative phrases. Recovery is not focused on such advisories as "You should not drink or drug." Instead, recovery is focused on a simple statement: "Just for today, I will not use or abuse." That statement allows you to make a choice and shift your perspective from what you cannot do to what you can and will do.

When you make choices based on optimism, you empower yourself in ways that enable you to see your life as one that is filled with opportunities and growth.

Today I will change my interpretation of what I have been given from the negative to the positive. I will begin each day with a positive outlook, and I will bring positive energy into all that I do and say.

God gave you a gift of 86,400 seconds today. Have you used one to say "thank you"?

—William A. Ward

Thinking that you are thankful for something a person has done for you or for a gift you have received is not the same as expressing your gratitude. It is taking without giving back. Unexpressed gratitude, it has been said, "is plain, old-fashioned ingratitude."

Even when you pray to your Higher Power, you may forget to add at the end of your prayer, "Thank you." Even when it seems that your prayers go unanswered, you need to trust they have been heard. So to express gratitude to your Higher Power following a prayer conveys your understanding that a divine power is always there for you and always ready to listen to your thoughts and needs.

Begin the day by thinking of those things you often take for granted, and then offer thanks for them. Make today the time when you express long-overdue gratitude to the human angels in your life. Throughout the day, add the words "thank you" whenever others assist you. And be sure to remember to include an expression of gratitude during your prayers to thank your Higher Power for being there.

I will use the words "thank you" for all of the gifts I receive today, be they big or small.

The difficult things of this world must once have been easy;
the great things of this world must once have been small.
Set about difficult things while they are still easy; do great
things while they are still small.

—Taoism

Before you entered the program, your life was likely filled
with chaos and disruption. Because your top priority was
your addiction, everything else became secondary. Today
you are free from your addiction, but you may still live
with chaos and disruption. You may not pay attention to
things until they reach a crisis stage.

Handling events before they get out of hand is like
practicing preventive medicine. Rather than be rushed
to the hospital with a heart attack, it is better to eat right
every day and exercise. Taking such action can avert future trouble or keep a bad situation from growing worse.

Today resolve to be a troubleshooter rather than a
troublemaker. Think of those things you usually put off
until the last minute. Consider what tasks you have not
yet completed. Pay attention to those who need your
attention. Ask, "What needs to be taken care of today?"
Then step up and face your responsibilities.

I would rather handle things effectively than move from one
crisis to the next. Today I will take care of my personal and
professional responsibilities while they are still manageable.

Just because you have a . . . handicap . . . doesn't mean that you can't be happy; it just means that it takes a lot of work to figure out how to do that.

—Jodie Foster

One day a blind woman prepared to cross a street. But as she did, her cane made contact with a car parked in the crosswalk. "Who owns this car?" she demanded in a loud voice. "This car is in my way. Can't anyone notice I am blind?" A man tapped her on the arm. "I am blind, too," he told her. "But my dog and I would be happy to take you across the street."

The woman drew her arm back from his touch. "This is not right," she snapped. "Yes, it is wrong," agreed the blind man. "But why not cross the street safely with us?"

Having a visible handicap, or an invisible one such as an addiction, can be stressful. You have to work extra hard doing things most people take for granted. Yet rather than bemoan the difficulties and challenges you face, you can be thankful for those who offer help by providing a guiding arm, holding a door open, or offering a seat in a crowded meeting.

Today I will accept the assistance of those who reach out to me.

In general, any form of exercise, if pursued continuously, will help to train us in perseverance.

—Mao Tse-Tung

One of New Zealand's greatest runners, Murray Halberg, once won an alarm clock in a race. The problem was, the prize was for second place. Every day thereafter, Halberg never had a problem waking up and training. The clock symbolized his not-fast-enough performance and gave him the incentive to push himself harder in his training.

As much as you understand the value of daily exercise, you may find it hard to keep up your motivation and commitment. One day without exercise turns into three, then into a week, until months go by without engaging in any physical activity. But when you think about exercise as something as valuable to you as your recovery, you can figure out ways to stay committed to daily workouts. A workout buddy or group exercises can provide fellowship of like-minded individuals.

If you prefer to exercise alone, you may find it helpful to keep a daily log of what you do. Think of this as your exercise "inventory." Or you can sign up for the services of a personal trainer at a local gym or YMCA, who can function as your physical health and well-being "sponsor."

Today I will consider ways that will help to develop my motivation and dedication to exercise each day.

The search for happiness is one of the chief sources of unhappiness.

—*Eric Hoffer*

Think about all of the components that go into creating a glowing campfire. There is the pit that must be dug in order to contain the fire. There are the sticks of varying sizes that must be gathered together and organized in the pit. And then there is the spark from a match that is needed to ignite the sticks. From this creation of a campfire are many by-products: something that cooks food, something that warms the body, something that produces an exquisite aroma, and something that provides light in the darkness.

Happiness can be seen in much the same way. It is a by-product of all of the positive and enjoyable things you gather together each day. It is the effort you exert into seeking the treasures of life. And it is the spark you add to your day-to-day existence.

Happiness is an outcome of the effort you put into life. It exists in the harmonious relationships you create, in the sense of purpose that awakens you in the morning, and in the feeling of connection to all of life.

Today I will remember that happiness is not something to strive for; rather, it is something I create. It is the outcome of purposeful living.

To fall into a habit is to begin to cease to be.
—*Miguel de Unamuno*

Sometimes it may feel as if your habit is constantly in your thoughts. You may find yourself driving by old haunts or running into people from your past. Or a scene from a movie or television show may spark a mental journey down old habit memory lane.

Such times of remembrance—whether they cause you to feel pain, regret, sadness, yearning, or even happiness—are natural. Even though you have let go of your habits, they are still a part of your psyche and memory bank. That means that they will always be with you, even when they are no longer your constant companions.

That is why it is so important to identify yourself in meetings as someone who has an addiction. Through this acknowledgment you weaken the hold habits have on you and strengthen your resistance to temptation. You are also striving to minimize those times when memories of your habits gain unexpected entry into your mind. Telling yourself and others, with openness and honesty, that you are an addict confronts your habits head-on. It says, "I recognize what my habits are, and I will not let them rule my life or ruin my day."

Expression, rather than suppression, will help to free my mind from the control of my addictions.

Total absence of humor renders life impossible.
—*Colette*

What one person considers funny can be quite different from what another appreciates as humor. Think about fellow addicts who, despite having a very tragic story that brought them into the program, can, with their wit and wry way of telling a story, bring laughter to a meeting. Then think about those who continually shed tears at meetings or with whom conversations always turn to the dark side, the things that cannot be done, and the impossibilities of life. Which person do you choose to be around? Which person seems to impart the greatest advice?

There are certainly those in meetings who act as if they are playing a room in Vegas. They provide entertainment, but after a while you may feel like saying, "Enough already." Too, there are those who rarely talk about anything with depth and keep what they say at a very surface level. With such people you may feel like asking, "But how do you feel?"

Striking a balance between being lighthearted and humorous and having a depth of feeling is part of the delicate dance of recovery. The greatest benefit comes when the two coexist. Feelings enable you to see the truth; humor keeps the truth from becoming too overwhelming.

Today I will strive to take things with a more lighthearted approach and outlook.

Long afterwards, she was to remember that moment when her life changed its direction. It was not predestined; she had a choice.

—Evelyn Anthony

It used to be that choices in life were quite limited. The purchase of a consumable product, for instance, often boiled down to this one or that one.

But today you exist in a world that has an over-whelming amount of choices. Do you want to drive to a particular destination? You can take any number of routes—toll road, highway, back roads, shortest route, fastest route. Do you want to order takeout for lunch? You can choose from Italian, Chinese, Thai, and more. Do you want to watch a movie? You can go to a multiplex or sit in the comfort of your living room and find a movie on cable TV or through an on-demand service.

While everyday life is much more complicated, the program offers clarity and consistency. It urges you to keep things simple in your recovery. The Twelve Steps are easy to understand and follow. Gathering in fellowship to share stories, experiences, and wisdom provides great support. Your choice to be in recovery is a simple one—one that you renew every day.

Today I choose to be clean and sober. I will show my commitment to this choice in all of my actions.

To do the same thing over and over again is not only bore-
dom; it is to be controlled by rather than to control what
you do.

—*Heraclitus*

Cartoonist Leigh Rubin conveys a humorous look at boredom in his comic drawing of a goldfish in a bowl, entitled
"Diary of a Fish." The diary runs from Sunday through
Saturday and conveys the same entries about how the fish
spent its day: It swam. It ate. It slept.

Now you may view your existence as one of dull routines, causing you to feel bored and disinterested in life.
When someone asks, "So what's new with you?" you may
let out a sigh and mumble, "Same old, same old." But the
things that once partnered with your addiction can be
transformed and refashioned to add freshness and richness to your life. Being spontaneous can open you up to
new experiences. Taking a risk can offer learning and
challenge. Doing something out of the ordinary can provide an opportunity to grow. Embracing unpredictability
can strengthen your ability to flow with life's challenges.

If you feel there is nothing special going on in your
life, do something different from what you did yesterday.
Even simple changes can provide enough stimulation to
make life more interesting and enjoyable.

Today I will make an effort to change the scenery of my life.

I generally avoid temptation unless I can't resist it.
—*Mae West*

Each time you run errands, you face a multitude of challenges to your recovery. Grocery store aisles with tasty junk foods and sugary treats tempt your desire to overeat. Liquor store displays with beverages in pretty bottles beckon you to drink. Shopping malls are filled with store displays trying to convince you to take out your credit card. Scratch tickets seem to reach out from their cases, teasing that you can be rich beyond your wildest dreams.

Those who are not in recovery are tempted just the same. However, their lives are not ruled by an addiction. They can easily turn away from unhealthy foods or purchase a single bottle of wine and make it last for a week. They can stick to their spending limits and avoid money games with nearly impossible odds of winning.

So how do you handle such temptations? Recovery teaches that it is not enough to simply stop an addiction. You also need to develop an understanding and acceptance of how your addiction caused you—and others— great harm. The more conscious you are of the power of your addiction, the greater your willpower can be to ignore the temptations around you.

My will to overcome my addiction is greater than any temptation I face.

Religion is for people who are afraid they'll go to hell.
Spirituality is for people who have been there.
                                                    —*Teen Anon saying*

Many times you may read newspaper stories in which neighbors describe someone who has committed a despicable crime as one who attended church regularly. You may wonder, "How could someone who believes in God act out so horribly?"

Consider the meaning of spirituality. Is closeness to God measured by the number of times you go to church? Is reading religious teachings the same as applying such knowledge in everyday life? Spirituality is not measured by who you are, but by how you live. Sinning, and then asking God to forgive your sins, conveys an attitude of self-importance—that because you have reached out to God, you earn a "free pass."

But asking for forgiveness and then changing your actions so you can protect yourself and others from harm is putting God's help into action. Getting down on your knees and asking God for help is the first step in connecting with a Higher Power. But rising up and doing everything you can to follow a path of good and appropriate behavior is putting God's guidance into action.

It has been said, "No God, no peace; know God, know peace."
Today I accept that God's will and God's knowledge need to be
my will and my knowledge.

There are no atheists on turbulent airplanes.

—Erica Jong

Before you came into the program, your relationship with a Higher Power may have been fleeting or peripheral. You may have felt your prayers went unanswered because problems remained. Maybe you only reached out to God when you experienced a great loss, such as the death of a loved one.

Once you entered the program, you may have flinched whenever you heard the word *God* or were encouraged to join in reciting the Serenity Prayer. Maybe you were reluctant to open the Big Book because it resembled a religious text. Perhaps the openness with which members talked about a Higher Power made you feel uncomfortable because you had not developed such a relationship.

When you make the decision to turn your life and your will over to the care of God—however you define and understand that Being—it is your belief that provides you with a new path in life. Your Higher Power will always be there for you, no matter what path you take. But the path that most directly leads to a Higher Power is the one that helps you the most.

I believe in a Higher Power. I turn my life and my will over to a Higher Power and ask for guidance in making choices to improve the quality of my life.

APRIL

Made a searching and fearless moral inventory of ourselves.
—*Step Four*

A prayer is a humble and heartfelt communication with a power greater than yourself. A prayer can admit a weakness, communicate a need, or convey praise and gratitude. Prayers can unburden your heart, give you strength and courage, and deepen your faith and trust in a Higher Power. Use the following prayer as you work on your understanding and acceptance of Step Four.

Step Four Prayer

Higher Power, because of my addiction I have made many mistakes. I have committed many wrongs. I have hurt others. I have not lived up to my potential. There is no one to blame, for I alone have done these things. But I am ready to embark on a journey that will bring me deeper into my self. I am filled with purpose, even though I know I will see many things for which I am not proud.

Through your help, Higher Power, I will also see the good in me. I will see that I am a human being with flaws and imperfections. But I will also strive to see my strengths and talents. I am ready to make an inventory of my self. I ask for the honesty and the strength to complete this task. Higher Power, thank you for listening to my prayer.

An ice-packing plant in Chicago burned down years ago.
This building had all the material inside capable of ex-
tinguishing the fire, but it was in unavailable form; it was
frozen.

—Allen Unruh

Experiencing any form of loss—of a job, a habit, a loved
one, health, financial stability, and more—can be trau-
matic. But how you react to the trauma determines how
long you will feel its effects. When you deny or suppress
painful feelings, you keep the misery deep within you.
In essence, you freeze your emotions, but you also freeze
that moment. So when you suppress sadness rather than
openly grieve, you may experience emotions from the
loss for a longer period of time.

You may justify emotional freezing because you feel
you need to be strong for others or because you think you
will not be able to handle those feelings. But emotional
pain is normal to feel with any loss. The more deeply you
care, the more profoundly the loss will affect you.

First acknowledge that it does hurt like hell to lose
someone you love or something you treasured. It is healthy
to admit you cared so much. Then, you must grieve. You
need to let your tears flow and allow yourself to feel.

I respond to the pain of my loss in a healthy way—by expressing,
not suppressing, my grief.

Rough weather makes good timber.
—*Appalachian adage*

When you journey up a mountain path, you see many types of tree growth. In the lower part of the mountain are small saplings just starting their growth as well as towering trees. Higher up, trees are smaller. Some cling precariously to the side of the mountain, growing out of a small patch of earth between cracks in a rock.

Journey up the same path after a spring snowmelt and you may see a different view. In the lower regions, once towering trees have been felled by the power of raging water, and small saplings have been snapped at their base. But up higher, small trees are still firmly in place, steadfast in their grip between the rocks.

The lesson in this is that the strongest can survive. Like the trees, you are ever-exposed to the storms and difficulties of daily life. Will you be overwhelmed by life's adversities, easily felled by such things, or will you develop an inner strength and resiliency that will enable you to work through each difficulty? Today recognize that challenges in life are inevitable. Brace yourself for them, hold firm to your position, and never let them dislodge you.

I am a survivor who can withstand the difficulties in life. I do this with strength and with dignity.

We should be careful to get out of an experience only the wisdom that is in it . . . lest we be like the cat that sits down on a hot stove-lid. She will never sit down on a hot stove-lid again . . . but also she will never sit down on a cold one any more.

—Mark Twain

Think about a time when you became sick after eating something. How soon after you felt better did you choose to eat the same thing? Maybe it was weeks, months—or perhaps you have never eaten it again. Your experience convinced you to avoid that food, even though it may have been harmless.

Abstinence from your addiction does not necessarily translate into abstinence from all of the things associated with it. You may have engaged in your addiction at parties, but that does not mean you can never attend another party or that you can no longer go out with friends and have a good time. A former habit of gambling on sports does not mean you can never enjoy watching another game.

While it is important to make choices that support your need to be free of your addiction, be sure that the choices you make are not too all-encompassing.

I will reflect on what experience has taught me to make choices that will be inclusive, rather than exclusive.

Honesty has come to mean the privilege of insulting you to your face without expecting redress.

—Judith Martin

A comedian tells a story about a dying man who calls his wife to his side. "Honey, I have something to confess," he tells her. "For many years I have not been faithful to you. I needed to tell you that before I died." The wife smiles down at him. "Baby, I know you have not been faithful to me."

"You knew?" the man asks. "Yes," she replies. "That is why I have poisoned you."

As laudable as honesty is, it does have a downside. The truth can be hurtful and even harmful. Before you choose to be honest with another, first consider whether your words will make only you feel better. Do you need to say something simply to get it off your chest, or will you convey helpful information for the person receiving the information? When you think before you speak, you may discover that leaving something unsaid might be the best option. But if you are confronted with a direct question, it is best to answer with honesty even if the truth may end up hurting the other person. Lying will not serve you well if, in the future, the truth comes out.

I will be honest with others, but will temper my honesty with compassion.

Though it sounds absurd, it is true to say that I felt younger at sixty than I had felt at twenty.

—Ellen Glasgow

The aging process has been described as a "slippery slope," "all downhill from here," and "the beginning of the end." But such phrases are not necessarily negative. Imagine that the slippery slope represents an ascent rather than a descent. Climbing to the top of a vista enables a much clearer view. So perhaps aging can be seen as a time to rise up and see all that is around you.

"It's all downhill from here" can represent a time of smooth sailing—one that is free from the anxiety, in-experience, and confusion of youth, when you experience life with less angst and greater gusto. "It's the beginning of the end" can offer a time for new opportunities and challenges. As one decade of your life draws to a close, a new decade opens up before you.

There are those who, as they age, seem to fade away and others who seem to have more spring in their step and a brighter twinkle in their eyes. You are, as another phrase conveys, "Only as old—or as young—as you feel."

I will not act my age or behave in ways that others think I should. I will embrace my years with a positive outlook.

Solitary shots should be ignored, but when they come from several directions, it's time to pay attention. As someone once said, "If one calls you a donkey, ignore him. If two call you a donkey, check for hoof prints. If three call you a donkey, get a saddle."

—Marshall Shelley

You may have grown up in a home where a parent frequently said, "You're stupid" or "You'll never amount to anything." But did every single person in your life—all of your family members, your teachers, your neighbors, and your friends—say the same things? Chances are the negative messages came from one or two sources.

Such negative statements, especially from people whose acceptance and approval are important to you, can have a lasting impact. But remember, such statements do not define who you are unless you let them. Chances are those saying such things have low self-esteem and feel more comfortable by criticizing you than by taking a look in the mirror.

Focus on doing things to help you feel better about yourself. Work toward strengthening a healthy level of self-esteem so you are better able to prevent outside influences from shaping or dictating how you feel.

I will not adopt negative messages. I will not give them the power to define who I am or to destroy who I am becoming.

Each morning the day lies like a fresh shirt on our bed. . . .
The happiness of the next twenty-four hours depends upon
our ability, on waking, to pick it up.

—Walter Benjamin

At times you may need to look back and reflect upon your actions and behaviors of the past, or look ahead so you can develop goals for the future. But the only place where you truly exist is in the here and now.

To fully appreciate each day, begin by having few expectations. While it is important to consider what you need to do at work or at home, and to plan ahead to fulfill certain projects or responsibilities, strive to be flexible about how you expect the day to go. This will help alleviate disappointment from unmet expectations and make you more open to new discoveries.

Start your day with a prayer—one of thankfulness for the day's beauty, freshness, and promise. Do what needs to be done to prepare for your day. Then head out the door in a positive frame of mind. Take on the day as if it were your last on earth. Embrace it fully. Live it fully. What lies ahead of you is a gift for you to unwrap and enjoy.

I will begin the day with a positive attitude and with an openness to experience all that lies ahead.

The little reed, bending to the force of the wind, soon stood upright again when the storm had passed over.

—*Aesop*

Plants flourish in a garden that receives the right amount of sunlight and water, as well as a well-balanced soil. Manure and compost can be excellent fertilizers, although it is ironic that something so repellent is vital to sustaining life. The same holds true with misfortunes, failures, and disappointments. Such things are as beneficial to you as manure and compost are to a garden. They facilitate the growth of positive things. Fortune can arise out of misfortune, success can rise up from failure, and fulfillment can be more fully appreciated through the experience provided by disappointment.

In Chinese language the symbol for the word *crisis* denotes a duality: "a moment of danger and of opportunity." This symbol conveys that every crisis can be viewed as both an enemy—a threat to your vital resources—and an ally—an experience that challenges you to make change.

Whenever you feel intimidated by any of life's crises, accept the challenge. Greet it like a reed in the wind. Bend through the adversity until it has passed. Then stand upright once again, a stronger person for the experience.

I will accept the challenges during times of adversity so I may weather them and grow stronger in the process.

True solitude is the din of birdsong, seething leaves, whirling colors, or a clamor of tracks in the snow.
                                    —*Edward Hoagland*

For most people, the first and only choice in life is to be with someone or to have someone be there for you. There is no second choice or any "second-best" scenario. You are either in the Land of We, or you are alone. And who *wants* to be alone? Who *chooses* to be in the Land of Me?

Many important paths presented to you during your journey in recovery and in life are narrow, winding, steep, and hard to negotiate. They cannot be traveled by walking hand-in-hand with another. These paths must be explored walking single file—in solitude, silence, and singular contemplation. To avoid these paths simply because they require solitude prevents you from developing self-reliance. Without them, you cannot test your wings.

Recovery teaches you not only how to be alone, but also how to *choose* to be alone. Choosing to be alone builds self-reliance. No one else can do this for you. You must learn to explore your own visions and expand your personal horizons on your own—and when you are alone. In doing so, you become vitally connected to understanding your own capabilities.

Today I will choose moments of solitude so I may test my wings.

Dreams pass into the reality of action. From the action stems the dream again; and this interdependence produces the highest form of living.

—*Anais Nin*

Steve Ross, who put together the Time Warner merger and left millions in his estate when he died, structured his life around being a dream maker. When he was a teenager, he was summoned to his father's deathbed and given this advice: There are those who work all day, those who dream all day, and those who spend an hour dreaming before setting to work to fulfill those dreams. "Go into the third category," his father told him, "because there is virtually no competition."

The biggest roadblock to realizing a dream is the fear you will fail. The second biggest roadblock is the fear you will succeed. Both can keep you mired in the same spot, neither advancing nor retreating from your dreams. But dreams are your hopes and desires for the future. They are symbols of your commitment to who you can become.

So today, go ahead and dream—and then take the steps that will help you to move closer to your dream. You have the power to make a dream come true, but only if you try.

Today I will focus on one of my dreams. I will do at least one thing that will help make this dream a reality.

They also serve who only stand and wait.

—*John Milton*

Volunteers at the Grupo Ecologico de la Costa Verde in Mexico know the value of patience as they guide hatchling turtles back to the sea from their sandy beach nests. Crossing the sand is a crucial part of the imprinting process that brings the turtles back to lay their eggs at the place of their birth.

Moonlight illuminates the course the turtles must take, but they can easily become misdirected by the lights of civilization. Yet they must get to the ocean on their own to complete the imprinting process. So as the time of hatching draws near, volunteers stand and wait for hours near the nests at night until the turtles break free from their shells and slowly emerge from the sand. Then volunteers gently turn the turtles in the right direction and follow their progress, inch by inch, over a period of several hours until the turtles make it to the sea.

The same process can be applied to your recovery. Skimming through the Big Book and rushing through the Twelve Steps will not hasten the restoration of your sanity, health, and wholeness. Your rebirth takes time and requires dedicated patience.

Today I will resist rushing and instead take my time in all that I do. Having patience with myself and with others can be directly applied to the process of my recovery.

We all have big changes in our lives that are more or less a second chance.

—Harrison Ford

Imagine you have a map in your hands, one you have used to guide you through the years. It shows all of your old routes of thinking, feeling, and behaving.

Recovery provides you with a new map, with an unfamiliar destination and different routes. Rather than discard your old map, you may still bring it out from time to time and think how much easier it would be to follow. But until you set forth on the course provided by the new map, you will never know what opportunities await you. You will never understand that your new destination may be more promising and enjoyable than the old one.

Take, for example, the story of Jill Elikann Barad. She wanted to be a surgeon, but fainted her first time in the operating room. After wandering from job to job, she ended up at Mattel where she refashioned a toy that had seen better days. She recreated Barbie and ended up president of the company. "The idea of trying everything is important," she said. "Your experiences come together and make you multidimensional." When you change your map, you change yourself and transform your world into something better.

Today I will trust the map of recovery to guide me in all that I do.

Living our pre-AA active daily lifestyle was akin to switching seats on the Titanic.

—*Anonymous*

Instinctively, every living thing struggles to survive in a world that is not always pleasant and often falls short of being ideal. Even those who stood on the decks of the sinking *Titanic,* who knew in their heads and hearts that their deaths were imminent, clung desperately to any floating object in the hope that they would be rescued.

Recovery presents challenges that can seem overwhelming. You may ask, "How can I survive this?" You may feel, especially in the first few days, as if you are going to die. You may feel that you will fail. You may feel circumstances will never change for the better. But you have survived stressful and difficult times in the past. Although you used drugs or alcohol to numb traumas, past events taught you that you are physically, emotionally, and spiritually much stronger than you think.

Progress in recovery is not made by staying in the same circumstances and expecting them to change, but by changing yourself in order to change your circumstances. You are going someplace, and it may not always be easy to get there. But you have within you the strength to take you there.

The tools of the program give me the tools I need to be strong and to endure.

Mercury and the Woodsman

A woodsman was chopping trees for firewood, but lost his grip and watched the axe sail into a nearby river. He began to weep, for without his axe he could not keep his house warm or cook food.

Mercury decided to help and dove into the river. He brought up a golden axe. "Is this your axe?" Mercury asked, but the woodsman shook his head. Mercury dove again and brought up a silver axe. "Is this your axe?" he asked, but the woodsman again shook his head. Then Mercury brought up a weather-beaten wooden axe. The woodsman told him, "That is my axe." Mercury rewarded the woodsman's honesty by giving him two more axes.

The next day, the woodsman told his story to a friend. The friend went to the river, tossed in his axe, and began to weep. Mercury dove into the river and brought up a golden axe. The man eagerly held out his hand for the axe. But Mercury knew the man was lying and returned the golden axe to the water, leaving the man with none.

The moral of the story: *Honesty is the best policy.*

When you embellish the truth or make up stories, the less trust others will have in you.

I will be truthful in my words and actions at all times.

What is the use of climbing Mount Everest? If you cannot understand that there is something in man which responds to the challenge of this mountain and goes out to meet it . . . then you won't see why we go.
—*George Leigh Mallory*

In experiments with deer mice in captivity, researchers discovered the animals exhibited behaviors that favored decision making. For example, the mice were able to control the lighting in their cages. The mice preferred dim lighting, but if researchers made the cage completely dark, the mice would make the light as bright as possible. If the researchers turned the lights up bright, the mice would make the cage dark. "They cared about choice more than comfort," wrote the researchers. "When given the opportunity to manage their environment, they battled fiercely for control."

When you were using, your habit held you captive by its power over your life. But when you resolved to be free from your addiction, you regained control of your life.

Your daily commitment to the program is one of choice. Abstinence provides a foundation from which your freedom emanates and from which you can make choices—both in your recovery, and in your life.

Today I am grateful for the release from the imprisonment of my addiction. I am free from its control, and free to make choices.

I don't understand people who hide from their past. Everything you live through helps to make you the person you are now.

—Sophia Loren

Two monks were walking when they came upon a woman waiting to cross a stream. One of the monks picked up the woman in his arms and carried her across the stream. The monks then resumed their walking. About a mile down the road, the other monk scolded the first. "We are celibate," he said. "We are not supposed to even look at a woman, let alone pick one up and carry her across a stream. How could you possibly do that?" The first monk replied, "I put that woman down a mile back. Are you still carrying her around with *you?*"

Even though the past is gone, it brought you to where you are today. Without it, you would not be able to envision and work toward a better future. The Steps of the program teach that your past is an integral part of your recovery. You need to remember those you have harmed and make amends to them. You need to admit that your life was unmanageable. And you need to use the past as a platform from which you can seek forgiveness from your Higher Power.

Today I embrace and accept the past as a valuable teacher.

If one is lucky, a solitary fantasy can totally transform one million realities.

—Maya Angelou

Laura Hillenbrand tells about a time when she watched some laborers working on an electrical box. One of the men walked into her side yard, looked around, and then jumped onto a swing her father had hung from a tree. The man, she wrote, "swung peacefully with the biggest grin on his face. Then he jumped off and went back to work."

A well-ordered, predictable day-to-day existence can provide you with much-needed parameters for lessening the chaos you have felt in the past. But strict adherence to a well-ordered existence can leave little room for curiosity, wonder, play, and adventure, which can add lightness to your life.

When you were a child, daydreams provided release from boredom and predictability and gave you the opportunity to ponder "What if" questions. It did not matter where your daydreams took you or if they would come true. You still have the opportunity to daydream today—and even to make your daydreams come true. You can imagine riding a horse across a grassy field—and sign up for a riding lesson. You can imagine being a brave person—and then transfer that energy into your actions today.

Today I will let my daydreams come so I can see a world full of joy and possibilities.

He has not learned the lesson of life who does not every day surmount a fear.

—*Ralph Waldo Emerson*

In his book *Stairway to Success,* Nido R. Qubein reports that a naval aviator once told him that many pilots die because they choose to stay with a disabled aircraft. He writes, "They preferred the familiarity of the cockpit to the unfamiliarity of the parachute, even though the cockpit was a deathtrap."

Whenever you choose to remain with what is familiar, what you have previously tried, or what you already know does not work, you will continue to experience the same outcomes. After all, when you keep doing the things that have never worked with the expectation that things will turn out differently, you are setting yourself up for certain defeat.

Like the pilots, you may feel much safer staying in a familiar environment than by taking the leap and venturing out into the unfamiliar. But if you have not tried something before, how do you know it will fail? It is only when you leave what is familiar and try something you have never tried before that you have the greatest possibility for success. There will be times in your recovery when you simply must face your fears and take the leap.

Today I can feel fearful before I try something new, but I will try it anyway.

Peace is when time doesn't matter as it passes by.
—Maria Schell

Prayer and meditation are used together so often that you may think they are essentially the same thing. But prayer is more of a direct outreach and communication with a divine being, while meditation encourages you to "go within" to create stillness and serenity.

There is no right or wrong way to meditate. Those who exercise—especially long distance runners—often think of their workout as a form of meditation. Others make a ritual out of their meditation by setting aside the same time each day, listening to soothing music, or chanting. Some use deep breathing techniques or yoga poses. Others listen to guided meditation tapes or meditate regularly with others.

But no matter what form your meditation takes, the purpose is to allow time for relaxation and for letting go so you can let your thoughts and emotions run free. You feel and observe what is within you and, in so doing, learn more about your innermost thoughts and feelings. When you do, you can better understand your fears, doubts, insecurities, regrets, and resentments. With this understanding, you can use the tools of the program to decrease the hold these emotions have upon you.

Meditation gives me the chance to learn more about myself. Today I will still my mind to open my mind.

The present is the point of power.

—Kate Green

Think of a recovery challenge you know you need to work on. If you look back to the past, you may consider that what you are currently facing is the same thing you have faced before and were unable to handle it. So you may use that as an excuse to avoid taking action now. If you look ahead to the future, you may consider putting off what you need to do today. Both approaches end up with the same result: you will not be able to handle what you are facing in the present. Do this for all the things on which you need to work, and you end up with an enormous accumulation of things you must eventually handle.

Living in the present moment means looking at what needs to be done in the present and taking care of those things. Taking action when action is needed provides you with more time, because as you take care of what you need to do today, you will have more time to handle the tasks of tomorrow. What have you been putting off in your recovery?

I will not let the things I need to do pile up. Today I will take care of something that needs my time and attention.

Our feelings are our most genuine paths to knowledge.
—Audre Lorde

There may be times when your emotions overwhelm you. You may wish you simply could not feel. But what would that mean—to live without any feeling? You would not feel sadness or happiness. You would not feel tired, and you would not feel refreshed and energized. You would not feel joy or love, or experience the unique connection between people. And you would not feel pride, confidence, compassion, or a whole range of feelings that add to the experience of living.

Feelings provide you with valuable information. Some of that information can be lifesaving. For example, the ability to feel physical pain helps you to avoid further injury. Other feelings are more subtle. Feelings of sadness give you information that there is something you need to grieve. When you feel fear, the message is that something or someone is causing you to feel cautious. When you feel love, you are urged to open your heart to another.

Without your feelings, you would not have any knowledge about yourself. You would have a life free of emotions, but your existence would be robotic. You would not be able to connect with anything or anyone, and your world would be silenced.

Today I will let my emotions teach me something about myself.

Without faith, nothing is possible. With it, nothing is impossible.

—*Mary McLeod Bethune*

Have you ever seen the wind? You can see a kite flying up above, a sailboat navigating waters with air-filled sails, birds dipping and turning as they navigate wind currents, or leaves shivering on trees. Such things let you know the wind exists.

Faith is like the wind; it is something you feel but cannot see. Faith is not comprised of logic and reason, but a trust in something greater than yourself. Faith exists when you can see the beauty of life all around you—in budding flowers, a cloudless sky, a majestic ocean. It provides you with the strength to face a challenge you feel is insurmountable, and yet you conquer it. It is there when you feel that daylight will never come, and dawn breaks.

Faith is the belief that most things are possible. It gives you strength to steer the strong winds of change and allows you to find comfort in the calming breeze of God's presence. Faith is trust that good will triumph over evil, that your sins can be forgiven, that your wrongdoings can be righted, and that the storms of your life can be navigated.

I have faith that I am being guided in my life by a presence greater than myself. Through this faith, I trust that anything is possible.

I was thought to be "stuck up." I wasn't. I was just sure of myself.

—Bette Davis

Do you remember the children's story about the little engine that could? By chanting "I think I can, I think I can," the little engine succeeded in traversing a difficult line of tracks and was filled with pride.

Confidence is built by beginning any task with a frame of mind based on "I think I can." Phrases such as "I should," "I ought," or "I might" are not confidence-building words because they express doubt in your abilities and leave the door open to the failure you are likely to expect. Know that you may not always succeed on the first try, but what you learn from that attempt is not failure. Rather, you gain knowledge on how you can approach the task again, and come closer to achieving success.

Remember that the greatest challenge in your life has been entering a program of recovery. You are like the little engine that could—and did. Each day you are clean and sober, you have lived by the words "I think I can." Continue to build your confidence by remembering what it took to get to where you are right now. With this confidence, you *can* get to where you need to go.

Each day I build confidence in my abilities to face and conquer challenges.

Striving for excellence motivates you; striving for perfection is demoralizing.

—Harriet Braiker

Beavers are often considered perfect engineers. The dams they create out of sticks and branches, green vegetation, and mud can still raging rivers and create a unique underwater living environment. They are dedicated workers that immediately take action when humans or natural elements conspire to destroy their dams. Even dams that have been broken down repeatedly are rebuilt.

Even beavers are not perfect as their dams do break. It might be better to think of them as tireless in their quest to create optimal survival conditions. Their dams are not works of beauty, nor is there one perfect dam-building pattern. But each dam is purposeful and functional.

Similarly, how you approach recovery determines the level of your success. If you strive to do everything perfectly, chances are little or nothing you can accomplish will result in the perfect outcome you desire. But if you work tirelessly at your recovery, to build and rebuild whenever necessary, and to create the best possible life for yourself, then you will accomplish much. Success is measured by your dedication to see your work through to completion, even if completion comes after several tries.

I will strive for achievement and success in all that I do, rather than for perfection.

When you cease to make a contribution you begin to die.
—*Eleanor Roosevelt*

Do you consider yourself to be charitable when you give away old clothing and the things you no longer want? Do you feel a sense of righteousness when you write a check to a nonprofit organization? While these are good and laudable things to do, such actions keep you at a distance from those receiving your charity. It is one thing to pack up a bag full of clothing and put it into the chute of a metal container; it is entirely another to offer your time and provide direct care—the greatest gift those in need can receive.

George Sand once wrote, "Charity degrades those who receive it and hardens those who dispense it." It cannot be easy for someone who has next to nothing to accept the material goods of another.

To be of greater use to others, set aside time to interact with the elderly at a senior center, offer tutoring services to homeless children, or serve meals at a shelter. Such things can open your eyes to the needs of others so you can see the difference your contributions truly make.

Today I will consider ways in which I can truly contribute to those in need. Then I will devote time to providing my attention and care.

Love doesn't just sit there, like a stone, it has to be made, like bread; re-made all the time, made new.
—Ursula K. Le Guin

Most people consider love as a word that describes romantic feelings or those of a sexual nature. But love is the opposite of hate and, in that context, can be thought of as an emotion that replaces feelings of animosity. It is an emotion that can sometimes be refashioned in situations where it can be helpful. With this definition in mind, think how different your life would be if you could see the positive in every challenge, if you loved everyone and everything in it.

Consider that when you feel hatred for something or someone, it affects your entire emotional outlook. It is hard, for example, to hate your job and have a positive attitude in other areas of your life. But if you reframe this hate with love, you lessen negative feelings and keep negativity from spilling over into other areas of your life.

While you may really hate your job, by thinking about loving it you can consider things about the job that are positive and, in so doing, change your outlook about the job—and in other areas of your life.

Today I will replace hate with love so I can let in positive rather than negative feelings.

If life is a bowl of cherries, what am I doing in the pits?
—*Erma Bombeck*

An excellent illustration of optimism comes from Portia Nelson, in her book of poetry, *There's a Hole in My Sidewalk: The Romance of Self-Discovery.* In her poem "Autobiography in Five Short Chapters," Nelson describes a hole in the sidewalk that confronts her each time she walks down the street. The first time she walks down the street, she falls into the hole. The second time she pretends she does not see the hole, but falls into it nonetheless. The third time she falls in, calling the tumble a habit. The fourth time, she walks around the hole. In the fifth and final chapter, she walks down another street.

Nelson, who achieved fame as a singer, songwriter, and actress, wrote the book of poetry as a breast cancer survivor. Later on in life, throat and tongue cancer robbed her of her voice, but not her talent for songwriting and scoring musicals and films.

There are thousands of people who, each day, approach a multitude of problems, afflictions, and difficulties with an optimistic outlook. They refashion their lives so they can continue to live with a positive attitude and enjoyment.

Today I will not allow the circumstances of my life or the challenges I face to destroy my cheerfulness or my ability to reinvent myself.

Proximity was their support; like walls after an earthquake they could fall no further for they had fallen against each other.

—*Elizabeth Bowen*

Native American women often were responsible for a chore that had considerable value to the survival of the tribe—planting. Without crops to grow and harvest, there would be little food to eat in the winter and the tribe would be in danger of starvation. If a woman was sick and unable to begin the spring planting, she would invite all of the members of the tribe to a feast and ask them to plant the fields for her.

The ailing woman knew her tribe would be there to help her, and she made certain everyone had a full belly so they could work hard in the fields. Both sides benefited from the arrangement of mutual support.

The program offers similar mutual support. When one member is feeling weak, the others share their strength. Even when one has experienced a temporary relapse and returns, the group welcomes the member with open arms, providing much-needed acceptance. Without such support, the infrastructure of the group would not be as strong. Without such connection to one another, there would be many individuals, but no whole.

I am thankful for the support I am given and the support I give to others.

Our lives teach us who we are.

—*Salman Rushdie*

If someone were to ask you, "Who are you, without your job title?" or "What do you know about yourself?" or "What are the qualities that make up who you are?" such questions might be difficult to answer. What is within you is what your addiction has long suppressed. What is within you is what you need to discover, or rediscover, in working through Step Four.

You may not realize that you are filled with ideas and creativity. You have a depth of feelings. You are a storehouse of memories. You have talents. You have experience. You are so much more than you could ever imagine. You have wisdom that goes beyond textbooks and degrees as well as strengths that have yet to be discovered.

To grow wiser means to know better who you are. That is the purpose of Step Four. When you immerse yourself in a searching and fearless moral inventory as part of your work in the program, you will discover things about yourself that you had not realized or have long suppressed. You will discover truths that you have long covered up with lies. And you will experience greater understanding about yourself in ways you never have before.

I am ready to find out who I am so I can discover who I can be.

MAY

Admitted to God, to ourselves, and to another human being the exact nature of our wrongs.

—*Step Five*

A prayer is a humble and heartfelt communication with a power greater than yourself. A prayer can admit a weakness, communicate a need, or convey praise and gratitude. Prayers can unburden your heart, give you strength and courage, and deepen your faith and trust in a Higher Power. Use the following prayer as you work on your understanding and acceptance of Step Five.

Step Five Prayer

Higher Power, I have undertaken a searching and fearless moral inventory. I have learned much about myself, and I have come face to face with the effects of my addiction.

Higher Power, thank you for the strength you have given me so I could accomplish this task. Your guidance has helped me see the wrongs I have committed. I now understand what is right.

I ask for your forgiveness for the harm I have done. I pray that you will look upon me with kindness and mercy. With your help, I can admit—with complete honesty and respect—the exact nature of my wrongdoings to you and to someone I trust. I humbly ask for your guiding light to show me the path ahead. Through your guidance, I will make progress in my recovery. Higher Power, thank you for listening to my prayer.

When the way comes to an end, then change—having changed, you pass through.

—*I Ching*

A Zen parable relates the story of a young monk who enters the monastery. Eager to begin his new life so he can attain spiritual fulfillment, he asks the head monk to provide him with some guidance. The head monk asks, "Have you eaten your breakfast?" "Yes, I have," the young monk replies, to which the head monk says, "Then go wash your bowl."

Fulfillment can be thought of as the outcome of executing something in a way that brings closure to it. With such fulfillment comes a sense of achievement that helps build self-confidence and facilitate change.

When the young monk is told to eat breakfast and wash his bowl, he learns that spiritual fulfillment is something that will not be attained immediately or may never even reach a point of completion. Fulfillment is ongoing and something he must tend to each day. Your recovery can be seen in much the same way. One form of fulfillment comes when you have reached the end of a day in which you have remained free from your habit. Another comes when you do the work required in the Steps.

Each morning I renew my energy and seek fulfillment through the program, then reflect upon my accomplishments at the end of the day.

*People have a hard time letting go of their suffering. Out of
a fear of the unknown, they prefer suffering that is familiar.*
—*Thich Nhat Hanh*

Each time you engaged in your habit, a link on a chain
was created. Over time, more and more links were added
until the chain that bound you to the habit was strong
and it prevented you from moving about freely. It impris-
oned and enslaved you.

The process of letting go in recovery is one in which
you remove, one by one, each link in the chain of your
addiction. If you came into the program knowing your
decision to be free from your habit was the right one,
you started your recovery with a deep determination and
conscious commitment. And you have discovered that,
by letting go and letting both your Higher Power and the
program work through you, you have kept your focus
strong. You have been able to slowly break free from this
chain.

But if you entered the program kicking and screaming
or thought of your recovery as something you would do
to prove that you could take a break from your habit,
then you may be finding it harder to break free. Until you
completely surrender your will and let go, you are still
enslaved by your habit.

*I will let go and completely surrender. Through this action, I will
find greater freedom.*

One sits uncomfortably on a too comfortable cushion.
—*Lillian Hellman*

After a long period of spring rain that keeps you indoors, you yearn for sunshine and fresh air, to be doing something other than sitting around the house. You want change. After several hours spent in front of the computer or the television, you are eager to do something different. You want change. After eating the same leftovers for three days, you want to eat something different. You want change.

Staying in one place for too long deprives you of challenges and new adventures. Change provides welcome relief from monotony. But add too much change, and you can become overwhelmed. That is why it is important to seek a balance in the changes you are making.

With balance, you can experience both times of monotony as well as times of challenge and activity. What you change and when you change is within your control. To ensure balance, remember that change is not accomplished in one day, but over an extended period of time. Consider ways in which you can devote time to making changes and times when you take a break so you can start anew. Welcome the changes you need to make and remember that without them, your life would be stagnant.

I welcome change but do not let it overrun my life.

Confusion is a word we have invented for an order which is not understood.

—Henry Miller

Recovery is a process of gaining better understanding of the truth about your addiction and how it affected your life and the lives of others, the truth about how the tools of the program work, and the truth that arises from gaining greater knowledge and understanding.

You may find that many things in the past that you once accepted as truth are now untrue, such as lies you told yourself or things that were covered up by others. Sometimes it may seem that you are trying to re-learn so many things that it is easy to become confused and overwhelmed, and to feel a bit lost.

It is easy to lose your way as you follow the path to recovery. It is not unusual to feel frightened and alone. At such times, others in the program will be there for you. They will pay attention to your confusion and be honest with you. Your Higher Power will also listen to you and guide you toward the truth. All you need to do is ask for guidance from others and pray for God's guidance, and you will find the truth.

When I feel lost, the truth of others, the truth of the program, and the truth of my Higher Power will lead me back to safety.

But buds will be roses, and kittens, cats. . . .
                                          —*Louisa May Alcott*

Think of how a tree grows. From a tiny seed it splits the soil, spreads its roots, and begins its skyward climb. Over time, the trunk widens, the bark becomes firm and thick, the branches spread ever outward. Season after season, the tree continues its growth until, years later, a massive tree has formed.

You are, in many ways, like a tree. But before you entered the program, you were not a very hardy tree. You were rooted in soil that provided you with little nourishment. You were trying to grow within a forest that deprived you of life-sustaining water and sunshine. Your growth was stunted, and your survival was always in doubt.

Recovery, however, has transplanted you to a soil that is rich with nutrients, in a forest with ample room to grow. The illumination is now plentiful so you can grow strong and tall. Your roots are now firmly entrenched in the ground so you can withstand stormy weather. The longer you are in recovery, the deeper your roots will be. You now are part of a forest of fellowship that encourages the growth of one so that all may grow together.

The love and nourishment given by those in the program encourages my growth and strengthens me.

The weak in courage is strong in cunning.
—*William Blake*

At times you may feel that recovery is so hard that you just want to give it a rest. You want to say, "I am over and done with it." You may convince yourself that because you are doing so well—after all, you have not engaged in your habit for a while—you are now safe. Or perhaps you have practically memorized the Big Book or heard the slogans and said the Serenity Prayer so many times that you think, "Yes, I have it. I get it." And so you may stop going to meetings or doing the work you need to do.

But just because you have stopped your habit does not mean you are "cured." Just because you think you know everything there is to know in recovery does not signify completion. To think anything different is to practice self-deception. It is denying that your recovery is a life-long, daily commitment.

Your recovery today can only be done today. You always have the option to return to your former life, but to make that choice means you risk losing everything you have gained. So resolve that, just for today, you will continue to persevere on your road to recovery.

Just for today, I will continue to do the work of my recovery.

There's folks 'ud stand on their heads and then say the fault was i' their boots.

—George Eliot

Who do you blame for where you are today? Perhaps you blame your parents because they were addicts and passed on the disease to you. Maybe you blame a family member for giving you your first drink or experience with a drug. Or maybe you blame a friend who encouraged you to toss aside your studies and responsibilities so you could join them in partying or acting out.

But when you use your recovery as a time to blame others or to seek a scapegoat to point to for causing your addiction, you are only hurting yourself. Blame serves no useful purpose. It is a set of blinders you put on so you cannot see that your recovery is your responsibility. Recovery is not about blaming, but about fixing. Blaming anything or anyone for your addiction only prolongs your misery and keeps you from focusing on how to achieve a better way of living.

Whether it was genes, choice, or circumstances that got you to where you are today, it truly does not matter. You alone are responsible for your recovery.

Today I will not play the blame game. I accept that I am an addict and will do the work I need to do so I can be a recovering addict.

Attention is a tacit and continual compliment.
    —Anne-Sophie Swetchine

When soldiers are ordered to attention, they stand erect and completely still. Their eyes are focused ahead. They are silent. Their attention is completely centered on their leader so they can respond without hesitation to the commands they receive. When you listen to another, your focus needs to be like that of a soldier at attention. Your mind must be free from the clutter of your own thoughts so you can give full attentiveness to the words of another.

There may be times when you are thinking about other things or formulating your response—interfering with your ability to truly listen to others. Or there may be times when your own burdens are all you can handle. To listen to another is an effort you may not be able to make.

But do this often, and you may miss out on the opportunity for human connection to ease your loneliness or isolation. You may lose learning from another's experience, which may be useful in your own life. And you may miss out on nuggets of wisdom that can ease some of the burdens you are carrying.

Today I will put aside my own thoughts and truly listen to the words of another. I will give my undivided attention so I can gain a different perspective and outlook.

My mother wasn't what the world would call a good woman.
She never said she was.

—Boxcar Bertha

Chances are you did not grow up in a home with a mother who was a Carol Brady, June Cleaver, or Claire Huxtable. If you did, you were blessed with love, attention, and care. Your mother was there for you. She made you feel important and noticed, and helped you build your confidence and self-esteem.

But if your mother was an addict herself, abusive, or an enabler to your father's addiction, you lost out on knowing what it felt like to be mothered. If you lost your mother due to divorce or death, such circumstances similarly deprived you of an experience of growth through her guidance. Losing out on the opportunity to build a long-term relationship with your mother is a loss that may never go away.

But no matter what the relationship was or is with your mother, she is still your mother. Have you used the time since you left your childhood home to better understand your relationship with her? Have you been able to let go of what you did not get and accept that you can find love and support in adulthood? Or are you still looking for the mothering you never received?

Today I will forgive my mother and let go of any resentment I might still be feeling toward her.

Rage cannot be hidden, it can only be disassembled.
—*James Baldwin*

In her book *The Tao of Inner Peace,* Diane Dreher tells about a time when she was working as a medical receptionist. One day the office was particularly busy and workers were installing new carpeting. During their lunch hour, the workers forgot to unplug an iron and it burned into the floorboards. Dreher rushed to the smell of smoke and quickly unplugged the iron. When the doctors returned from lunch and smelled the smoke, they erupted in anger. Long after Dreher had unplugged the iron and averted an even worse disaster, others were operating as if a great disaster was in progress.

Anger is one of those emotions that can spark quickly. It is not always a bad emotion to express, particularly when it provides warning of possible danger or sets personal limits and boundaries. But anger that lasts for minutes, hours, days, or even years after the source of the anger has passed is unhealthy.

Anger that does not have an on-off switch or that festers over time can easily distract you from taking an appropriate course of action. It absorbs valuable time in the present that can eat away at your growth. And it can spill over into other emotions, which can increase your stress level.

I take steps to release my anger before it escalates or does more harm than good.

*I have always wagered against God and I regard the little
I have won in this world as simply the outcome of this bet.*
—André Breton

What kind of relationship did you have with God in the
past? Maybe you prayed only when you were down in
the dumps or down on your luck. Perhaps your prayers
were filled with "I wants" rather than humble requests
for guidance. Maybe your conversations with God were
filled with anger and resentment over all that was wrong
with yourself and your life. Because you received no answers and your life did not get better, you began to doubt
that God even existed.

You might view your use and abuse in the past as "good
times." But each time you engaged in your habit was like
placing a bet on a roulette wheel; sometimes you experienced a good outcome, but more often than not you lost.

In recovery, there can be no wagering with your Higher
Power. You cannot build a connection to God by bargain-
ing. You cannot come to a greater understanding of God's
will if you want your will to have the loudest voice or to
come out on top. And you cannot fulfill the purpose of
your existence when your sole purpose is to fulfill your
needs.

*I will silence my desires and needs so that I might better hear
what God is telling me.*

People need joy quite as much as clothing. Some of them need it far more.
—Margaret Collier Graham

Have you ever met those who seem to emit a glow all around them? They seem to exude a brightness that illuminates even the darkest times. They can find the joy in most anything. When they walk into a room, you can almost feel the burdens of those around them being lifted. These people are not the life of the party—they *are* the party! What makes some people have such a lightness of living? How can they always seem to be able to find the silver lining in any dark cloud?

Those who have this inner light have learned how to develop a sense of joy and wonder with the world. They are able to sift through what is important in life and what creates distractions so they can extract what is most beneficial to them and discard what is not.

You can develop a similar lightness within you—one that enables you to experience more joy in your life. You do this by developing the ability to pay greater attention to those things that provide you with the most benefit and positive energy, and less attention on petty arguments, silly conflicts, or meaningless distractions. You can then be joyful by keeping your life light, open, and free.

I will nurture the glow within me.

If you can't feed a hundred people, just feed one.
—Mother Teresa

A pebble dropped into a pond reverberates in ways that are hundreds of times bigger than the pebble itself. From the point of entry into the water, ripples emerge and extend outwards. Fish dart in the direction of the sinking pebble in the hope of obtaining a bit of food. A duck feels a small disturbance and turns. And when the pebble lands on the pond's floor, it displaces tiny grains of sand as it settles in.

All this happens, just from one tiny pebble.

The slogan "Keep it simple" reminds you to avoid complications and overanalysis so you can stay focused on your recovery. But it also reminds you of the importance of performing simple acts of kindness for others in the fellowship. Things you might not even think about because they are so small may turn a person's day for the better. When you allow someone to go through a door before you, offer to pour a cup of coffee for another, or smile at a stranger, you are not saving hundreds of addicts. But perhaps, like the pebble in the pond, your simple action will have profound and positive repercussions in the life of another.

Today I will remember that small, simple actions can make a big difference.

The Hares and the Frogs

One day the hares were discussing how they could hardly ever relax because of their fear of other animals.

Just then they felt the earth tremble and saw a herd of wild horses stampeding their way. They scampered about in a panic and soon were trapped near the edge of a lake. They decided they would rather leap into the lake and drown themselves than continue living in a state of perpetual panic. But just as they were about to leap, they startled some frogs that promptly hopped into the water.

The hares scanned the lake and saw that the frogs had disappeared. "Perhaps," said one hare, "things are not as bad as they seem."

The moral of the story: *There is always someone worse off than you.*

There are many others who are facing their own set of difficulties and challenges. To think that you are the only one who has problems, what you are going through is unique, or no one could possibly understand the hardships you face minimizes the needs of others. The program is for the good of all, not for the good of one. Rather than stay locked in your own mind-set and bemoan what you are facing, reach out to others.

I will remember there are others who also require attention, comfort, and care.

A request not to worry . . . is perhaps the least soothing message capable of human utterance.
—Mignon G. Eberhart

There is a fine balance between worrying in a healthy way and worrying in an unhealthy manner. Healthy worry provides you with an essential alert that enables you to take appropriate action. For example, worrying about a food allergy you have can make you more rigorous in avoiding foods that would trigger a reaction. But unhealthy worry, such as obsessing about something that may or may not happen, can make you feel as if you are drowning and clinging to yourself at the same time.

Feeling nervous, anxious, or filled with dread from time to time is not unusual. But feeling such things most or all of the time can make it difficult to focus your energy anywhere else or difficult to think more rationally about your worry so you can put it in perspective.

When you take the time to figure out what you are so anxious about, you might discover that your worry is not based on a reality but on what you imagine or fear might happen. Think instead about how you could best handle a situation so it does not get to that point.

I will not spend my time today in useless worry. I will take action that will lessen my anxiety and fear.

Spilling your guts is exactly as charming as it sounds.
—Fran Lebowitz

There is a difference between sharing your information with others and spilling your guts. When you provide intimate and highly personal details of your life to those with whom you do not have a close relationship, you are not deepening the relationship but, instead, may be making others uncomfortable.

While the program encourages you to look at yourself, your actions, and your behaviors with total honesty, it does not mean that you need to share every little thing you uncover with others. Telling the story of how you came into the program is one that others would like to hear, but you need to do this in a way that eliminates some of the more graphic and intimate details that can make others feel uncomfortable.

The program teaches that when you listen to others, you take what you need and leave the rest. The goal of communication in recovery is to provide others with experiences and knowledge that will be of benefit to their own recovery. By taking the time to think about what you should share before you speak, you have a better chance of providing something of value—and not something others will discard in the trash can.

I will think before I speak. I will be open and honest in ways that benefit others.

If what I am watching evaporated before my eyes, I would remain.

—*Anne Truitt*

When you become so absorbed in an intimate relationship that all you want to do is spend time with that person or have that person spend time with only you, you are overly needy. When you think about people, places, and things more than you do yourself, you can become so dependent upon them that you would be lost without them.

Caring deeply about others is not the same as not being able to live without them. Loving your job is not the same as immersing yourself in work every waking hour or while you are on vacation. Such behaviors deprive you of developing or strengthening a conscious contact with yourself or with a Higher Power. You may forget that you exist apart from whomever or whatever it is you are focusing on. You may neglect to do the things you need to do for yourself and in your recovery. And you may become detached from your connection to a far bigger universe.

Today you need to reframe your interactions in ways that leave you with time for yourself. You can begin by imagining your life without the person, place, or thing you obsess about and say, "I will still exist."

I will practice conscious detachment from people and habits so I can attach to myself.

No day is so bad it can't be fixed with a nap.
—*Carrie Snow*

When the batteries wear down in a flashlight, first the light dims. You may shake the battery and, for a short time, the light may glow. But soon it will go out completely. By simply adding new batteries, you restore the light.

The same is true for your own level of energy and capacity for accomplishment. Work too hard, stubbornly refuse to leave a task unfinished, or burn the candle at both ends, and eventually you will be worn down. Your thinking will become confused and your body will feel exhausted. But by getting a good night's rest, taking a short nap, or even taking a break, you can restore your energy so you can start anew.

Rest is not a matter of doing absolutely nothing. It simply means slowing your pace, becoming less active, and changing your focus to something different. Rest is a requirement for human restoration. Although you may not literally feel your body being rejuvenated when you break away from intense activity or fall into a deep sleep, you know how different you feel when you arise. Rest allows the time to release tension so you can return to a normal, balanced state.

Today I will remember to recharge my batteries through rest so I can shine brightly throughout the day.

Prayer does not use any artificial energy, it doesn't burn up any fossil fuel, it doesn't pollute.

—Margaret Mead

When you are hungry, you eat. When you are tired, you sleep. When you feel bored, you seek stimulation. When you injure yourself, you give your body time to heal. When you do not understand something, you seek knowledge. You can take care of such things without really thinking about them. But how well do you take care of your spiritual needs? More often than not, you may ignore them as they do not cry out for attention like your other needs do.

But without prayer, you may not be able to handle stress as effectively as you could. You may be able to cope with life and do well in remaining free from your habit, but you may not be able to develop a sense of inner peace.

Prayer is something as essential to you as eating. It provides you with nourishment that develops a feeling of being fulfilled. It restores your soul and provides healing energy. It offers answers that can help ease confusion. And it can lighten your outlook so that your burdens do not seem so heavy.

I will make time today for prayer and peaceful connection with a Higher Power. When I pray, I will be cultivating inner peace and adding enrichment to my life.

If you let yourself be absorbed completely, if you surrender completely to the moments as they pass, you live more richly those moments.

—Anne Morrow Lindbergh

When you were a child, you wanted the days to rush by to get to a birthday, holiday, or school vacation. Each day seemed to pass so slowly. When you were older, you looked forward with eagerness to getting your driver's license, going off to college, or getting your first job. At times, it may have seemed the future would never come.

When you were older still, you may have looked forward to your wedding, to the birth of your first child, to buying your first home, or to a longed-for promotion. To achieve those things, you may have spent most of your present time planning for the future.

It is not always easy to live by the slogan "One day at a time." It becomes doubly hard to stay focused on the present when you feel all you have to look forward to is another day without your addiction. Living one day at a time is, perhaps, one of the hardest things you face in recovery. But within each day lies hope. To live each day, each minute, and each second means to be ever hopeful for a better tomorrow.

All I have is today. I will appreciate each moment of it.

Everyone who is born holds dual citizenship, in the kingdom of the well and in the kingdom of the sick.
                                        —Susan Sontag

Recovery facilitates healing much like applying salve and a bandage to a wound help healing. Such healing helps you to become more aware of the negative influences in your life so you can stop the flow of negative energy.

Healing in recovery involves learning about your disease as well as becoming more aware of how this addiction affected you and the lives of others. Healing in recovery also involves making positive changes in your life. For example, you can assess the relationships in your life to determine if they are detrimental to your recovery.

To heal in recovery, you need to take action to bring about change. You can let go of the people, places, and things that are no longer beneficial to you and allow into your life those people and things that will encourage your healing. The program is a journey you undertake that leads you out of one land and into another. You entered the program with a passport to the kingdom of the sick and were given a passport to the kingdom of the well.

Today I have a choice between sickness and health. I choose health, and use the program to heal my sickness.

I believe that he was really sorry that people would not believe he was sorry that he was not more sorry.
—Samuel Butler

How much can people believe in what you say? In the past, you most likely made promises you did not keep or said what you thought others wanted to hear just to get them off your back. You may have told others you were sorry for something you had done. But your apology may have sounded less than sincere if it was snapped at another in anger—"I said I was sorry!"—or spoken with sarcasm—"Well, sor-ree!"

Just because you tell someone you are sorry may not be enough. You can certainly say those words—and deliver them by using a tone of voice and body language that convey your regret—but you also need to take action to rectify the wrongs you have committed. Your words, combined with your actions, build trust.

Ask yourself, "Am I expressing that I am truly sorry simply because I am frustrated, or am I saying that I am sorry because I understand the harm I have done?" Then back up your words with actions that reflect your apology.

I want others to trust me. Today I will pay attention to the words I am saying and the actions I am taking to back up those words.

But the beginning of things . . . is necessarily vague, tangled, chaotic, and exceedingly disturbing.

—Kate Chopin

You may be someone who has entered the program not once, but several times. You may have left because you did not view your problem as *that* bad. Or you broke away because you thought others in the program were a bunch of lunatics or that the program was some form of religious cult. Perhaps you were not strong enough to resist the pull of your habit. Whatever your reason, relapse is something that is all too familiar to addicts. Sometimes the program is not a "one and done," but a process of starting over multiple times.

But any relapse usually begins in much the same way: with the expectation that things will be different this time around. You may be able to use less than you had in the past. But you are still using nonetheless. And, even though you think you may be in control *this time,* the control will never be in your hands. It is and always will be with the habit.

So, today, which will you choose: to submit to the lure of your addiction and see if, this time around, things will be different, or to appreciate a new day that is filled with promise and purpose?

Today I will be free from my habit. I am committed to my recovery.

Immature love says: "I love you because I need you."
Mature love says: "I need you because I love you."
—Erich Fromm

In the past, you may have viewed any loving relationship as a sort of joint bank account that you could draw from repeatedly. You most likely contributed little to the account, but used its resources whenever you could. You depended upon this account and may have often taken for granted that it would always be there for you. But money in a joint bank account cannot last long when one person is depleting and not replenishing its funds.

Love thrives when there is a balance of give and take between two people. If one takes, the other is left without. But when one gives, the other is enriched. When two people contribute in this way, security is built and the needs of both can grow.

Recovery offers a time in which you can replenish the depleted accounts that supported you in the past. You can now be a contributor, a giver, and a provider of love. You will still be able to withdraw from these accounts, but with more consideration for how much you are taking for yourself and how much you are giving to others.

I invest in those I love by giving them time, attention, and care.

There is something infinitely healing in the repeated re-frains of nature—the assurance that dawn comes after night, and spring after the winter.

—Rachel Carson

Imagine opening the morning paper and reading the following headline: *Today has been cancelled due to lack of interest.* Perhaps you are overjoyed at this headline. You were not looking forward to the day anyway. In fact, you would have preferred to stay in bed.

Now imagine opening the morning paper and reading the following headline: *Tomorrow has been cancelled due to lack of interest.* Perhaps you really were not looking forward to today, but to think that tomorrow will not come can make you think twice about how you will spend today.

No matter what lies ahead of you today, if you think of it as something you have to endure just so you can get through it, then chances are you will get very little out of it. Even if today were cancelled, you might not miss it. But if you can think of this time as the only time you have—one in which there is no understanding of a tomorrow that has not happened—then you have the opportunity to experience a deep connection with every minute in it.

Today I will connect with everything and everyone around me.

Gardening is an exercise in optimism. Sometimes, it is the triumph of hope over experience.

—*Marina Schinz*

Look at a garden that is flourishing, and what you will see is exquisite beauty. It is a marvelous outcome of a gardener's labor of love. But what you do not see is all that went into the creation of the garden. You do not see the aching knees and back, the dirty fingernails, or the soiled clothing. You do not see the constant weeding, insect control, and soil enrichment.

What drives the gardener to work so hard at something that may only be for the benefit of a few? For some, it builds closeness to God. For others, it is a visual oasis as well as a useful one that sustains bees, birds, and other living things. A garden can provide a sense of purpose and accomplishment, or satisfy a desire to nurture another living thing. But, mostly, gardeners garden because each new season holds promise. As Marina Schinz says, "This hope for the future is at the heart of all gardening."

Recovery is a similar garden of hope. Each day holds promise and a hope for a better future. To grow as one means to grow together.

Recovery is the garden in which I grow and flourish. It provides me with hope and promise for a better future.

It made me gladsome to be getting some education, it being like a big window opening.

—Mary Webb

The learning that comes from school or college can impart great knowledge. With such knowledge comes the ability to read and write and to add and subtract. Such knowledge can teach someone skills to work in a trade or to save lives.

While having a diploma or certificate can provide you with a big salary, a nice office, or a fancy car, having an education does not necessarily mean that you have the ability to make appropriate decisions or that you will live without sin and with good moral character. Education is not an end to itself. It is like learning to drive a car. You can study the rules of the road, familiarize yourself with a vehicle, and pass a written test. But when you actually get behind the wheel and drive, you learn so much more about how to be a better driver.

The program provides you with the knowledge you need to learn more about your addiction. But it is not until you engage in abstinence and employ the Steps of the program that you can more fully understand what it is you need to do to live your life without your habit.

The recovery program is my school. I will attend to my studies each day so I can effectively apply what I learn.

The challenge for a conductor is not to get the orchestra that you ideally want—the challenge is to take the orchestra in front of you and draw from them something which exceeds their own expectations of what they could be.
—Roger Nierenberg

The program of recovery does not give you recovery. Rather, it teaches you how to recover. It does not give you a better life. Rather, it gives you the tools you need so you can improve your life. It offers you a wealth of knowledge and a fellowship that, together, give you the support you need to make it through each day clean and sober.

No matter what you set out to do in life, starting out with a firm idea in mind of what to expect or about how things will go only sets you up for disappointment. It is like deciding to learn the game of golf with the expectation that you will play as well as a professional golfer in six months.

Instead, focus on one desire: to learn by doing. Then, strive to do the best that you can by applying what you have learned. What you may discover is that you have exceeded the expectations you did not have!

Today I will let go of how I expect things will turn out. Instead, I will learn as much as I can.

When I played drunks I had to remain sober because I didn't know how to play them when I was drunk.
                                                        —*Richard Burton*

Would you board an airplane if you knew the pilot had just knocked back a few in the airport bar? Would you consent to surgery if you smelled liquor on the breath of your surgeon? Would you write a check for a down payment on remodeling work to a contractor who reeked of marijuana?

When you were using, you may have believed that a pill or booze or some other substance enhanced your skills—you were stronger, smarter, funnier. But now you know that these things were far from the truth. Being inebriated or high may have made you the life of the party, but it also probably made you the butt of jokes, destroyed your career, ruined your marriage, or put your life or the lives of others in jeopardy.

Today you can draw your strength, intelligence, humor, and other positive elements from a new habit: recovery. Even though you may feel confused or weak at times, those are not the symptoms of a bad habit. Those are the experiences of someone who is engaging on a journey of self-discovery. Your life is much more manageable now because you are in control, not your habit.

I live my life today with the new habit of being clean and sober.

Nothing is so difficult as not deceiving oneself.
                                        —Ludwig Wittgenstein

Look in the mirror and stare at yourself. Think about what you see. Refrain from any desire to wish for something to be different. See yourself for how you look at this particular moment.

The same critical eye with which you see what you really look like is the same view you need to take in your work on Step Five. After having completed a searching and fearless moral inventory in Step Four, you are now ready to admit to God, to yourself, and to another human being what you have found.

It is one thing to confess such things to your Higher Power and to personally accept responsibility. It is entirely another to admit such things to someone else. That is why it is important to choose this person wisely. While you may be tempted to talk to someone whom you have harmed, that is better saved for Step Eight. Instead, work on Step Five with your sponsor. The foundation of trust and honesty in this relationship will provide you with a safe space in which to admit your wrongs.

Today I will work on Step Five with my sponsor. If I have already done so, I will reflect upon what I have done in the past to see if there is anything I have left out.

JUNE

Were entirely ready to have God remove all these defects of character.

—*Step Six*

A prayer is a humble and heartfelt communication with a power greater than yourself. A prayer can admit a weakness, communicate a need, or convey praise and gratitude. Prayers can unburden your heart, give you strength and courage, and deepen your faith and trust in a Higher Power. Use the following prayer as you work on your understanding and acceptance of Step Six.

Step Six Prayer

Higher Power, I am ready to learn from your infinite wisdom so that, with your help, I can remove my defects of character. These defects have resulted in considerable discomfort and pain. They have prevented me from moving forward. They have kept me from knowing a better way of living and from becoming a better person.

Higher Power, I have looked deep within me. I have seen my defects. I confess these defects to you. I am ready for your help in removing these defects. I humbly pray for your guidance so I can release these defects and become a better person. I ask for your help so I will always be a seeker of truth and remedy in my life.

Higher Power, I am open to your guidance. I trust in you. Thank you for listening to my prayer.

Golf without bunkers and hazards would be tame and monotonous. So would life.

—B.C. Forbes

What would life be like if every relationship was perfect and every day was filled with great satisfaction and went according to plan? A stress-free life would be like playing a golf course free from sand traps, trees, and difficult holes. While you might enjoy the ease of play, you would not learn how to make the tough shots.

There is no such thing as a life—or even a day— without some stress. Each day offers different variables— weather conditions, traffic volume, miscommunications, and malfunctions. Similarly, you feel different each day— some days you may be more tired or more energized than others. The most you can reasonably expect on any given day is the unexpected.

Instead of longing for today to be stress-free, begin your day as an eager student seeking answers: "What can I learn today? How can I grow? What will I be given that will test my knowledge and skills?" When you see each day as an opportunity for growth, you will be more capable of going with the flow and learning what you are capable of when you are put to the test.

Today might be a hole-in-one day, or it might be filled with many hazards. I will let the day unfold and learn from every experience I am given.

In the old days, if a person missed the stagecoach he was content to wait a day or two for the next one. Nowadays, we feel frustrated if we miss one section of a revolving door.
—Modern Maturity

The pace of life is faster than ever. New technologies facilitate round-the-clock manufacturing. Courtship has been upended by online matchmaking sites. E-mails, texting, and instant messaging have replaced the enjoyment of long phone conversations.

This sense of time urgency can spill over into your recovery, making it seem as if it is moving at a snail's pace. You may arrive at a meeting late and only half-listen to what others are saying as you keep one eye on the clock and the other on your text messages. You may put off reading the Big Book because you believe you do not have the time.

While a speedy recovery is sought for poor health, having a need for speed in recovery from your addiction will not help you get better faster. In fact, the deliberate day-by-day pace of recovery imparts a valuable lesson: take time in all that you do for a greater appreciation of the efforts you make and of what those efforts help you to achieve.

Today I will break out of the whirlwind of doing. Rather than operate in a perpetually frantic mode, I will take the time to appreciate and notice what I am doing.

So I close in saying that I might have had a bad break, but I have an awful lot to live for.

—Lou Gehrig

While much about Lou Gehrig's battle with amyotrophic lateral sclerosis was kept out of the public eye, today we know the debilitating effects of the illness that robbed him of his career in professional baseball. We understand more clearly how the disease creates a powerless person inside of an ever-weakening body.

Even Gehrig's patience, strong will, and positive attitude could not cure him of his illness. Each day his body broke down a little more and made even the simplest of actions extremely difficult to perform. Yet he coped with pride and dignity, and drew strength from those who cared about him. In his farewell speech before thousands of fans, he proclaimed a statement that, even today, has the power to both humble and awe: "I consider myself the luckiest man on the face of this earth."

Will you do the work in recovery that you need to do with pride and dignity, or will you have a defeatist attitude? Will you triumph over your addiction, or will you let your addiction get the better of you?

Today I will remember that there are others who face greater challenges and hardships, and they do so with a positive attitude.

*When I found out I thought God was white, and a man,
I lost interest.*

—*Alice Walker*

Out of all the work that you need to do in recovery, one
of the hardest tasks may not be abstinence but the development of trust and belief in your concept of a Higher
Power.

Within the program, the terms *God* or *Higher Power*
simply signify something greater than you. It is up to
you, in your recovery, to determine how you personally
develop a greater understanding of a spiritual presence in
your life. Maybe you feel, as Alice Walker writes in *The
Color Purple,* that "God ain't a he or a she, but a It."
Perhaps, for you, a Higher Power is not a being but a
feeling or an essence—the unfolding of a sunrise or the
sound of ocean waves lapping the shoreline.

The form your spiritual guide takes or the name you
apply to it is not as important as the substance of what
this guide symbolizes and how you can embrace its guidance and wisdom. Belief in something other than yourself
and greater than yourself is where your spiritual awakening begins. Where this essence takes you is your spiritual
journey.

*Today I believe in something greater than myself that will re-
store me to sanity and empower me to become a better person.*

It's an indulgence to sit in a room and discuss your beliefs as if they were a juicy piece of gossip.

—Lillian Hellman

As someone who regularly attends a particular meeting, you may think you know how others at the meeting view that fellowship. Because you have gone to the meeting for so long and know most, if not all, of the people, you may not realize how hard it might be for a newcomer to feel welcomed. You may also not be aware of how often group discussion strays from the topic of recovery and into areas of gossip, judgment, and criticism.

You may not consider that because the meeting has had the same attendees for a long time, you or others in the group may have discouraged those who dropped in, did not like what they saw or heard, and left.

Just as each individual needs to undertake a searching inventory, so too is there a value in the members of a particular fellowship conducting an analysis of how the group presents itself to others. Is each member on the lookout for newcomers and available to make them feel welcome?

Today I will look at one of my meetings from an outsider's point of view. I will work harder to make newcomers feel welcome and to redirect topics of discussion when they go astray.

The monsters of our childhood do not fade away, neither are they wholly ever monstrous.

—John le Carré

When you were young, you may have insisted upon sleeping with your bedroom light on. You were frightened of the monsters you imagined were hiding underneath your bed or who would enter your bedroom the moment the lights went out. Over time, you outgrew your need to sleep with a light on and came to understand that stories of monstrous beings were just that—stories. But then addiction entered your life, becoming the monster you had once feared, taking over your life. Try as you might to get out of its grasp, it would not let you go.

Freedom from your addiction released you from the monster's grip. While your life today may be a far cry from a happily-ever-after fairy tale ending, you have regained the joy, serenity, and rational thinking that your monster once took from you.

Although your monster may still come back to haunt you, you understand how it operates. Rather than be controlled by stinking thinking, doubt, insecurity, and fear, you comprehend the power of the Serenity Prayer. This prayer offers you protection and enables you to develop the courage you need to face those things you can change.

Today I will use the Serenity Prayer for the courage and wisdom I need so I can face my monsters and overcome them.

If I can't be beautiful, I want to be invisible.
                                    —*Chuck Palahniuk*

Very few people choose to go to their first meeting. Some were given the directive to attend. Others became so sick and tired of feeling sick and tired that they figured meetings could not make matters any worse. Maybe you came into the program because you made a promise to someone that you would attend meetings, or maybe a friend invited you.

No matter how you came to your first meeting, you can expect to feel a wide range of emotions just by walking through the door. You may feel angry at the mess in your life, or ashamed of the label "alcoholic" or "addict." You may feel frightened and alone, or an overpowering sense of hopelessness.

Until you become more comfortable, you may not want to say anything or have anyone acknowledge your presence. But retreating into a shell or imagining that you are wearing a cloak of invisibility will not make your discomfort go away. What is more helpful is to be open to the welcomes of others, to introduce yourself, and to let the words you hear sink in. Over time, meetings will become the best part of your day.

Even when I do not feel like going to a meeting, I will. There is value to each meeting I attend.

We do not have to become heroes overnight. Just a step at a time, meeting each thing that comes up, seeing it as not as dreadful as it appeared, discovering we have the strength to stare it down.

—*Eleanor Roosevelt*

How do you define courage? When you think of the word, your mind might conjure up images of soldiers in battle saving comrades, of doctors serving the needs of populations in third-world countries, or of someone who has lost the use of a leg learning how to walk again.

But perhaps courage is less about heroics and more about having the commitment to make things right. Making the decision to follow a path of recovery is courageous. As rock singer Bono once said, "My heroes are the ones who survived it wrong, who made mistakes, but recovered from them." That is what you are doing today. Admitting you have a problem takes incredible courage. Making a commitment to be clean and sober reflects courage. Taking stock of the things you have done wrong and striving to make amends takes courage.

Courage is based on doing more than you think you are capable of doing, and going farther than you thought you could go.

Today my actions will reflect courage. I will go above and beyond all the challenges that face me.

I read somewhere that everybody on this planet is separated by only six other people. Six degrees of separation between us and everyone else on this planet. The President of the United States, a gondolier in Venice, just fill in the names.
—*John Guare*

Six degrees of separation—a concept originally conceived by Frigyes Karinthy and made popular by playwright John Guare—refers to the idea that socialization in the modern world has resulted in ever-increasing connections. It becomes apparent that people are more linked with one another than they realize.

Facebook, Twitter, blogs, and other social media provide places for discovering and enhancing such connections. They are like technological coffee shops where people feel comfortable gathering together to share their personal lives. But sometimes this sharing can be too open and too personal. The pseudo-anonymity afforded by social media sites can present serious issues with privacy. This is especially true for members of Alcoholics Anonymous.

It is especially important to safeguard the anonymity of others on any social media sites you frequent. While you may choose to discuss thoughts, feelings, and opinions of your own, you should never include the names of other program members or information about them or their lives.

Today I will respect the confidentiality of others in the program.

My defenses were so great. The cocky rock and roll hero who knows all the answers was actually a terrified guy who didn't know how to cry.

—John Lennon

When you choose to suppress, rather than express, your feelings, they have a tendency to emerge in other ways. You may be able to keep them under control for a while, but eventually they will build up like the steam in a pressure cooker and reach a point where they need to be released. This is especially true when you are afraid. Fear can sometimes escalate into a panic attack, particularly during stressful times.

Whenever you feel fear, remember that you are not the first or only person to feel scared or anxious in recovery. Then ask yourself, "What am I afraid of?" By taking a more rational, analytical approach to your fear—even by making a list of those things that scare you—you will gain greater understanding of what frightens you.

Perhaps you are afraid you will fail in your recovery. Maybe you are terrified to think about your childhood and stir up memories you have long suppressed. Or maybe you are anxious about making amends to someone. Identify what it is you are afraid of—and then conquer your fear by taking action.

No matter what I do today, I will not allow myself to be paralyzed by fear or anxiety.

Efficiency is intelligent laziness.

—David Dunham

The invention of the modern sandwich is attributed to John Montagu, the Fourth Earl of Sandwich. As the story goes, Montagu was hungry but did not want to stop playing cards. He ordered his servant to bring him meat between two slices of bread so his fingers would not get greasy and he could continue to gamble while eating.

Whether truth or legend, what is considered to be accurate is that Montagu held a number of important positions of power throughout his lifetime. Yet he was viewed as so incompetent and corrupt that it was suggested his epitaph read, "Seldom has any man held so many offices and accomplished so little."

Do you approach your recovery with determination, or with laziness? After attending 90 meetings in 90 days, you may begin tapering off from such diligence. Upon completion of your work on one of the Steps, you may focus your attention outside the program. Or as you accumulate days free from your habit, you may go about your day-to-day life thinking you are "cured."

Recovery requires your time and attention. It requires you to do all of the work necessary to develop your knowledge and skills so that you can become not just a sober person, but a better person.

Today I will do the work I need to do in recovery.

What lies behind you and what lies in front of you pales in comparison to what lies inside of you.
— *Ralph Waldo Emerson*

Imagine that today represents the starting line to a race. Behind you are the months of training that infused your mind, body, and spirit with great strength and stamina. Ahead of you lies the finish line, at a point you cannot yet see.

You understand that as you race from the starting line to the finish line, you will face many challenges. But no matter what lies ahead of you or what the conditions will be, trust that you have the strength to face it—and to conquer it. Recovery shows you that you have, within you, a strength you never realized you had. This strength is so powerful that it can overcome an addiction. This strength is so dedicated that it can overcome dishonesty. This strength is so determined that it can overcome negativity.

Recovery is a platform from which healthy living springs. What you learn in the program and how you grow in the program is applicable to everything you do. Embrace everything you have learned in your recovery. Let this lead you to the finish line in any task you undertake today.

Recovery is my training program for life. It strengthens me so I can face and conquer any challenge.

It is one thing to learn about the past; it is another to wallow in it.

—*Kenneth Auchincloss*

There may be times when you wish you could simply forget about your past. The memories of who you once were and the life you once lived can be painful. You may feel there is little to be gained by such reflections, other than to remind you of all the things you messed up, all the relationships you damaged beyond repair, and all the embarrassment you caused yourself and others.

But there are times when you will need to reflect on what has gone by. Your past is part of the definition of who you are today. Without it, you would have no way of measuring your present-day progress.

Through the information you gain from such reflection on past times, you will have a better understanding of what has served you well and what has not. You will be able to identify mistakes and missteps so you can avoid making the same ones today. It is okay to look back when you keep your past in perspective. Use your past as a teaching tool that will impart lessons to be used now, and in the future.

I will spend some time studying my past so I can apply this knowledge to create a better future.

The Crow and the Pitcher

A crow dying of thirst came upon a pitcher that had once been full of water. He shoved his beak into the pitcher and discovered that there was very little water left. But he was determined to get it.

Time and again he thrust his beak into the pitcher, but could not reach the water. He was about to drop dead from both thirst and despair when he spotted a pile of pebbles nearby.

The crow picked up one in his beak, and dropped it into the pitcher. He took another, and did the same. Each time he dropped a pebble into the pitcher, he noticed that the water level rose slightly. Energized by this discovery, he continued his efforts until the water level rose to where he could reach it.

Then the crow drank the water, which saved his life.

The moral of the story: *Small actions can have big results.*

Recovery is a process that involves taking small steps, but sometimes progress is hard to see. At such times, take heart. Resist the temptation to give up. Instead, trust that your steady and dedicated effort is taking you ever closer to your goal.

There will be great leaps in my recovery, and there will be baby steps. I will trust that everything I do is serving a useful purpose in my progress.

Love and fear. Everything the father of a family says must inspire one or the other.

—*Joseph Joubert*

When you were growing up, your father may have been someone you feared or someone who provided you with great comfort. He may have been there for you when you really needed him, or he may have been so caught up in his own addiction or overly devoted to things outside of the home that he had little time to spend with you.

While parents can be some of the greatest influencers in life, they are—just like you—imperfect human beings. They are on a journey of discovery to find out who they are as an adult and who they need to be as a parent. They must tend to their own growth as well as to the growth of their children. Sometimes parents succeed in these endeavors—and sometimes they fail.

No matter how you feel about your father, it is far better to forgive him for his failures or shortcomings than to hold onto anger or sadness. It is far better to give credit for those things he was able to give you rather than regret that you did not get everything you wanted from him.

Today I will think about my father with compassion and understanding.

Nobody wants their problems solved. Their dramas. Their distractions. . . . Their messes cleaned up. Because what would they have left? Just the big scary unknown.
—*Chuck Palahniuk*

Do you live your life as a fire setter, a fire fighter, or a fire preventer?

When you are a fire setter, you simply cannot live without having some sort of drama going on. When you are a fire fighter, you are someone who thrives on being needed and who enjoys trying to resolve an issue or a problem. When you are a fire preventer, you live in a constant state of fear that chaos or disagreement will be sparked, and so you devote your energy to doing everything you can to ensure fires can be kept to a minimum.

No matter which group of fire bugs you identify with, all share one thing in common. They provide distractions that keep you from doing the things you need to do in your life. You are like someone who pulls a fire alarm before a big test is handed out, expecting that activating the alarm will cancel the test. But once a false alarm is declared and the students and teachers return to the classroom, the test will be given. Pulling the alarm has only delayed what has to be faced.

Today I will pay attention to the things I need to do—and just do them!

It is inevitable when one has great need of something one finds it. What you need you attract like a lover.
—*Gertrude Stein*

Eons ago, hunter-gatherer societies ensured their survival through the roles each member fulfilled. Those who gathered procured seafood, roots, and edible vegetation; those who hunted, tracked, and killed animals. Each person played a significant role. When everyone worked together, the efforts of both hunters and gatherers ensured the health and well-being of the entire clan.

It is this same way in the fellowship of recovery. Each person plays a vital role in helping others feel that they are on the right path. You support others when they feel weak or tempted. They, in turn, do the same for you. You share your experience so that others can learn. They do the same.

It is the fellowship's unity in abstinence that helps to strengthen each person's commitment to recovery. Sometimes all it takes is one member of the fellowship falling off the wagon to tempt others to do the same. But even during those times, the jitters of one can be soothed by the others. You will be able to find whatever you need, whenever you need it, in the fellowship of recovery.

I am part of a wonderful fellowship that provides a strong foundation of support for all of its members.

Rejoice when the going gets tough, when everything turns mean. It is time to shout and clap our hands—if only in the privacy of our own minds.

—Joyce Sequichie Hifler

Changing your life from use to dis-use does not happen overnight. It is one thing to put down the drink and make the decision that you will no longer abuse your body. It is entirely another to live without the addiction.

Living without your addiction is where the work in recovery really begins. This work is all about adjustment: adjusting how you think and how you behave, adjusting your way of feeling, adjusting how you interact with others, and—ultimately—adjusting your way of living. The slogan "Easy does it" serves as a reminder to approach your recovery in a relaxed manner. It encourages you to be patient with the adjustments you need to make. It reminds you to be gentle with yourself and not to burden yourself or take on more than you can handle.

Whenever you remind yourself, "Easy does it," you can transform the challenges you face from steep mountains into gently rolling hills. You can dry your tears of frustration. You can be filled with joy because you are where you need to be: on the road to recovery.

Today I will use "Easy does it" whenever I feel that I am trying to take on too much.

You have put me in here a cub, but I will come out roaring like a lion, and I will make all hell howl!
                                                                    —Carry Nation

Prisons take away freedom; so do cages in a zoo. Such enclosures are designed to decrease individuality and increase dependency and obedience. Your addiction can be viewed similarly; it is a jail that has kept you captive. It has prevented you from thinking about anything or anyone else. It has numbed your feelings. It has severed your ties to a spiritual presence. It has taken away your ability to make choices. And it has deprived you of all of life's beauty and experiences.

Addiction enslaves you, but recovery liberates you. It opens up all of your senses so you can experience a wide range of sensations. It clears your mind so you can think both rationally and creatively. It opens your world to possibilities. It encourages you to dream. It increases your knowledge.

Addiction requires your obedience, but recovery releases you. With such freedom comes the ability to discover what is within you. It gives you the power to choose and to take action. And it expands your horizons in ways that will enable you to see that the only limitations you have today are those you create for yourself.

Today I will celebrate my freedom from addiction.

How would you go about taming a wild horse? You wouldn't whip it back into a corner. You'd pat it on the nose and give it some carrots. . . .

—*Steven C. Hayes*

The way you treat or view yourself today is likely the way you were treated in the past and repeats the messages you were told by others. You may have little confidence in your abilities and explode in anger at yourself whenever you make even the smallest of mistakes. Or you may regularly talk about yourself in negative terms, using such phrases as "I'm so stupid" or "I'm never going to amount to anything."

You would not tame a wild horse by beating it or screaming at it. Instead you would move about it slowly and talk to it calmly. You would treat the horse with respect and kindness for however long it would take, until the horse finally saw you as someone who would not mistreat it.

You need to treat yourself in the same way. When you show yourself kindness and respect, and when you are patient with yourself, you will gradually shift how you think about yourself. You will be able to see that you have more positive qualities and abilities than you thought.

Today I will treat myself with kindness and respect so I can learn to see the good in me.

You can always trust information given you by people who are crazy; they have an access to truth not available through regular channels.

—Sheila Ballantyne

Sometimes you may feel that your sobriety is going really great. You may rarely think about your addiction or experience any cravings.

Other times you may feel that all you do is think about having a drink. You drive by a liquor store, and your hands squeeze tightly on the wheel. It takes all of your power not to turn into the parking lot. Or you see a beer commercial on television and think about it so much that you can almost smell it and taste it.

Even though you are striving for total honesty in your life, sharing such thoughts with those who are not in the program is not a good idea. Telling your spouse that a beer would sure taste great with dinner or making a joke about almost stopping at a liquor store will not instill trust in your commitment to sobriety. Even confiding in a friend who is not an alcoholic how much you wish you could drink again will deprive you of the support you really need. Only another recovering alcoholic will truly understand the peaks and valleys of sobriety.

I trust that those in recovery will provide me with the support I need to overcome a craving.

There is more to life than simply increasing its speed.
                    —*Mohandas "Mahatma" Gandhi*

Our society favors gadgets designed to help people reach their goals while exerting the least amount of effort in the shortest period of time. So, you can stay in touch with friends and family through instant messaging. You can watch your favorite movie by downloading it onto your computer. You can trim inches off your thighs and bottom simply by walking around the house in specially engineered sneakers. With so many time-saving devices in existence, you may wonder why your recovery cannot move with similar rapidity.

The truth is, instant messaging does not offer you the same give-and-take exchange as does a conversation over a cup of coffee. Watching a movie on your computer does not give you the opportunity to meet up with friends at the movie house. And specially designed body-trimming sneakers do not provide you with truly aerobic exercise.

Recovery has been, and always will be, a process that takes time. There is no special mechanism that will accelerate your rate of progress, nor are there any magic sneakers that will reshape your mind, body, and spirit. Recovery provides you with the tools, but you need to do the work.

The tools of recovery are not magic, but are guaranteed to work through time and effort.

While you have a thing it can be taken from you . . . but it is yours then forever when you have given it. It will be yours always. That is to give.

—*James Joyce*

A new faculty member arrived at her office at a college and her assistant offered to give her a tour. As soon as they headed out the door, the assistant stooped to pick up some trash. Walking down a sidewalk, he removed a large branch. He picked up a pen on a stairway. "You must live in a very neat home," the professor commented.

"Force of habit," he replied. "You see, my sister lost her eyesight in an accident last year. Because both of our parents are gone, I dropped out of school and found this job so I could help take care of her. I've gotten so used to thinking ahead about what path she is going to take that I'm always on the lookout for things that might trip her up. I apologize for taking time from your tour, and promise I will stop doing that for you."

The professor thought for a moment. "Please don't," she said. "In fact, let's walk around the campus and do this together."

Today I will give to another in ways that will help to make the journey through recovery easier.

Don't worry about the world coming to an end today. It is already tomorrow in Australia.

—*Charles M. Schulz*

On one of those days when it seems everything that happens is an uphill struggle, nothing happens on time or when you want it to, your boss is in a particularly foul mood, and others are making demands of you, you may want to cry out, "Will this day never end!"

The reality is, it *will* end. The sun will eventually set and night will fall. "Good riddance," you might think. But saying goodbye to one bad day does not guarantee that all of the catastrophes that occurred in it may not once again rear their ugly heads.

If your struggle is uphill, you may need to face a particular challenge. If time goes awry, perhaps you need to employ greater patience. If your boss is ornery, you may need to learn how to be less reactive. And if others are making demands of you, perhaps you need to learn how to say no. It has been said that God does not give you anything that you are not ready for or incapable of handling. So too it is with everything about to unfold today. Are you ready for whatever comes your way?

Today I will greet the day with an optimistic attitude and take this attitude with me throughout the day.

My idea of an agreeable person is a person who agrees with me.

—*Benjamin Disraeli*

In the past, it may have seemed as if you were at odds with everyone. No matter what you said or did, it never seemed to be the right thing. A big part of such discord was a result of your habit. Because you were enslaved by your addiction, your thoughts and actions preserved a direct path toward your habit—and away from others. As a result, you were constantly caught up in arguments with those who did not understand the hold the addiction had on you. Try as you might, you could not force others to see your point of view.

But recovery shows you that there are others who share many of your thoughts. They have been down that same Habit Road multiple times, and they have often fought the same battles with others that you did.

Finding a connection with others who understand how you got here and what you are facing makes the journey that much easier. While not every person in recovery will agree with you, what is most important is that those in the program with whom you have bonded share a common connection.

My recovery journey is made easier through my connection to others who understand what I am going through.

There is always a "but" in this imperfect world.
—Helen Keller

Often there is not a day that goes by without some tragic or upsetting news story. An act of terrorism, a natural disaster, or a school shooting can dominate the air waves and make it seem as if all there is in the world are tragedy, loss, and immeasurable sorrow. At those times when the world seems to be crashing down around you, you may be tempted to look at your addiction from a different perspective.

You may consider, for instance, how minor your addiction is compared to everything else that is going on. So you might tell yourself, "Okay, I think I have a problem with alcohol. But maybe my problem isn't so bad after all." Or you may think, "But all I did was just knock over a trash can when I was drunk. It's not as if I killed someone."

Maintaining sobriety can be an extremely difficult task. But you make it more difficult whenever you spend more time trying to find excuses than doing what it is you need to do in your recovery. While it is true that sometimes there is too much tragedy and negative news, such things should not be taken as reasons for you to take a break from your recovery.

Today I will not excuse myself from my recovery.

There never was a night that had no morn.
—*Dinah Mulock Craik*

When he was serving as a Green Beret medic in Vietnam, Doug Peacock carried with him what he called his "landscape of hope." It was an old road map of the Rocky Mountains, and he took it with him always. Whenever he could, he would take out his landscape of hope and study it. He would look at the roads that had been carved out years ago into the mountains and stare into the empty spaces between those roads. He tried to imagine the rugged wilderness, the smell of pine, and the stillness at the highest altitudes. He held onto the hope that he would someday be able to leave the horrors of war behind him and experience the wilderness for himself.

Upon his discharge, Peacock journeyed through Wyoming and Montana, camping and living off the land. Grizzly bears were some of his companions, but mostly he experienced solitude. Over time, Peacock was able to let his landscape of hope become his reality. He devoted his life to saving the untamed domain of the grizzly and transformed his hope into a reality.

What can you imagine for yourself today? What will you hope for?

Today I will create a landscape of hope to guide me.

There are some people who see a great deal and some who see very little in the same things.

—T.H. Huxley

When you are asleep, you are at peace. Your body is stilled and your mind—even when caught in a dream—is quieted. But from the moment you open your eyes in the morning, you are greeted by a nonstop cacophony of sensual activity. Are you aware of all of the activity around you?

You may see daylight but not notice whether it is raining or sunny. You may be stalled by traffic but not hear its sounds. You may drink coffee but not take in its freshly brewed aroma. Throughout the day, you may hold conversations, participate in meetings, make decisions, run errands, eat lunch, work against deadlines, and juggle activities. You may do all these things with total awareness and immersion in each activity, or you may rush through your day paying it only peripheral attention.

But the more in tune you are with everything and the more willing you are to embrace the action around you, the more capable you are of seeing the transitions and transformations within each day—and the better able you will be to more fully appreciate and respond to your life.

Today I will learn more about myself and all of the things in my life by developing greater awareness.

Your thorns are the best part of you.

—Marianne Moore

What is hidden within the cocoon spun by a caterpillar is a mystery. Yet within that cocoon is something that lives and will eventually be revealed in a different living form through a marvelous transformation.

Life is made up of many mysteries and, whether you realize it or not, you are one of them. Your life before you entered the program was full of all of those things that make up a good mystery—suspense, the unknown, deception, and conflicts. But your work in recovery helps you to unfold the mystery of who you are. The more you know about yourself, the greater your understanding will be. And, through this understanding, you are more capable of transforming yourself.

Step Six brings you to the point where you are ready to have God remove your defects of character. You have become aware of your own mysteries by making a searching and fearless moral inventory of yourself in Step Four, and you have admitted the nature of your wrongs to God and to another human being. You have, with honesty and courage, looked deep within yourself so you can see those things that you need to change. You can rise up with a greater lightness of being and transform your life into something better.

Today I am ready to be transformed.

JULY

Humbly asked Him to remove our shortcomings.
                                                    —*Step Seven*

A prayer is a humble and heartfelt communication with a power greater than yourself. A prayer can admit a weakness, communicate a need, or convey praise and gratitude. Prayers can unburden your heart, give you strength and courage, and deepen your faith and trust in a Higher Power. Use the following prayer as you work on your understanding and acceptance of Step Seven.

Step Seven Prayer

Higher Power, I devote my life in recovery to you. I treasure your guidance, and humbly ask for your help. You are my creator. You have given me life so that I may live it with purity and respect. But I alone have created my many defects of character. I have allowed them to grow because I have paid more attention to my addiction than to you or to others.

Higher Power, I have made many mistakes. I have harmed others. And I have distanced myself from you. I pray to you now to help me remove these defects of character so that I may commune with you with a greater willingness to listen and follow your guidance, and so that I can be more useful to you and to others who share in my journey. This I ask in your name.

Higher Power, thank you for listening to my prayer.

A fool sees not the same tree that a wise man sees.
—*William Blake*

When you were a child and were asked, "How deep is the ocean?" you may have spread your arms as wide as you could to signify the ocean's massive size. When you were a bit older and asked how big something enormous was, you might have answered, "It's as big as infinity." You had learned a word that would signify what your arms had expressed. But when you were using and were asked, "How much did you have to drink?" or "How much money did you take out of the bank to gamble?" you may have answered, "Not much" or "Just a little." The reality was, you had more than a few drinks. The truth was, you withdrew more money than you wanted to admit.

While lies and an altered vision of your universe may have helped you change your perspective so you could continue to use and abuse, this perspective was foolish and far from reality.

Today you know the value of honesty, and how it enables you to see and speak the truth. As hard as it may be to accept the truth, growth springs from such knowledge. You can become wiser and, in so doing, become more in touch with reality.

I will see the world as it really is, not as I want it to be.

All work and no play make Jack a dull boy.

—*Proverb*

While the above proverb is familiar to most through one of the more chilling scenes in *The Shining,* when the discovery of reams of paper on which the proverb is written repeatedly captures the main character's descent into insanity, it originated at a time when children were required to work as hard as adults. It served as a warning to parents that working their children too hard would deprive them of other experiences.

Working too hard at anything—even your recovery—may prevent you from experiencing other things in life. The holistic focus of recovery urges a balance in everything in your life, and that includes setting aside time to have fun and play.

Removing your addiction from your life has given you many gifts. One of these gifts is more time. Use the time in which you formerly used to become more adventurous, learn something new, or try out a recreational activity you have always wanted to do. You can even engage in activities that you never got to experience as a child—running through a sprinkler on a hot day or simply lying on your back in a field, looking up at the clouds.

Today I will have fun in my addiction. I will do something for no other purpose than sheer enjoyment.

Nature never said to me: Do not be poor; *still less did she say:* Be rich; *her cry to me was always:* Be independent.
—*Sebastien-Roch Nicolas de Chamfort*

You may think that recovery has taken away your freedom because you can no longer do the thing you most want to do—engage in your habit. Because you are in recovery, you may feel that you have simply gone from wearing one set of shackles to donning another.

But you awaken each day in recovery with a choice that is yours to make: to use or not to use. What you choose is up to you, and so this reflects that you do, indeed, still have your freedom. All of the actions you take today will be based on this choice. All of your choices will not only guide your life in the direction you have chosen to travel, but also symbolize your independence from dependence.

Today you have immense freedom. You can choose to be clean and sober. You can choose which tools of the program you will use. You can choose which meetings to attend. You can choose a sponsor. You can choose to share your story with others. You can choose to reach out to a Higher Power. And you can choose the changes you would like to make.

I will celebrate the independence recovery gives me.

Memory itself is an internal rumour.
—George Santayana

There is a difference between minor forgetfulness—walking into a room and forgetting why you went there or not being able to recall the name of someone you just met—and the more significant memory loss that results from an addiction. Alcohol abuse can often result in fragmentary memory loss. You may not remember something that happened while you were drunk until prompting provides you with clues. Or you may experience blackouts, when you are incapable of remembering what happened during a previous binge no matter how much you are prompted.

Prolonged alcohol abuse can lead to the development of alcohol dementia. Poor nutrition during the time when you were actively using can lead to memory loss as well as decrease your ability to learn new information or solve problems. In recovery, it is essential that you exercise regularly, improve your nutrition, and take vitamin supplements to develop a healthy body and improve your memory. Engage in memory-building activities and learn something new each day so that your brain gets healthy exercise as well.

Taking control now of any memory issues brought on by your addiction will strengthen your mind for the future.

Today I will exercise my brain by using memory-enhancing techniques.

In stillness the world is restored.

—Lao Tzu

To be able to sit and let your mind wander is a form of meditation. You can close your eyes and simply focus on your breathing. Pay attention to what it feels like to take in a deep, cleansing breath of air and then slowly release it along with the toxins from your body.

When you combine focused breathing with imagery—creating a picture in your mind that replicates the gentle action of taking in the good and releasing the bad—you make your meditation more powerful. Imagine ocean waves coming to shore and then slowly receding. Or think of a morning glory slowly opening up to sunshine, and then gently closing as daylight dims.

While meditating, you can also release tension from your body. Begin with your hands. As you expand your lungs, slowly squeeze your hands into fists. Then, as you exhale, open your fists and relax your hands. Do this with each muscle group in your body, and you will feel a wonderful relaxation spread throughout your entire body. You may also enjoy greater focus and concentration, a more positive outlook, and renewed energy.

I begin my day with a meditation consisting of focused breathing, imagery, and muscle relaxation. I will use this same meditation at night to help me unwind from the day's activities.

*I am beginning to learn that it is the sweet, simple things
of life which are the real ones after all.*
                                    —*Laura Ingalls Wilder*

It is often advised in meetings to check your baggage at the
door. What this means is that too often there is a tendency
to drag everything around with you in recovery: your
past, your childhood issues, everything and everyone you
have lost, your anger or sadness, your inability to forgive
yourself and others, and more. Such things can weigh you
down to such an extent that they can prevent you from
moving forward.

Similarly, the greater the number of physical things
you carry around with you, the more overwhelmed you
may feel about life in general. Take time to look into your
closets and go through your bureau drawers. Peer into
your garage, basement, and attic. Then ask yourself, "What
do I really need?"

Mother Mary Madeleva once said, "I like to go to
Marshall Field's in Chicago just to see how many things
there are in the world that I do not want." So too can you
start to use a critical eye in reviewing the possessions that
stuff your life.

*I will take the time to assess not only what I need to carry
around with me in recovery, but also the things in my life.*

Mama exhorted her children at every opportunity to "jump at de sun." We might not land on the sun, but at least we would get off the ground.

—Zora Neale Hurston

Starting from when you were a child, you may have been pushed into goal-setting. You may have been asked to think about what you wanted to be when you grew up. As you grew older, the questions may have become more persistent: "Are you going to college? What are you going to major in? What do you want to be doing with your life?" Even in your first job interviews, you may have been asked, "Where do you see yourself five years from now?"

But the program is not based on goal-setting. While it is important to have a single commitment—not a goal—of achieving abstinence each day, if you create definite goals for your recovery you may set yourself up for failure. You will not be open to testing your strength, to trying new things, to meeting new people, and to giving yourself the freedom to recover at your own pace.

The pace to recovery has been likened to peeling an onion—a layer at a time, not all at once, and not with a preset idea of which layer will be removed at a particular time.

I will set goals in my life, but I will let my recovery unfold.

For nearly 30 years, I have been saying Alcoholics Anonymous is the most effective self-help group in the world. The good accomplished by this fellowship is inestimable. . . . God bless A.A.

—*Ann Landers*

For more than seventy years scientists, psychologists, doctors, and others have tried to figure out why Alcoholics Anonymous works. While not everyone who enters AA is cured, for those who stay it can be a life-transforming experience.

What makes AA work? It could be that the program helps develop a spiritual awareness that gives AA members greater meaning and purpose to their lives. Perhaps it is the consistent message of the Big Book, AA's sacred text. Maybe it is the Twelve Steps and their logical progression to recovery. Or perhaps the admission "I am an alcoholic" develops a greater acceptance and understanding.

While we may not truly comprehend how the program works, we can witness the power in its fellowship. Such unity provides much-needed emotional support and lifts the spirits of each person, so that one and all understand, "I am not alone." And, when AA members share their story in the public forum provided by a meeting, both the speaker and listener are engaged in a dialogue that can lead to greater self-awareness.

I keep coming to AA because it works.

Habit has a kind of poetry.

—*Simone de Beauvoir*

A habit is simply a manner of behavior that falls into a pattern. It can be a set time for doing things, a particular way of doing something, or a tradition or custom. Exercising at the same time of day, taking your dog for a romp in the park each afternoon, vacationing with your family at the same place every summer, attending church on Sunday, or going out to dinner on Friday nights are examples of good habits. While such things are not physically addictive, when they are absent from your life you may feel emotionally or spiritually empty. Without them, you can miss the pleasure and enjoyment they bring.

You can even convert something you do not like doing into a good habit. Perhaps you dislike doing laundry or mowing the lawn. But when you seek out the positive elements in such activities—all your clothes smell fresh and clean or you have the opportunity to get outdoors and make your yard look nice—you can convert them into habits you enjoy.

The more bad habits you replace with good ones, the less likely you will be to engage in the bad habits—and the more likely you will be to develop their positive replacements into lifelong good habits.

I will develop something I really like to do into a good habit.

The actions you take during your first three months in a new job will largely determine whether you succeed or fail.
—Michael Watkins

What would happen if you were hired to run a company and then, on your first day, without taking the time to learn about the company, you came into the office with firm ideas about how you will run the business?

In his book *The First 90 Days*, Michael Watkins outlines success strategies for new leaders who often lack in-depth knowledge of the climate and the challenges of the organization they are entering.

The first 90 days in your recovery—whether this takes place in a treatment facility or program or by following the advice to attend "90 meetings in 90 days"—are just as critical. This start of your recovery represents a major transition in your life, and the way you begin will often determine whether you will succeed or fail. The recovery initiation period of 90 days, combined with early abstinence, provides you with the chance to develop awareness of your strengths and weaknesses and make maintaining abstinence easier. When you take the time to learn about the tools of the program and form relationships within the fellowship, you will learn that while your recovery is up to you, you do not have to do it alone.

I will learn all that I can about the program so my path in recovery will be easier.

It is easier to live through someone else than to become complete yourself.

—Betty Friedan

While recovery is all about relationships—with others in the fellowship, with your sponsor, with your Higher Power, and the one you must build or rebuild with yourself— there are some relationships that should be avoided.

Whether you are new to recovery or have been involved for some time, becoming involved in a romantic relationship can be dangerous to your sobriety and your work in the program. When you first become involved in an intimate relationship, most other relationships get pushed to the back burner. A new romantic interest can provide you with a "rush" of energy that can replicate a "high," and the relationship may then become your substitute "drug." Romance can be a detour that may take you away from your much-needed journey of self-discovery.

This does not mean that you can never become intimately involved again. While some suggest people wait between six months or even a year before pursuing romance, it is best to build a strong foundation in the recovery program and with your Higher Power first. Make the choice to reach a point in your recovery in which you feel you can contribute as an equal partner to an intimate relationship.

I will enter the dating scene cautiously, without losing focus on my recovery.

*I am in that temper that if I were under water I would
scarcely kick to come to the top.*

—*John Keats*

Everyone gets the blues or feels down from time to time.
But if you feel down or blue on most days and have felt
this way for an extended period of time, you may be suffering from depression.

It may bring you comfort to know that depression is
quite common among alcoholics and drug abusers—
both during their addiction as well as in their recovery.
Common symptoms include such things as finding little
enjoyment in life, even with those things or people that
used to bring you pleasure; having trouble sleeping at
night or getting out of bed in the morning; having a general disinterest in anything; experiencing a significant
weight loss or gain; feeling intense fatigue and a general
disconnection from yourself; experiencing feelings of sadness that do not go away; or having suicidal thoughts.

Even if you discover from this assessment that you are
experiencing few or none of these symptoms and just feel
down from time to time, it is still a good idea to talk with
a therapist. A mental health professional can provide help
for how you are feeling and also become a valuable member of your recovery support network.

*I will utilize all of the resources available to me so I can better
understand how I am feeling.*

We've removed the ceiling above our dreams. There are no more impossible dreams.

—Jesse Jackson

There are "if only" dreams in life and "what if" dreams. When you were using, your dreams were most likely "if onlys," such as "If only I didn't spend so much money gambling, I would be able to go away on vacation" or "If only I didn't drink, I would be spending more time with my partner and kids."

"If only" dreams are based upon regret and fault-finding. They are perfect mechanisms for self-blame—a sure-fire method for ensuring your dreams cannot come true.

"What if" dreams, on the other hand, are based upon possibilities and hope for the future. They focus on the things you want to do *and will do* to make a dream come true. "What if I saved a little bit of money each week— then I could go away for a weekend" or "What if I set aside one night during the week and one weekend afternoon to spend time with my kids—then we could get to know each other better." When you think of your dreams as "what ifs," you free them of any limitations. You make yourself an active participant in making them happen.

I will dream, and then I will act upon these dreams to make them happen.

The Fox without a Tail

One day a fox became caught in a trap. In his struggle to free himself, he left his tail behind. On his way home, he devised a way to head off being made the butt of jokes. He trotted back into the forest and called together all of the foxes.

"Foxes are much more attractive when they do not have a tail," he said as he wiggled his stump. "Observe how sleek my appearance is. No longer will I have to pull burrs out of my tail. I am free—and you can all be free, too! It is time for all foxes to cut off their tails."

"Nonsense!" an elder fox yelled out. "If you had not lost your own tail, my friend, you would not be urging us to lose ours as well. You must deal with your loss on your own."

The moral of the story: *Do not trust all of the advice given by others.*

Many in the program offer helpful support based on their experience. There are also those who give advice. Sometimes this advice is well-meaning and useful; other times it may seem suspect. Listen to the support, guidance, and advice you are given. But never let such information have a negative impact on your recovery.

I will listen to the advice I am given, but will make decisions that are right for me.

My aim in life has always been to hold my own with whatever's going. Not against: with.

—Robert Frost

Once there was an old man who needed to transition from his beloved home into an assisted care facility. Before he moved, a home care worker visited with him. "This must be very difficult for you," she remarked. "It's not hard at all," he said to her with a smile.

When moving day arrived, the home care worker drove him. "This must be very difficult for you," she said. The old man smiled at her. "It's not hard at all."

The woman grew concerned. She had taken many people to the facility, and most were far less cheery. "Let me tell you about this facility," the woman said as she escorted him through the lobby. "I love it here," the old man replied as he looked around him.

"I'm really worried about you," she began. "I've never seen someone so cheery about leaving his home and coming to this facility." The old man patted her arm. "I make it a point of asking God to give me the strength to accept each moment as it comes. So when I asked this time, He assured me that no matter where I live, He is always with me."

I greet this new day with acceptance of all that will happen.

Progress always involves risks. You can't steal second base and keep your foot on first.

—*Frederick B. Wilcox*

The great things in the world happened as a result of risk taking. Explorers and adventurers discovered new lands. Inventors tinkered and created amazing inventions. Businesses sprang from simple visions. Great diseases were conquered by those who risked experimentation.

The accomplishments of these and so many other people all started from the same place: a willingness to take risks. They did not shy away from risking everything, even without the guarantee of a positive or beneficial outcome.

Beginning your recovery is also taking a risk. But what differentiates your risk from those of the greatest risk takers is that your outcome is assured of being positive and beneficial. Think of the great number of people who use and abuse and do nothing to change their circumstances. Then think of all those—yourself included—who are waking up each day ready to take the risk of finding a better way of living. You may begin your day with the fear that you may fail, doubt that you might not succeed, or dread over the difficult things you must do. But remember that the risk you are taking in your life today guarantees a better future.

What great thing will I accomplish today in recovery by taking a risk?

If you mess up, 'fess up.

—*Author unknown*

Self-respect is developed, in part, from your ability to accept and take full responsibility for your actions. Even when you make mistakes or behave badly, your willingness to own up to your part in such things makes you a better person. Your humility in being able to ask for forgiveness displays the depth of understanding you have for the hurt or harm you may have caused others.

But until you can take responsibility for your actions and place this responsibility squarely on your shoulders, you may spend the majority of your time looking for someone or something else to blame.

When you blame others you not only show them little regard, but you are, in essence, giving up on yourself. You may think that you are saving face by pointing a finger in another direction, but what you are really doing is pointing the finger at yourself. You are saying, "Look at me. I am someone who would rather find a scapegoat than take responsibility. I am not a person you can trust or respect." And whenever you cannot trust or respect yourself, it will be hard for others to feel that way about you.

The power to grow self-respect is within me. I will own up to the problems that are mine and fix them.

I have had, and may still have, a thousand friends, as they are called, in life, who are like one's partners in the waltz of this world—not much remembered when the ball is over.
—*Lord Byron*

In the online world, you may have dozens of friends through connections facilitated by social networks and forums. Chances are you have never met these friends. You could be standing behind one in a grocery store line and never know that the two of you have been exchanging daily e-mails. While your online friends may give helpful advice and may "be there" for you whenever you are online, it is important to distinguish between those who are true friends and those who have "friended" you.

True friends are there in times of misfortune as well as times of gladness. They can be helpful when you are sick or need a hug. They may understand you better than you understand yourself. They love you, even when you do not love yourself. They will tell you the truth, even when you do not want to hear it.

While your online community can be of value to your life, just be aware of how much time you devote to those people so you do not take away time and attention from your true friends.

I will limit my online friends so I have more time to devote to my true friends.

I don't believe in ageing. I believe in forever altering one's aspect to the sun. Hence my optimism.
—*Virginia Woolf*

You may have joined the program at a more mature age than most of the people you see at meetings. You may even question why, at your age, you are in a program of recovery.

Yet no matter what your chronological age, it is important to be willing to change and to never lose your dedication to that commitment. At those times when you doubt whether you belong in the program, think of all of those years in which you were miserable. Reflect on all of the things and people you lost from your life because of your addiction. Consider your current state of health and how drugs and alcohol ate away at your body and mind. And think about how hopeless and disconnected you once were from a spiritual life.

Recovery offers hope for a better life for anyone of any age. It does not matter if this better life for you consists of one day, one year, or several years. The peace and serenity that comes from being clean and sober can make a huge difference in your life.

I am older than most of those I meet in recovery. But I am growing younger in mind, body, and spirit each day.

The conversation whipped gaily around the table like rags in a high wind.

—Margaret Halsey

The recovery program is based on communication and dialogue that enables members to become fully engaged in their recovery. It is not a place of silence or withholding, but of freely expressing one's thoughts and of talking with others. The person who opens the meeting with a story does so in order to encourage discussion. The more others share in response to the story, the greater will be the exchange of information and knowledge.

Yet communication can be hard when you have spent your life avoiding discussion or suppressing your feelings rather than expressing them. While alcohol or drugs may have made it easier for you to be more open with others, the goal of drinking or drugging was to get drunk or high so meaningful discussion could be avoided and feelings could be numbed.

Freedom from addiction provides you with freedom of expression. Your participation in discussion brings about greater self-awareness as well as a deeper understanding of others. Too, the more you converse with others, the more fully developed your social skills can be—skills that can be valuable in many other areas of your life.

I will engage in conversations and share my feelings with others so I can learn more about myself and develop more confidence.

Nine-tenths of wisdom consists of being wise in time.
                                        —*Theodore Roosevelt*

Choosing to enter the program is a wise decision. But how you choose to go through your process of recovery requires wisdom. You will need to make decisions along the way that are right for you. The basis of making these decisions depends upon whether you approach your recovery with folly, or with wisdom.

It is folly to think that you must work on everything all at once. Trying to take on too much too soon can scatter your attention. Wisdom comes from the understanding that you need to take things one step at a time.

It is folly to think you can handle your recovery on your own. Wisdom comes from refusing to go it alone and accepting the help and guidance of others.

It is folly to think that you can work through your recovery with speed. Wisdom comes from the understanding that recovery is not a timed event but one that requires a slow, dedicated pace to learn from the past and formulate strategies to overcome each day's challenges, and then celebrating accomplishments.

It is folly to think that everything you do in recovery will be perfect. Wisdom comes from accepting that failure may happen and applying that experience to find what could work.

I will approach my recovery with wisdom.

Each of us has something to give that no one else has.
—Elizabeth O'Connor

Have you ever looked at others and wished you had their qualities and talents? Have you ever thought that your life would be better if you could be just like them? Admiration of others is not necessarily a bad thing. What you admire in them can help you to focus on similar things you would like to develop in yourself. But when admiration goes too far it can dominate your thinking, turn your focus away from yourself, and develop into jealousy.

When you are jealous of what others have, you take precious time away from yourself. Rather than count your blessings, you count theirs. Instead of considering your worth, you consider theirs. Rather than feel secure in yourself, you see their security. Jealousy is, quite simply, an emotion based on fear. It is a feeling that you will never measure up, never be loved, never achieve success, never develop talents and skills, and never do anything as good as someone else.

Rather than spend your life looking outwardly at others, turn your thoughts inward. Visualize jealousy as weeds that must be removed. Place your energy on what things you would like to change in yourself, and take action.

I will remove the weeds of jealousy from my mind so I can make myself into a beautiful, flourishing garden.

I have a "carpe diem" mug and, truthfully, at six in the morning the words do not make me want to seize the day. They make me want to slap a dead poet.
—Joanne Sherman

How you begin the day often sets the tone for how you approach the rest of the day. Get out of bed groggy, and you may find yourself slogging through the morning and afternoon. Hit the snooze button several times, and you may spend the rest of the day wishing you could put everything on hold. Start out late, and your day may be off-schedule and filled with stress. Snap at others right from the start, and you may come off like a snapping turtle throughout the day.

Just as the recovery program teaches you a different way to live your life, you can apply new ways of doing things to transform your morning attitude. Take care of some chores in the evening so you're not overwhelmed in the morning. Use meditation and positive thinking before you fall asleep to develop a good frame of mind for the morning. Go to bed earlier to get extra sleep.

You can wake up in the morning feeling like an ogre, or in a positive frame of mind. The choice is yours.

I will practice good evening rituals so I can more fully appreciate the start of the day.

I am filled with confidence, not that I shall succeed in worldly things, but that even when things go badly for me I shall still find life good and worth living.
—*Etty Hillesum*

It can be impossible to achieve your goals and aspirations when you have little confidence in yourself. Whether your confidence is low because of the continual criticism you received as a child or a result of the accumulated failures, losses, and disappointments you experienced in your life, it can be reassuring to know that your confidence can always be built or rebuilt.

To begin you need to accept responsibility as the builder. While others can provide you with support, they don't have the tools and materials.

To create this structure, you will need a large bucket of positivity. Negative thoughts are like bent nails; they go nowhere. So discard them and replace them with positive thoughts. You will also need assorted pieces of wood. A structure is composed of many smaller pieces of wood, not one enormous piece. So set small goals that can be easily achieved. The more you achieve, the greater your confidence will be. Finally, you will need a fresh coat of paint. When you take time on your outward appearance, you can feel better about yourself.

Today I will focus on building myself into a structure of self-confidence.

I cannot meet with a single day when I am not hurried along, driven to my wits'-end by urgent work, business to attend to, or some service to render.

—*George Sand*

If asked to describe each of your days as if they were pictures in a coloring book, what colors would you use? Perhaps gray would suit days filled with sadness or despair. Maybe fire-engine red would signify the urgency and stress you sometimes feel. And a brilliant blue would be used when your thinking is clear and your future seems bright.

But while your days may be filled with a multitude of colors, there is one color that is often neglected: white. White is a perfect complement to any color you choose. White space provides breathing room and gives you the opportunity to see and appreciate all of the colors. When you add white to each of the days in your coloring book, you are creating a space in which you can free your mind and welcome peace and serenity. And you are allowing space with no clutter, no stress, and no confusion.

Think of those days that are filled to the brim with appointments, activities, meetings, deadlines, and endless rushing. Add some white space to those days to give yourself the opportunity to experience serenity.

Today I will use white as part of the palette of my day.

*"It's a question of discipline," the little prince told me. . . .
"When you've finished washing and dressing each morning, you must tend to your planet."*
—Antoine de Saint-Exupéry

Most consider procrastination to be the action taken to avoid an unpleasant task—for example, rather than mow the lawn you watch the baseball game. Recovery can fall into that category of an unpleasant task. You might think, then, that being in recovery means you are not a procrastinator. After all, you joined the program even though you knew it would not be easy. But even if you never procrastinated before you entered the program, you may find it is something you now do quite well.

Perhaps the process of working the Steps seems so daunting that you have delayed getting started. Or, since you were so adept in the past at ignoring your shortcomings and fears, the program's requirement that you come to terms with them has you backing away.

You may become more adept at procrastination whenever you compare the pace of recovery to the pace of your life. It is far easier to do those things that will have an immediate reward than attend to those that will require diligence and attention over an extended period of time. By understanding the reasons why you are procrastinating, you can be more capable of overcoming it.

Today my motto is: Action, not procrastination!

In solitude, where we are least alone.

—*Lord Byron*

In solitude, you are never alone. Solitude is a time in which you can engage in many connections. You can take a hike through a forest and hear the sounds of the birds and the air rustle the leaves on the trees. You can look around you at the greenery and growth of living things and feel the crunch of the earth beneath your feet. The experience of all of these things makes you feel a part of them—not apart from them—thereby shifting your feelings of disconnection to connection.

Solitude is a time when you can choose to look inwardly rather than outwardly, when you engage in self-examination, contemplation, and discovery. It can be a time when you remove yourself from the voices of others and the sounds of everyday life so that, in the silence that remains, you can hear your own voice.

Solitude is also a time for connecting to your Higher Power, when you seek greater knowledge to better understand your purpose. It can be a time of prayer asking for the strength to overcome obstacles so you can meet all of the challenges you must face.

Today I will not consider myself alone and lonely, but at peace in a solitude that provides connections and comfort.

All changes, even the most longed for, have their melancholy . . . we must die to one life before we can enter another.

—Anatole France

In the movie *Defending Your Life*, those who die are put on trial. Where they go next—to a joyful afterlife or back to earth to do it all over again—is determined by a panel of judges.

As the main character is on trial, he falls in love and realizes he will most likely not be with the woman in the after-life because they made different choices in their earthly lives. When the judges confirm this, he takes an enormous risk. He refuses to lose out on the opportunity to be with the one he loves and goes against the judges' decision to be with her in the after-life.

The program teaches that in order to gain a new way of life, you must release your former one. By developing a greater understanding of the harm your former life has caused, you are more capable of seeing the mistakes you made, the risks you did not take, and the opportunities you let slip away. And then you have a choice: return to your former life, or enter into a new way of living.

Today I will let go of my former life and develop a new way of living.

Whatever there be of progress in life comes not through adaptation but through daring. . . .

—*Henry Miller*

When you were a child your parents may have measured your growth by drawing a pencil line on a wall above your head. Each time a line was added, you had a way of measuring your progress. When you started school, your report card showed your grades from term to term and provided a greater understanding of how you were advancing in your education. You had another way of measuring your progress.

There are many times in your life when you can measure your progress quite clearly. But how do you measure your progress in recovery? You can certainly feel what it is like to be clean and sober. You can receive recognition for the amount of time you have accrued through key anniversary dates. And you can know where you are in your work on the Twelve Steps.

Rather than strive to see where you are, focus instead on how far you have come from the life you once lived and from the person you once were. Reflect on the quality of the relationships you have today. Consider all of the risks you have taken that you might never have undertaken. Then ask yourself, "Who do I like better: the person I once was, or the person I am now?"

Today I recognize and celebrate my progress.

If any one of you is without sin, let him be the first to throw a stone at her.

—*John 8:7*

Writer Annie Dillard relates in her book *Pilgrim at Tinker Creek* a conversation an Eskimo has with a missionary priest. The Eskimo asks if he would go to hell after he died if he did not know about God and sin. The priest replies that if he did not know about such things, he would not be faced with hell. Why, the Eskimo then asks the priest, did he tell him about God and sin?

You may feel the same way in your work on Step Seven. Once you are confronted with the sins and transgressions you committed in your life as an addict, you may end up feeling much as the Eskimo did: that you were better off not knowing about your shortcomings.

But it is through this knowledge that you can learn to accept responsibility for your actions and learn how to treat yourself and others with greater respect and kindness. Through greater recognition of your shortcomings comes a sense of humility. You can recognize that you are not perfect, that you are not without fault, and that you will sometimes fail.

Step Seven teaches that I am not alone when I face my shortcomings. My Higher Power is there to help me to become a better person.

AUGUST

Made a list of all persons we had harmed, and became willing to make amends to them all.

—*Step Eight*

A prayer is a humble and heartfelt communication with a power greater than yourself. A prayer can admit a weakness, communicate a need, or convey praise and gratitude. Prayers can unburden your heart, give you strength and courage, and deepen your faith and trust in a Higher Power. Use the following prayer as you work on your understanding and acceptance of Step Eight.

Step Eight Prayer

Higher Power, I pray for your guidance. You have helped me to recognize and remove my defects of character. I come before you ready to take on the challenge presented by Step Eight. I need your strength to guide me as I make a list of all I have harmed. I will take responsibility for the errors of my ways. I will do everything I can to face up to those I have harmed and to confess my sins against them. I seek your forgiveness for not living a life of love.

Higher Power, I ask for your strength so I may look into the eyes of those I have harmed and find the courage to speak with honesty and regret. I ask for your strength so I may listen to whatever is said to me without anger or defensiveness. Higher Power, thank you for listening to my prayer.

Those who flee temptation generally leave a forwarding address.

—*Lane Olinghouse*

You may recall the fable about the wind and the sun, and how they argued about who was stronger. One day they saw a man clad in an overcoat walking down a path. The wind bragged it was so strong it could remove the man's coat. So it blew powerful gusts, but the man clutched his coat tighter. Then the sun had its turn. It began to beam its rays down on the man. The man grew warm in the sun's heat and removed his overcoat.

One can easily believe the sun is the winner. Yet there is another way to look at this story. When you see it as one that symbolizes the power to resist temptation, both the wind and the sun become temptation. One surrounds the man with frightening energy; the other merely lets its presence be known.

Before you came into the program, your habit was like the sun—it did nothing more than offer itself to you, and you succumbed to its power. But in recovery, temptation is like the strong wind. It will always be swirling about you, striving to force you to yield to its power. Even though the winds of temptation will continually challenge you, take heart. You are much stronger than you think.

I will resist temptation today because I am strong. I am more powerful than any temptation.

God grant me the serenity to accept the people I cannot change, the courage to change the one I can, and the wisdom to know it's me.

—Author unknown

This variation of "The Serenity Prayer," originally penned by Reinhold Niebuhr, serves as a reminder that recovery does not begin—or end—simply when you stop using. While this is certainly the most vital change you need to make, what is of equal importance is changing yourself. Ask yourself, "Who am I without my habit? What talents and abilities have I suppressed or not realized? What can I achieve when I give myself the opportunity?"

If you take away your habit but stay the same person you were when you were using, you run the risk of losing your commitment to recovery. As it is sometimes said in AA, "Nothing changes if nothing changes."

Changing yourself works best when you break it down into a series of small changes. Did you lie a lot when you were using? If so, you can learn to be more truthful. Did you feel more tempted to use when you were tired or stressed? If so, then you need to make changes in your life that will add more time for relaxation and rest.

Recovery represents a time in which I become more aware of who I am so I can change for the better.

*Those who think they have not time for bodily exercise
will sooner or later have to find time for illness.*
—Edward Stanley

A good number of the world's greatest athletes have experienced career-ending injuries. Some approached such injuries with a defeatist attitude. Because they could not engage in the sport they loved, they gave up completely on exercise. Others, however, used a positive attitude to rebound from their injuries so they could discover a different activity they could enjoy.

Finding an exercise you enjoy can be challenging as you get older. Injuries may present limitations. The stamina you once enjoyed in your youth can take away some of the ease with which you once played a sport. There may be other limitations as well. The busier your daily schedule is, the harder it can be to find time for regular exercise.

Just because you cannot engage in your favorite exercise does not mean you cannot or should not exercise at all. And using a busy schedule as an excuse for not exercising will end up working against your overall health in the long run. Removing an unhealthy habit begins a cleansing process that will make you feel better. But you need regular exercise to strengthen your body, tone your muscles, and build a foundation for a healthier future.

Today I will commit to being fit.

Resentment is an extremely bitter diet, and eventually poisonous. I have no desire to make my own toxins.
—Neil Kinnock

A Cherokee chief was quite proud of his young grandson, but many members complained that the young man was filled with anger and treated others with disrespect. So the chief called to his grandson. "What do you want?" his grandson snapped.

"Two wolves live inside of us all," the chief said. "One wolf is good. He helps you feel joy and love. He shows you the beauty of the world. And he creates in you compassion, understanding, and forgiveness. But there is also another wolf. He teaches you to see only evil. He causes you to feel anger and scorn. He is full of himself, and his powerful ego makes him feel superior. It is a fight to the death with these two, because one must be the winner."

The young man thought for a moment, then asked his grandfather, "So, which wolf will win?"

"The one that you feed," he replied.

When you hold onto anger, turn it upon yourself, or treat others with disrespect and scorn, your anger erects walls so high that you cannot see over them. But when you let go of your anger, you treat yourself and others with respect, kindness, and compassion. You build bridges to yourself and to others.

I will not let the wolf of anger win.

We tend to forget that happiness doesn't come as a result of getting something we don't have, but rather of recognizing and appreciating what we do have.
—Frederick Koenig

How you receive a gift conveys much about your ability to feel gratitude. This gift can be a material object, a kindness shown to you by another, one of your abilities, or a beautiful sunrise that starts your day. No matter how a gift comes to you, how you respond to the gift reflects how capable you are of being grateful for everything you have been given.

Gratitude consists of three parts: the recognition of something you have been given, an appreciative attitude for having received it, and the ability to express your appreciation.

But gratitude is not just about receiving. The more grateful you can be for what you have in your life, the more willing you can be to give to others. This builds a habit of gratitude that begins with you and can extend outward to others. What results is a beautiful continuum to gratitude: as you take in the gifts you are given and are filled with gratitude for them, you can reach out to spread this gratitude to others.

Each day I will think of three things for which I am most grateful. I will spread this attitude of gratitude to others.

God brings men into deep waters, not to drown them, but to cleanse them.

—*John Aughey*

A woman who had great faith rented a boat with the intent of crossing a lake. "Be back within the hour," the boat rental owner advised. "A storm is coming." The woman smiled, "God will protect me."

When she was partway across the lake, the storm rolled in and her boat capsized. Soon she saw the boat rental owner steering a boat toward her. "Get in," he shouted, but the woman said, "God will save me."

Sometime later, the woman heard a helicopter and saw a long cable extending down toward her. "Climb up," the pilot shouted, but she refused. "God will take care of me."

It was not long before the woman was standing, dripping wet, before God. "Why did you let me drown?" she asked. "I have faith in you. I thought you would save me."

"Who do you think sent the boat and the helicopter?" God asked.

Remember that your Higher Power can be a lifesaver, but only when you can grab hold and take action on your own. Reach out to God whenever you are in need, but also take responsibility for finding what you are looking for.

Today I have faith in a Higher Power and also in myself.

A lie may take care of the present, but it has no future.
—Author unknown

When you were using, you most likely knew that you had a problem with drugs or alcohol but you were afraid to acknowledge this truth to yourself. So you may have lied to yourself and told yourself that things were not that bad. You convinced yourself of one big lie: that you could, in fact, stop anytime you wanted to. You just did not want to.

You also lied because you were afraid of what others would think of you. Perhaps they suspected you had a problem with drugs and alcohol. But you created lies to convince them they were wrong and told more lies to cover up your addictive behaviors.

Yet here you are in recovery. Your lies may have bought you a little time and postponed the inevitable, but they never changed the fact that you were an addict. And now, in recovery, you have learned that you can experience greater freedom and peace when you no longer lie, cover up, or act in secrecy. Today you can acknowledge, with total honesty, that you are an addict. Recovery helps you to see the value in honesty. Your truthfulness sets you free from your former life.

The program teaches me honesty and releases me from fear so I will speak truthfully.

Only through our connectedness to others can we really know and enhance the self. And only through working on the self can we begin to enhance our connectedness to others.

—Harriet Goldhor Lerner

How many times do you compare yourself to others and think, "I'll never be good enough." When you look at others and recognize their strengths, but then look at yourself and see only your weaknesses, you are creating a form of comparative measurement in which the worth of others rises while your self-confidence drops. By the same token, if you choose to look only at the faults of others as a way of boosting your self-confidence, you are judging your own self-worth through a false comparison.

When you can enjoy your life without comparing it to the life of others, you can develop a greater connection to those around you. You can learn from them and use their experiences to influence yours in positive ways. The greater your ability is to forge connections with others, the more you will be able to see how much you share in common with them.

When you can look at your own strengths and see your own value, and look at others in the same way, you have the opportunity to build a shared experience with them.

Today I will not compare myself to others, but connect with them.

To change one's life: Start immediately. Do it flamboy-antly. No exceptions.

—William James

Did you know that a mayfly, an aquatic insect, has a life span that ranges from thirty minutes to nearly a day? So when you hear people say, "Life is short," it may seem to be a false statement when you compare the life span of a human being to other living creatures.

You may live for many more years, but each of these years is made up of precious moments. Squander these moments, put off doing something that needs immediate attention, or take for granted that you will have plenty of time to do what you need to do in the future, and you may find—at some point in your life—that you have wasted the time you had.

Strive to live each day as if it were your one and only beginning. Imagine that you are like the mayfly, with only a single twenty-four-hour period in which to fully appreciate your life and to take care of all of those things that need tending. Start now on your new beginning, and you will be that much farther down that road tomorrow.

I only have one today. How can I make it into a new beginning?

So many people in this world have come to believe that they are locked into their life pattern . . . yet, new perception choices can truly set us free.

—Chelle Thompson

Sometimes the transition of letting go of the person you once were can be unsettling and highly emotional. You may even feel at times as if you have lost your identity. As you learn more about your addiction, develop greater awareness about the behaviors you exhibited when you were using, pray to a Higher Power—perhaps for the first time in years—or hear yourself admitting or saying things you might have never aired in the past, you may feel that you have no idea of who you are anymore.

Just as you may feel unsettled with the "new you," so too may others feel off-balance in their interactions with you. Recovery is a bit like wearing a new pair of shoes for the first time. Before they are broken in, you will be conscious of something that feels quite different.

But being out of touch with who you once were is not necessarily a bad thing. You are still somebody. Recovery is simply giving you an "upgrade" so that you can refine your self-image in ways that make you feel better about yourself.

Who I am becoming represents a magnificent work in progress.

Diseases of the soul are more dangerous and numerous than those of the body.

—Cicero

An Irish proverb advises, "A good laugh and a long sleep are the best cures in the doctor's book." A Danish proverb says, "Fresh air impoverishes the doctor." And an Arabic proverb states, "He who has health has hope; and he who has hope has everything."

What each of these proverbs focuses on is the idea that your overall health can be measured—and affected—by more than just the attention you pay to your physical needs. Without a healthy mental outlook, emotional stability, and regular attention to your spiritual development, your health can be affected. Stress, loneliness, depression, and a sense of disconnection from life can chip away at even the healthiest of bodies.

You can begin today to take small steps that will help to increase your overall health. Set aside time to meditate, pray, or simply clear your mind from the hustle and bustle of the day. Volunteer to help those who are less fortunate. Spend time with your children, your friends, or a loved one. Make these things part of your daily routine, and you may find that you not only feel better about yourself, but you also feel better on the inside.

Today I will pay attention to my mental, emotional, and spiritual health.

When you come to the end of your rope, tie a knot and hang on.

—Franklin D. Roosevelt

In the past, you may have attempted to use your own power to climb out of the deep, dark well of addiction. The only equipment you had to help in your escape was a frayed rope attached to a weak anchor. Even when you exerted your greatest effort to inch your way up the slippery sides of the well, the rope would unravel or the anchor would slip and you would fall back down to the bottom.

But when you are ready, the program offers a sturdy ladder that is held firmly in place by many others. The strength of this ladder offers you the opportunity to finally escape from your prison. It is up to you to make the climb.

As you draw ever closer to the top of the well, when you can fully release yourself from your addiction, you will be greeted by strong hands and encouraging words. These are the hands and voices of your rescuers, who were once trapped in that same well. They know how hard it is to make the climb. But they are committed to helping you so you do not lose your grip or your determination.

The ladder of recovery is strong. I trust that it will hold me and lead me to a place in which I can grow.

The block of granite which was an obstacle in the pathway of the weak becomes a stepping-stone in the pathway of the strong. That block of granite is often nothing more than a decision.

—Thomas Carlyle

Trails through national parks and forests are often clearly marked and well-maintained. But sometimes a heavy snowmelt or downpour can turn a trickling stream into a tricky obstacle that needs to be navigated in order to continue following the trail.

When this happens, hikers can turn around and postpone their hike until another day. They can attempt to create their own trail by rambling through—and possibly destroying—delicate forest undergrowth. They can slog through the water, soaking their footgear and creating discomfort for the rest of the hike. Or they can utilize the resources available to them, such as by positioning large rocks as stepping-stones to cross the stream.

How you navigate the trails of your recovery can be seen in similar terms. You must choose how to navigate these trails, both in times when the footing is good and when it is not. Be like the hiker who thinks first about how to handle the challenges, so you can continue safely along your journey.

Today I will make choices that will keep me on the path of recovery.

The Fox and the Cat

One day a fox and a cat were discussing the methods they used to avoid their enemies. "I have many clever ways to escape," bragged the fox. "I only have one," replied the cat.

Just then they heard a pack of hounds headed their way. The cat immediately scampered up a nearby tree. But the fox froze. He thought about digging a hole. He considered that he could jump into a pond and swim to safety. He figured that he was so quick on his feet that he could create a very confusing trail for the hounds to follow. As the fox continued his internal debate, he remained immobilized. So the hounds easily caught him.

The moral of the story: *Better to have one safe way than a hundred unproven ones.*

How many times in the past did you strive to convince yourself that you did not have a problem? And yet no amount of excuses saved you from your problem. The program is your one and only safe way to escape from the ravages caused by addiction.

Today I will be like the cat, which used one sure way to ensure safety.

We have two ears and one mouth so that we can listen twice as much as we speak.

—*Epictetus*

A Zen story tells of four monks who had made a vow to meditate for two weeks without speaking. They decided that each night they would gather in a dark room, light a candle, and meditate in silence.

One night the candle flickered, and then went out. The first monk immediately cried out, "Oh, no, the candle has gone out." The second monk said, "You have just spoken!" The third monk pointed out, "You two have just broken our vow of silence." The fourth monk arose, began a little dance, and said, "I win! I am the only one who did not speak."

It is through listening that you are able to develop a greater understanding for what others are going through. Your listening enables you to stop the urge to control others, to overcome prejudice and judgment, and to gain greater awareness of what is going on around you. While it takes courage to stand up and speak at a meeting or to admit your shortcomings to others, it also takes courage to sit down and truly listen.

I will listen to the words of others, the guidance of my Higher Power, and the sounds of silence. In doing so, I will gain greater wisdom.

Those that are most slow in making a promise are the most faithful in the performance of it.
—Jean-Jacques Rousseau

Each day you may hear hundreds of promises. Advertisers promise that your clothes will be cleaner, your hair will be thicker and fuller, or you will shed excess weight in a short amount of time. Similarly, politicians make campaign promises to end war, lower taxes, increase employment, and unite the two parties of government. The sad truth is, you have probably developed a thick skin to such promises. You know that the product you buy will most likely not deliver the promised results. You know that when the politician is elected, the promises made will most likely not be fulfilled.

Just as you do not trust the advertisers or politicians for the promises they make and do not keep, so too may others have lost trust and faith in the promises you made when you were using. In the beginning, they wanted to believe what you were saying. But, over time, you simply became an advertiser or politician making promises just to get buy-in.

In your recovery it is important for you to make promises and to deliver upon those promises. Make promises that you can and will fulfill, and you will be building a lasting foundation of trust.

Today I will deliver on any promise I make.

Addictive behaviors come in many forms and packages and they can all put us into slavery where we are no longer free to walk in what God has given us.
—Rodney Johnson

Those with addictive tendencies may not only be addicted to alcohol, chemical substances, gambling, cigarettes, or an excess of food, but also to a multitude of other things.

You may use technology so much that if you cannot get a signal for your cell phone or log on to your computer, your only focus becomes reconnection. You may be a daily exerciser who feels miserable when you have to skip a workout, so you end up creating misery all around you. You may focus solely on your work and not give time or attention to the needs of others—or even to your own needs.

Sometimes the most harmless or helpful habits can grow into addictions. If being without them—even for a short period of time—causes you discomfort, makes you lash out in anger and frustration at others, escalates your levels of stress or anxiety, or absorbs most if not all of your focus and attention, then your good habit may have developed into an addiction.

Today I will be aware of how being without a particular activity affects me.

No matter what accomplishments you make, somebody helped you.

—Althea Gibson

Once two people were lost in a desert. Hours passed into days. One morning, using their last reserves of strength, they made their way to a mountaintop so they could find shelter from the heat and die with some level of comfort. But when they got to the top, what they saw on the other side was astounding. It was a magnificent oasis of trees with ripened fruit and a crystal-clear waterfall.

They raced to the oasis and drank their fill of water and ate fruit until their bellies were full. Then one lay down on the lush ground and sighed with contentment. But the other began to make vessels in which to carry water and gather fruit. "What are you doing?" asked the one who was relaxing.

"I am returning to the desert so I can help others who are lost find their way here."

Recovery is based upon a fellowship that offers a mutually supportive alliance. It thrives upon the interdependency of its members and through a cooperative spirit that provides unity for achieving shared and personal goals. This, in turn, builds strength—both individually, and within the group as a whole.

Today I will help others, and they will help me.

Every survival kit should include a sense of humor.
—Author unknown

It may be hard for you to find anything humorous as you work on your recovery. After all, addiction is quite serious, and how it affected you and impacted your life may be far from comedic.

So when you hear others laugh at a meeting or listen as someone tells a lighthearted story of how she came to AA, you may feel as if these people are not taking their recovery seriously. You may think that your problems must be much worse than theirs because you cannot find the humor in them. Or you may believe that you must have lost much more in your life than others have. After all, how could they laugh if they had experienced devastations similar to yours?

And yet without being able to approach your recovery with some sense of humor, it may be harder to rise above your difficulties. Humor has a way of diffusing conflict, lightening burdens, and easing resentment and anger. Humor can also provide a useful defense against difficulties, challenges, and hardships so that you are better able to rise above them, rather than let them defeat you.

Humor helps to part the dark clouds in my life so the sun may shine. I will find humor in my recovery so I can approach it with a lighter heart.

I used to love night best but the older I get the more treasures and hope and joy I find in mornings.
—Terri Guillemets

No matter how challenging your day, when it draws to an end you can trust that a new day will dawn. With each dawn comes a clean slate. What has gone on before is in the past. What lies before you is the unknown. You have the opportunity to turn this unknown into something positive.

Rather than see the new day as no different from any other day, you have the ability to make it into something magnificent, something beautiful, and something unlike no other. You do not need to spend money or invest a great deal of energy into facilitating such a change. All you need to do is approach the day with a different attitude. Make one small change in your morning routine or replace dread with excited anticipation, and such changes can make a world of difference.

In the day that lies before you, if you trust that absolutely anything can happen, it will. Dawn ignites a flame of possibility that can enlighten and invigorate your entire day.

I awaken to this day filled with hope and anticipation.

Pick battles big enough to matter, small enough to win.
—*Jonathan Kozol*

Have you ever thought that you could be much stronger if only you did not have so many weaknesses? Everyone faces challenges in their lives and embarks on journeys into the unknown. But it is not just those who consider themselves to be strong who are able to succeed. It is also those who are well aware of their weaknesses and who can convert these weaknesses into strengths who also are able to succeed.

Perhaps you are intimidated by large projects or ones that come to fruition after a long period of time. First, create a plan to break down the project into several smaller projects. Or you can formulate a schedule that allows you to measure your progress at the end of each week. By making these simple changes, you can ignore your weaknesses, overcome a negative mind-set, and focus on your strengths.

You can apply this exercise for every challenge you face in life. To convert your weaknesses into strengths, first view what it is you need to do. Next, consider how to meet the challenge by developing a step-by-step plan that works to your strengths. Then use your strengths to carry through with your plan.

I can worry about my shortcomings, or I can work toward my strengths. Which do I choose?

Worrying is like a rocking chair. It gives you something to do, but it gets you nowhere.

—*Glenn Turner*

You may be someone who is in a constant state of worry. But where has all of your worrying gotten you? Worry prevents you from living in the present. It does not rob your time from yesterday—that is already over and done with—and it cannot take anything from tomorrow, because that has not yet arrived. What worry does is sap the life of the day you have before you.

While many people worry about a lot of things, worry is based predominantly on self-doubt. Worry is the voice in your head that prevents you from believing in yourself. Even though you have friends and family who truly think you are special, worry strives to convince you that you are not as good as others think you are. Worry is the "but" that butts into praise you receive, achievements you make, and the time you have before you. Today ease your worry by replacing some of worry's buts with positive thoughts of your own.

Whenever the voice of worry tells me I am not good enough, I will answer, "But I am good enough, and here are some things that prove that."

It wasn't raining when Noah built the ark.
—Howard Ruff

To stay clean and sober, it is vital to create a foundation of support that will help you to strengthen your commitment and resist the temptation to use or abuse.

Become active in your group by helping before or after meetings and make new friends. Together you can enjoy activities that are free from drugs or alcohol. Those who are clean and sober have experience and wisdom that support your recovery.

Use a daily book of meditations for guidance each day. Read materials available at meetings so you can stay focused on your recovery. Read—or reread—the Big Book.

From time to time you may need to attend events where alcohol is served or where your former drinking buddies will be. If you can invite someone from the program, you will have a supportive guest to be with you. If you cannot, arrange to get together with your sponsor immediately after the event.

Connect with your Higher Power through prayer and meditation. Share your feelings at meetings. Spend regular, quality time with your sponsor. Accept the support and guidance you are given, but remember that your recovery is your responsibility.

I will use tools of support for my recovery.

One must marry one's feelings to one's beliefs and ideas.
That is probably the only way to achieve a measure of
harmony in one's life.

—*Napoleon Hill*

Imagine that the four tires on your car symbolize your
spirit, your knowledge, your dreams, and your feelings. If
even one of these is out of balance, your car will not run
smoothly. It will need more guidance to stay on the road.
It will use up more gasoline. And, over time, each of the
other tires will wear unevenly.

In your recovery you may have three tires that are usually in balance with one another, and one that is not. If
you are holding onto feelings of resentment, anger, or sadness, it can be difficult to embrace the present. If you are
suppressing your feelings rather than expressing them, it
can be harder for you to stay focused. And if you believe
that the feelings of others are more important than your
own, you may have a difficult time accepting and gaining
a better understanding of what it is that you need. Your
tire of feelings is out of balance.

Even if it is hard for you to express your feelings, write
down how you feel. The more you can feel, the greater the
balance you can achieve in your life.

I will not ignore my feelings. I will let them out so I can feel
them.

Courage is only an accumulation of small steps.
                                        —*George Konrad*

In a Sioux Indian story about courage, the Great Creator gathers all living things together and presents them with a challenge. "I gave each of you courage," the Creator says. "But it is something I want humans to work hard to discover. Where can I hide it?"

The eagle spoke. "I am not afraid to soar high into the sky. I will place it among the stars." But the Creator said, "No. One day humans will fly into the skies and easily find this."

The dolphin said, "I am not afraid to dive deep into the ocean. I will deposit it on the ocean floor." But the Creator said, "No. One day humans will go far below the surface of the ocean and find it."

Then a tiny gnat spoke up. "I cannot soar into the sky or dive deep into the ocean or dig into the ground. Even so, I have courage. Why not place it inside of humans? Then it will be up to them to discover it themselves." And so it was.

Until you discover your courage, you will not be able to see how high you can soar and all of the things that you can accomplish.

I will seek the courage within me and use it to guide me in all that I do.

If happiness is activity in accordance with excellence, it is reasonable that it should be in accordance with the highest excellence.

—*Aristotle*

The hospitality industry has earned the nickname of the happiness industry because its ultimate goal is to make customers happy. These businesses thrive when they achieve excellence in customer service and experience.

Imagine that you are the concierge for a busy resort. From the moment guests arrive until their departure, you oversee all aspects of their experience. Even the most difficult and hard-to-please customers need to be treated with courtesy and respect. You must listen closely to your guests' requests and feedback so that you are able to meet all of their needs and correct any mishaps or missteps. All of the promises you make must be fulfilled. If one member in the organization does not perform up to your standards, you must offer appropriate correction and guidance. And you must be available to your guests at all times, and not pass off your responsibilities to others.

You may not realize it, but you are a concierge every day—to yourself. Treat yourself with courtesy and respect at all times. Ensure that your needs are met. And fulfill all the promises you make.

I will show myself the same respect, kindness, courtesy, and love that I show others.

You start by saying no to requests. Then if you have to go to yes, okay. But if you start with yes, you can't go to no.
—*Mildred Perlman*

There may be times when a friend, family member, co-worker, or others ask for your help, and you say yes when you really do not want to. There are some requests made of you that may add to an already full schedule, deprive you of the time in which you need to do something for yourself, or make you uncomfortable.

One of the first words you learn to say in recovery is no. You must say no to your addiction in order to stay on the right path. You must say no to someone who asks you to be a sponsor if you cannot devote the time and attention needed. You must say no to invitations to parties if the presence of alcohol or drugs will put your recovery at risk.

Yet outside of the program it may be more difficult to say no. You may feel guilty if you do. But your recovery must come first. This does not mean you must be selfish or say no to everyone. It simply means you need to make sure your needs are met first.

I will not say yes unless it is right for me to do so.

God gives every bird his worm, but He does not throw it into the nest.

—P.D. James

A young girl loved to ice skate at every opportunity. In the winter she would find a frozen pond; in the summer she used indoor rinks. As she grew older, she won several competitions. Some of the best coaches in the world noticed her and vied to lead her to Olympic glory. She selected a coach who had trained gold-medal Olympians and began working with him.

For the first few weeks, the coach had her focus on the basics of jumps. She begged him to let her practice ice dancing, but he refused. Finally she fired him and hired another, who led her to the Olympics. During the competition, she was locked in a fierce battle with another skater. Their numerical scores were so close that one tiny mistake could spell the difference between a gold or silver medal.

On the final day of competition, she thought back to her first coach, who had made her practice her jumps. She realized that he had provided her with a very valuable lesson. Perfecting even the simplest components of her routine could lead her to victory.

I devote focus to all that I do to be the best I can.

Ritual will always mean throwing away something . . . .
—*G.K. Chesterton*

A young student of Zen came upon a chapter in his reading that talked about how a cat must be tied up before the meditation ritual could begin. Confused, he sought an explanation.

Long ago, the Zen master told him, a spiritual teacher was about to begin his evening meditation with his pupils when a cat who lived in the monastery started to howl outside the door. Its howling was so distracting that the teacher ordered the cat to be tied up. After the teacher died, the cat continued to be tied up during a meditation session. Then, after the cat died, another cat was obtained so that it, too, could be tied up during meditation. Tying up a cat, the Zen master explained, had simply become part of the ritual. "But it serves no purpose," the young student pointed out. "You are right," said the Zen master and immediately tore the chapter out of the meditation book.

If a routine or habitual way of doing something in your life is no longer helping you, it may be time to get rid of it. You can replace it with a beneficial habit, or simply let it go.

I will hold on to those routines and habits that help me.

Even when we know what is right, too often we fail to act . . . putting off the unpleasant and unpopular.
—*Bernard M. Baruch*

Recovery increases your awareness of the ways in which you have hurt or harmed others. This includes reflecting on those times when you have inflicted physical, emotional, and spiritual pain. Because of this, Step Eight presents you with realizations that can lead to shame and asks you to face up to it.

The first part of Step Eight asks you to identify those people you have harmed, but this list represents only the beginning of your work. It is the second part—being willing to make amends to those you have harmed—that requires greater insight and contemplation. Writing down a name is not the same as remembering that you hit or yelled at this person in anger, that you repeatedly lied to this person, or that you caused this person to feel incredible sadness. You may see these images in your head and want to simply erase them forever. But you cannot.

Your willingness to make amends must be heartfelt, which means that you must go further than simply saying, "I'm sorry." How did your actions affect each person on your list? What harm did you cause? The more clearly you can identify those things, the more willing you can be to make amends.

I accept the challenges presented to me in Step Eight.

SEPTEMBER

Made direct amends to such people wherever possible,
except when to do so would injure them or others.
—Step Nine

A prayer is a humble and heartfelt communication with a power greater than yourself. A prayer can admit a weakness, communicate a need, or convey praise and gratitude. Prayers can unburden your heart, give you strength and courage, and deepen your faith and trust in a Higher Power. Use the following prayer as you work on your understanding and acceptance of Step Nine.

Step Nine Prayer

Higher Power, I have made a list of those I have harmed in my addiction. I have become willing to make amends to them all. I ask for your help now so that I may have the courage to make direct amends. I ask for your wisdom and guidance. I need to face those I have let down or mistreated and those to whom I have told lies in an effort to avoid giving up my addiction. I will not let shame lead me down a path of falsehood. I will speak with sincerity, openness, and honesty.

Grant me the wisdom to exhibit actions that are reflective of a person who has compassion and understanding. Let me be your humble servant who shows patience, kindness, respect, and love to everyone. Higher Power, thank you for listening to my prayer.

No one can look back on his schooldays and say with truth that they were altogether unhappy.

—*George Orwell*

When you were a child, you may have been filled with anticipation at the start of a new school year. Perhaps you shopped for new clothes and school supplies. Perhaps, in advancing to a new grade, you had greater opportunities for sports or clubs.

As an adult, you can view this time of year as a period in your recovery in which you return to a fresh start in the "school of sobriety." You can think of your meetings as classroom sessions and listen with greater attention to the discussion. You can resolve to gain deeper understanding about your addiction. You can review the Twelve Steps to determine what you have left undone and make up your mind to no longer put off Step work you have avoided. You can reread the Big Book and strive to gain greater knowledge.

When you think of September as an opportunity for opening yourself up to new discoveries, you can become more deeply involved in all aspects of your recovery: in your mind, your body, and your spirit. What you choose to do can help you to continue on your new path in life— one in which you are clean and sober.

I dedicate this month to renewing and strengthening my commitment to recovery.

Good for the body is the work of the body, and good for the soul is the work of the soul, and good for either is the work of the other.

—*Henry David Thoreau*

Police officers and those in the military wear equipment that offers critical protection from bullets and bombs. Deep-sea divers must wear gear that will insulate them from cold temperatures and regulate their internal pressure so they can ward off the crushing pressure of the depth.

Over the years, you may have fashioned your own protective gear. You may have created an outer shell designed to protect you from feeling your emotions, from opening yourself up to new opportunities, and from developing a spiritual connection. You may have kept yourself locked up within this shell, engaging in your habit while you kept the outside world from entering your life.

Your journey in recovery can be likened to entering a new environment. It is a safe place in which you do not need protective armor and where you can change how you approach life. By developing an attitude of acceptance, openness, and a willingness to take risks, you can free your body from the imprisonment of addiction. You can experience life in all of its richness and fullness and, in so doing, flourish.

I will shed my protective armor so I can grow with a positive, open, and welcoming attitude.

He was paralyzed with the impossibility of either belief or disbelief.

—L. M. Boston

A spiritual leader had embarked on a mission to spread the word of God. One of his followers served as a scout, ensuring the roads ahead were clear. One day the scout returned with bad news: torrential downpours had caused a small stream to swell beyond its banks and they could not advance. The leader instructed them to make camp. The next morning, the leader asked the scout to check on the stream.

"But we could not cross it yesterday," the scout answered.

"Please check," said the leader. So the scout went ahead and checked. He returned with the same news.

Each morning for a week, the leader asked the doubting scout to check on the stream. Once more the scout was sent to check, and this time he returned with good news: they could cross the stream. "There is a lesson to be learned in this," the leader said. "One doubt should not breed eternal doubt. God ensures that what was yesterday is not the same as today. And so it is with faith. To believe, you must replace doubt with faith. Each day you must awaken with faith because one day your faith will be rewarded."

I will be steadfast in my faith so I can overcome my doubts and fears.

Perhaps loving something is the only starting place there is for making your life your own.
—*Alice Koller*

Because you may have been hurt by feeling and expressing love in the past, you may have learned to equate love with pain and disappointment. Because the love you were shown may have been conditional, given to you only when a parent or a partner was in a good mood, you learned that love was inconsistent.

Without knowing love as a wonderful experience that builds you up rather than tears you down, you may have learned to fear the emotion. When others showed you love, you may have felt that there was something wrong with them or there was an ulterior motive to their love. You may have believed that love was never meant to last and doubted that you were even deserving of love.

Love is simply part of the foundation on which you build who you are as a person. It is a cornerstone from which you can learn and grow. Love that is neither felt nor expressed presents you with an incomplete life. Develop a love of your self, a love of a Higher Power, and a love for the goodness of others, and you will find there is nothing to fear in love.

Today I will express and feel love.

It has been said that a butterfly flapping its tender wings in an Amazon rainforest can cause a tsunami in Indonesia.
—*Author unknown*

One of the most amazing things about life is how interconnected and united everything is. One small imbalance or a minor improvement can affect entire ecosystems and the ways in which people live. This is also true for the fellowship within the program of recovery.

Imagine what would happen if one member decided to use the fellowship as a platform to encourage others to drink or use. Consider what might happen if one member presented the group with a different set of Steps to follow.

A fellowship that is not united in a common purpose, that does not follow the guidelines of AA, or that allows even one member to disrupt meetings may put the recovery of others at risk. This can harm the physical health of others, their trust and faith in the fellowship, and their connection to a Higher Power. That is why it is important to remember that you are part of a much larger fellowship. You play an important role in ensuring that your fellowship does not become a personal platform for others.

I will do my part to ensure my connection to AA follows the Traditions and Steps of the program.

A cruel story runs on wheels, and every hand oils the wheels as they run.

—Ouida

Social media have become a fertile ground for spreading lies and rumors, which can sometimes border on bullying. Such postings inflict emotional hurt and make life so miserable for the subjects of such falsehoods that they can have devastating results.

It is human nature to be drawn to gossip and innuendo. But to engage in it—even by listening—runs contrary to the need to be honest and respectful of others. You can let those who enjoy spreading gossip know that you will not tolerate listening to their rumors by asking them three questions.

1. "Is what you are going to share based on something that is truthful?"
2. "Is what you are going to share something nice or good about someone?"
3. "Is what you are going to share useful to know?"

By asking these questions, you create a means of turning aside rumor or gossip. You may also be able to raise the awareness of the speaker about the nature of gossip—that it is hurtful, rather than helpful.

I will not engage in gossip or rumor about others in the program.

Man's extremity is God's opportunity.

—*John Flavel*

Do you ever watch the news about some catastrophic natural disaster and expect to see people so devastated that they are nearly nonfunctional? And yet what you may see are people who exhibit calmness and even an eagerness to do whatever it is they need to in order to improve their situation. What you may hear is how deeply the people believe in God and the faith they have that things will get better.

When do you turn to a Higher Power for guidance and support? For some, it is when a major calamity strikes. For those who are addicts, it may be when they finally hit bottom and come to the realization that they cannot sink any deeper.

Through your helplessness and hurt, prayer to a Higher Power can help you begin the process of rebuilding. Prayer conveys your willingness to accept help. It gives you time in which to reflect upon your priorities and reevaluate them so you can consider new or different ways of doing things. It opens you up so you can learn better or more useful ways of navigating through a difficult period or trauma. And it builds a spiritual relationship that can last a lifetime.

I reach out to a Higher Power so I may learn how to rebuild myself and my life.

My evil genius Procrastination has whispered me to tarry
'til a more convenient season.
                              —*Mary Todd Lincoln*

While it may seem that as you grow older time moves faster, that is just a fallacy. Each person has the same twenty-four hours in a day. But how you make use of each day reflects whether you are a can-do person or a someday person.

If you are a can-do person, you make full use of your time. You know what you need to do and set about doing it. At the end of the day you likely experience a sense of accomplishment. But if you are a someday person—who prefers to get things done "someday"—at the end of the day you may feel that you have done very little. While you may have been a great someday person when you were using, recovery and procrastination are not good partners.

Consider someday as today. Think about something you have been putting off for a while—in recovery or in your personal or professional life—and break it down into small steps. You may feel uncomfortable about something you need to do, but then do it. Ask for help on tasks you find daunting or confusing rather than put them off. Then, at the end of the day, celebrate all that you have accomplished.

Someday has arrived! Today I will act rather than procrastinate.

There are people who live lives little different than the beasts, and I don't mean that badly. I mean that they accept whatever happens day to day without struggle or question or regret.

—*Celeste De Blasis*

Learning to live with what you were born with—from your appearance and innate talents to your failures and shortcomings—is a process of acceptance. Making an honest assessment of who you are—one that is focused on you and not based on comparisons to others—requires acceptance. No one is perfect. But sometimes you can feel disappointed when you know that you have not lived up to the expectations others have of you, or when you recognize how you have fallen short of achieving your goals. You may doubt you can ever become a better person.

Acceptance can be strengthened and developed by making good use of the tools available to you each day in the program—the Serenity Prayer, the Twelve Steps, belief in a power greater than yourself, and fellowship.

The program teaches acceptance, not perfection. Each day presents you with an opportunity to accept all of your qualities—both the good and the not-so-good—so you can gain greater knowledge about yourself. You can then utilize this knowledge to change those things that you can.

Working the program will help me to develop greater acceptance of myself.

Do what you can, with what you have, where you are.
—*Theodore Roosevelt*

A Chinese parable tells of a humble man who daily carried water from a stream to his home. He used two pots—one balanced on each end of a pole—to carry the water. One pot was perfect; the other had a crack in it. The perfect pot was proud of its ability. But the cracked pot was ashamed of its flaw. One day the cracked pot spoke as the man was filling it. "Why haven't you thrown me away?" it asked.

The man silently placed the cracked pot on his pole and slowly began the walk back to his home. Finally, he spoke, "Little cracked pot, please look along your side of the path. What do you see?"

"Flowers," the cracked pot answered.

"That is correct," said the man. "Each spring I plant flower seeds on your side of the path. Every day when we walk back to my home, your leak helps to water the seeds. Now there are flowers, which I can take home and put on my table. Without you being the way you are, there would not be beauty that I can enjoy on my journey home."

Today I will see value and beauty in all that I am and all that I do.

Many people are so concerned with adding days to their life that they forget to add life to their days.
                                        —*Harriet Meyerson*

How can you live in the moment when life is full of distractions or when your thoughts are constantly tumbling you forward into the future or causing you to slip backward into the past? Whether your thoughts move you forward or backward in time, such movement wastes the precious moments in the present you have been given and can influence the way you feel. Even though you may not have awakened feeling sad, thinking about the past may cast a pall over how you feel during the day. Or you may feel anxiety or dread about things that have yet to happen.

Living in the moment is not easy to do. Living in the moment means taking charge of your thoughts so you control them, rather than let them dictate what you think about and how you feel.

There are many techniques you can use to live more in the moment—from reminding yourself of what you are doing at any given time to meditating or enjoying a hobby. Practice living more fully in the moment, and you will be more capable of immersing yourself in and appreciating the day.

Today I will not let thoughts of the past or future intrude upon my ability to live in the moment.

It is easier to gaze into the sun, than into the face of the mystery of God. Such is its beauty and its radiance.
                              —*Hildegard of Bingen*

When you were a child, you may have thought less about yourself and more about the wonder of the world around you, asking questions such as, "Do fish sleep at night?" As you grew older, your questioning may have been based less on the world around you and more on all of the things you were anxious to have or do: "Why can't I have a puppy?"

When you became an adult, you may have thought little about your place in the world or the value of others and asked questions such as, "Why do you always have be on my case?" When you entered the program, you may have asked, "Why do I have to go to meetings?" But as the program gradually became a new way of life for you, your questions changed: "How did I manage to stay alive using when others I know died?"

Asking questions—even those that have no clear answers—helps you to look outside of yourself and to recognize that the world is vast and filled with many mysteries.

Even if I do not know all of the answers, I will continue to ask questions. The more I learn about life, the more I want to learn.

If you don't like how things are, change it! You're not a tree.
—Jim Rohn

Imagine that you have signed up for a white-water rafting weekend. As you head off down the river on your first day, your guide shouts commands and issues warnings of upcoming hazards. When the raft nearly flips over in a particularly rough patch of water, he says you are doing an awful job. By the end of the day, you feel like a failure.

But the next day you have a new guide. As you head out in the raft, the guide offers instruction to paddle with greater strength. As you negotiate gnarly twists in the river, the guide praises your efforts. Even when the raft is almost upended, the guide gives soothing guidance and positive feedback. You enjoy this day far more than the previous day.

Some people strive to instill fear in you and speak with anger and impatience. They rarely give praise or guidance. When you are around such people, you feel weak and uncertain of yourself. Others provide support and good advice. They recognize your strengths and give praise. When you are around such people, you feel strong and self-assured. Whom do you choose to be with today as you navigate the river of life?

I choose to associate with people who recognize my strengths and help build my confidence.

The Milkmaid and Her Pail

A milkmaid walked to the village with a pail of milk balanced on her head. She began to think about what she would do with the money she would make when the milk was sold, and decided she would buy some chickens. They would lay eggs, which would bring in a good price at the market. "Then I will use the money I earn to buy a new dress and hat," she said. "I will go to the market dressed so nicely, and all the young men will notice me. All the women will be jealous of me."

Eager to get on with her plans, she began to walk a little faster. "I will just look at those women, smile, and toss my head in the air." With that, she actually tossed her head. The pail fell to the ground and all of the milk spilled out.

The moral of the story: *Do not count your chickens before they are hatched.*

While it may be tempting to think being clean and sober means you can show others they were wrong about you, this is not the purpose of recovery. Recovery is a program that helps you stay clean and sober. Your work in the program is something you do for yourself.

I will not use my recovery as a means of retaliation or personal gain.

Today is life—the only life you are sure of. Make the most of today. . . . Live today with gusto.

—Dale Carnegie

Your tomorrows can be quite different from your yesterdays when you strive to be the best you can be today. What you choose to do right now can set the tone not just for the hours that lie ahead, but also the days, months, and years in your future.

In his poem "Just for Today," Kenneth L. Holmes details actions that can be taken by those in recovery to make the most of each day. These include: tackling the problems of today, not all of your problems; being happy; strengthening your mind; adjusting to what is and not what you would like; treating others well; focusing on yourself and not on others; following the program; meditating; and being unafraid. He writes at the beginning of his poem: "I can do something for twelve hours that would appall me if I felt I had to keep it up for a lifetime."

What can you do today that will help you become a better person now, and in the future?

Just for today, I will do something outside of my comfort zone.

We are most deeply asleep at the switch when we fancy we control any switches at all.

—Annie Dillard

Imagine that the front door to your home is blocked by a massive rock. Because of this rock, you cannot get out the door and no one can enter. All you need to do is move the rock, but it is much too large for you to handle on your own.

Now imagine that a dozen people arrive to help move the rock. If you are stubbornly independent, you will tell them, "I have it under control." They will leave, and you will still be held captive by the rock. But if you are self-reliant, then you know that even though you can manage many things in your life, the rock is too big for you to handle on your own. You welcome the assistance.

Over time, the burdens of being stubbornly independent can prove to be overwhelming. You may try to overcome your addiction alone, face your fears and sadness alone, and strive to be strong alone. Asking for help does not mean you are no longer self-sufficient. It means you are smart. When you are able to identify the rocks in your life that you cannot move without assistance and ask for help, you are letting go in a positive way.

Are there rocks in my life that others can help me move?

I have a right to my anger, and I don't want anybody telling me I shouldn't be, that it's not nice to be, and that something's wrong with me because I feel angry.
—Maxine Waters

For many people in recovery, anger has been and may still be a problem. If others have lashed out at you through verbal or physical abuse, or you have done the same to others, then you are well aware of how destructive anger can be. Anger can damage relationships, escalate emotions, cause unnecessary stress, and pose health risks.

Yet, anger can provide the spark and motivation for taking positive action; many beneficial outcomes have been born out of well-expressed anger. Anger also helps set personal boundaries. It can alert you to something that is not right, protect you, and energize you to take constructive action.

While anger may be an emotion that is uncomfortable for you to feel, you can practice becoming more comfortable with anger by releasing it in ways that are not hurtful to others. Express your anger first to your sponsor or a trusted friend. Write about your anger in a journal. Use exercise to decrease its intensity. When you treat anger as an ally, rather than an enemy, you can use it to effect positive change.

I will acknowledge my anger and release it in positive ways.

Go to meetings when you want to, and go to meetings when you don't want to.

—*Author unknown*

To use the excuse that you have not been able to find any recovery meetings that are right for you is a bit like saying you have not found a word in the dictionary that you like. Whether you live in the city, the suburbs, or in a rural location, there are a variety of meetings and formats. Some meetings are open to anyone who is interested in learning more about addiction. Others are closed, reserved for those who have identified themselves as having a problem with alcohol. Some are gender-specific (men or women only), some are for people of color, and some are for those who are gay.

There are discussion meetings that feature dialogue on a particular topic, meetings devoted to a speaker's story, and meetings that combine reflection on a speaker's story with open-topic dialogue. There are also Big Book study meetings and meetings that focus on the Twelve Steps.

There is no "right" meeting to attend or "right" way to run a meeting. Rather than criticize the meetings you have attended or avoid attending meetings, give another meeting a chance. As it is often said in AA, "Meeting-makers make it."

I will find something worthwhile in any and every meeting I attend.

Power? It is like Dead Sea fruit. When you achieve it, there is nothing there.

—Harold Macmillan

Once there was a simple man who was jealous of the king's power. He felt that if he had power greater than the king's, he would be a happy man. So he observed how the sun rose over everything and had the power to make things grow. So he became the sun and was happy for a few days.

But then a dark cloud blocked his light and his ability to oversee the land below. He considered the cloud to be more powerful than the sun, and so he became a cloud.

As a cloud he emitted great torrents of water that washed nearly everything away—except for a giant boulder. He considered the boulder to be more powerful than the sun and the cloud, so he became the boulder.

He stayed steadfast and unmoving as the boulder. But then the land dried out, and one day a stone cutter came to him and chiseled him into tiny pieces.

Your addiction once promised you great power. Now that you are in the program, you understand more clearly how powerless you were to resist the temptation presented by your addiction. You have become stronger than you realize.

I have more power in recovery than I did when I was using.

Just because you're not sick doesn't mean you're healthy.
                                        —*Author unknown*

By definition, an addictive behavior is something that so dominates your thoughts and actions that it becomes a focus in your life. This focus can affect you in ways similar to substance addiction and become just as habit-forming. Take away your ability to engage in something that has become a habit, and you may experience similar symptoms to withdrawal from a substance. Not only will you physically feel the deprivation, but you will also feel it emotionally through mood swings, anger, and depression, and spiritually through an overall sense of emptiness.

Whether you view such things as simply part of your personality, as compulsive behaviors that you can stop at any time, or as true addictions, anything that overtakes your life to such an extent that it excludes others or helps you avoid your responsibilities is not good for your overall health. While your dedication to your job may have brought great financial reward, it may have damaged your marriage or your relationship with your children. While your commitment to exercising every day is laudable, your inability to take a break even when you are exhausted will work against you. Good health requires balance in all that you do.

I will pay attention to my behaviors to ensure I have not replaced one addiction with another.

We'll never know the worth of water till the well go dry.
—Scottish proverb

Think of the process entailed in applying for a loan. First you have to fill out an application. Then you must make all of your financial information available. Finally, you must wait until the lending company has assessed the risk involved in loaning you the money. If you have a good credit history and income, your loan will most likely be approved. But if your credit history is not good and you are not making enough money to cover the loan payments, then your application will most likely be denied.

So many things in life are determined by a similar process of assessment before approval or disapproval is given. But this is not the way the program works. Nor is it the way your relationship with a Higher Power is developed.

In essence, there is no room for excuses in the program or with your Higher Power. You are worthy, even if you think you are not. You are loved, even if do not love yourself. You are accepted, even if you are not yet accepting of yourself. You are forgiven, even if you have not yet forgiven yourself. And you are approved, no matter how many times you have failed in the past.

I will not use any excuses to distance myself from the program or from a Higher Power.

Responsibility's like a string we can only see the middle of. Both ends are out of sight.

—William McFee

Dealing with your addiction can oftentimes present itself as a full-time commitment. It requires your diligence to stay clean and sober, to attend meetings, and to honor the responsibilities you have made in the program, such as by being a sponsor to a newcomer.

But sobriety can also present you with great challenges, especially when you have numerous other responsibilities to attend to. If you are a parent, then you need to take care of your children. If you have a partner who is ill, then you need to provide assistance. If you have an elderly parent, then you need to provide care or help with decision making. Added to your family responsibilities are your day-to-day tasks. So it is perfectly normal to feel overwhelmed. You may ask, "How can I do it all—and well?"

Sometimes the greatest awakening in the program is realizing how much your addiction has kept your responsibilities in the background. Today presents you with the opportunity to develop greater awareness of these responsibilities so you can begin to address them.

Today I will take stock of those things that need my time, attention, and care. I will develop a greater sense of responsibility to others.

It was as if I had worked for years on the wrong side of a tapestry, learning accurately all its lines and figures, yet always missing its color and sheen.

—Anna Louise Strong

In the movie *The Blind Side*, Leigh Anne Tuohy is a wealthy woman who has welcomed into her home Michael Oher, an impoverished and homeless young man. One of the most poignant scenes occurs when Leigh Anne shows Michael his room. When he says he's never had one, she assumes he is talking about having his own room. But he tells her it is the first time he has ever had a bed.

For Michael, the way in which the Tuohys live is foreign and quite unfamiliar. In staying with the family, what was once normal for him is transformed into a new normal in which he can thrive and grow.

Similarly, the program offers you a new normal. You unlearn what you have grown accustomed to before you adopt your new way of living. You engage in soul searching and reflection upon your past to let it go. You look at yourself—perhaps for the first time—with a different set of eyes. You acquire new knowledge about how to live without your addiction. And, by seeing things with greater clarity, you move on to a better place in your life.

Today I will embrace the new awareness I have about myself and my addiction.

I wait for a chance to confer a great favor, and let the small ones slip; but they tell best in the end, I fancy.
— Louisa May Alcott

No matter the building—from a ranch house to a sprawling mega-mansion to a skyscraper—every structure that is built to last is made by using a simple piece of string and a weight. Known as a plumb line, this string ensures that construction will take place along a straight line. Without alignment, building materials will not fit together well. Walls will be crooked, the roof line will be uneven, and the structure will not rest firmly upon its foundation. Over time, pressure will build on the unaligned parts, and the structure will either need massive repairs or eventually collapse.

Recovery can be seen in much the same way. If you make huge changes, you may find that you have not built the proper foundation. But if, instead, you concentrate on making small changes, you may find that your larger goals become more within reach. Make more small changes, and your larger goals come ever closer.

There is both wisdom and benefit to following the slogan "Keep it simple." By thinking about the small differences you can make rather than concentrating on one huge one, you are creating a strong foundation for future growth.

In whatever I do today, I will follow the slogan "Keep it simple."

Greed is a bottomless pit which exhausts the person in an endless effort to satisfy the need without ever reaching satisfaction.

—Erich Fromm

Once there was a greedy boy who wanted the biggest of everything. One evening his mother prepared two dinners: one with enormous portions and one with average-sized portions. She purposefully cooked the larger portions so they were not as tasty as the smaller ones.

When it came time to eat, the boy saw the biggest slice of meat and requested it. He asked for the biggest baked potato and the biggest ear of corn. His parents began to eat their small but very tasty portions. But the boy's meat was thick and tough. His potato was cold in the middle. And his ear of corn had hard kernels. When it came time for dessert, the boy picked the biggest piece of chocolate cake. But the cake was dry and tasteless, and the boy went unsatisfied.

Most people equate greed with money and material objects. But greed can also reflect an insatiable hunger— for love, appreciation, attention, or success. While it is okay to hope and pray for change in recovery, it is not appropriate to want more than others have, to make demands, or to take from others in order to get more for you. There is no room for greed in recovery.

Today I will appreciate all that I have been given.

When we blame ourselves we feel no one else has a right to blame us.

—*Oscar Wilde*

The origin of the word *scapegoat* can be traced back to ancient times. On the Day of Atonement, people would confess their sins to a holy man, who would then touch the head of a goat and recount the people's sins. Then the goat would be driven off, symbolically taking with it all of the sins of the people and thus releasing them from their past transgressions.

Similarly, if you approach the action of making amends with the expectation that you will be forgiven once you say you are sorry, then you may be sorely disappointed. There may be people you have harmed who will not let you speak to them. Even if they do, they may not be able to forgive you or even accept your apology.

Sometimes no amount of restitution can right a wrong. But rather than continue to heap more blame upon yourself or slip back into bad behaviors, you need to forgive yourself. Just coming to the realization of the harm you have caused another is the first step to being able to release your "goat" into the wilderness.

Even if others will not accept my amends, I will forgive myself for my past transgressions.

The things people discard tell more about them than the things they keep.

—Hilda Lawrence

Writers are known for a particular genre, athletes by the sport they play, actors for the roles they choose. Sometimes the nonfiction author wants to write fiction, the basketball player wants to play baseball, the comedic actor wants to play a serious role. With an already established identity, creating a new one requires others to accept a different way of defining someone.

You have similarly been pigeonholed by the identity you established in the past. The people in your life who knew you as someone who had a problem with alcohol or drugs may have a difficult time accepting you as a recovering addict. They may have a hard time with the "new you"—a person who is clean and sober, someone who no longer erupts in anger, and someone who is honest, respectful, and responsible.

Rather than strive to work harder to convince those who have pigeonholed you into your past identity to accept who you are now, what is most important is that you are able to let go of how you defined yourself in the past. There are those in the fellowship who see and accept you as you are now.

I am proud of who I am now, even if there are others who cannot let go of who I was in the past.

You receive through the same door through which you give.
The way to receive freely is to give freely.

—*Brad Jensen*

While you know the value of service and giving to others, you may feel as if you have very little to give. Because you live paycheck-to-paycheck, there may be no money you can give to charity. Because every minute of your day is filled with obligations, there may be no time you can devote to a worthwhile cause. Because you are immersed in your recovery, there may be no energy left to assist others. Even if these are your circumstances, there are a number of ways to give to others that may benefit you as well:

- *Give out five hugs a day.* A hug costs nothing. In giving someone a hug, you also receive one in return.
- *Give someone five minutes of your time.* Even if you are a perpetually busy person, giving someone your attention for five minutes will not throw your entire day out of whack.
- *Offer to help someone with a problem.* By offering to listen to what someone else is experiencing, you may find solutions that can help you work through a similar situation in your life.

I can be a giving person even though I may have little. I have more to give to others than I think.

Memory is the diary we all carry about with us.
                                    —*Mary H. Waldrip*

Recovery increases your awareness of how you have harmed others. For many, such realization can be a real shock and lead to intense feelings of shame, guilt, despair, and depression. If you stay immersed in such feelings, you may find it hard to move forward. Your emotional baggage from the past will always be with you. If you focus only on the relationships and people you have "broken" as a result of your addiction, you may find it hard to think about anything else.

Step Nine offers you an opportunity to remember what you have done to others and to try to repair as much as you can with them—the broken promises, the emptiness and abandonment you caused others to feel, and the relationships and responsibilities you ignored.

In doing such things, it is important to keep in mind that there is no guarantee you will able to fix everything in ways that restore happiness and reconnection to those relationships that your addiction damaged. Your actions may not lead to reconciliation or rebuild bridges, but they will help you release some of the emotional baggage that has been weighing you down.

I will make direct amends to those I have harmed. I will do so without any expectation of acceptance or forgiveness, but because it is the right thing to do.

OCTOBER

Continued to take personal inventory and when we were wrong promptly admitted it.

—Step Ten

A prayer is a humble and heartfelt communication with a power greater than yourself. A prayer can admit a weakness, communicate a need, or convey praise and gratitude. Prayers can unburden your heart, give you strength and courage, and deepen your faith and trust in a Higher Power. Use the following prayer as you work on your understanding and acceptance of Step Ten.

Step Ten Prayer

Higher Power, I reach out for your guidance so I may continue to recognize any mistakes I make and to correct them as soon as possible. I ask that you help me remember to make regular assessments of myself and to change those things that need to be changed.

I am open to your wisdom so I may become more fully aware of those times when I find myself slipping back into old behaviors and ways of thinking. I ask for your help to remain humble in my recovery. Even when my accomplishments are truly wonderful, I will always remember that they are a gift from you.

With your love, I will accept the work I need to do on myself. My recovery has great value and importance in my life, and I will continue to make it a priority. Higher Power, thank you for listening to my prayer.

Our deeds determine us, as much as we determine our deeds.

—*George Eliot*

If everything in life were easy, then everyone would be a success. Each of us has a certain set of skills, talents, and abilities. It is up to us to develop our strengths and to strive, to the best of our ability, to utilize these assets. Yet you may be someone who has created limitations and built imaginary ceilings in your life. Rather than move beyond these self-erected barriers, you may find comfort in hiding behind them. Until you challenge yourself—even in small ways—you will never know what you are capable of achieving.

You can learn how to extend the boundaries of your limitations by first making a list of all of those things you would like to do or learn. Then write down why you have not taken action to make these things happen. The first list expresses your desires; the second list conveys the roadblocks that are preventing you from achieving your desires.

Review your lists, and then select one desire you would like to pursue. Take actions that will help you move beyond the roadblock, and you may be surprised at what you really can do.

Today I will take action to move beyond my limitations.

Although it is generally known, I think it's about time to announce that I was born at a very early age.
—Groucho Marx

Your birthday or a special anniversary date can represent one of the most important days of the year for you. Not only does it give you the opportunity to reflect upon your achievements over the past year, but it also represents a time in which you can begin to write a new chapter in the story of your life. It is a time in which you can be reborn.

Just as a birthday presents a chance to reflect upon all of the years that came before and the opportunity to think about what you would like to achieve before you turn another year older, your anniversary in recovery offers a time to remember what brought you into the program and what things you would like to do as you continue on the path of sobriety.

While it is important to continually set goals, make changes, and welcome new adventures of discovery, special days in your life can engage you more fully with renewal. Look back at all you have achieved up to this point in time, and look ahead to all of the new beginnings that lie before you.

Today I will celebrate how far I have come in my life and in my recovery.

Just as you began to feel that you could make good use of time, there was no time left to you.

—Lisa Alther

In one neighborhood the houses had clean windows, the lawns were cared for, and the driveways were free from clutter. But there was one home that had peeling paint, a yard full of overgrown weeds, and a driveway filled with junk. One day a man knocked on the door of the unkempt house and said to the owner, "I will give you $86,400. But you must use it wisely." The owner gladly accepted the money and shut the door.

Later that evening the man knocked on the door. "Please tell me what you did today," he asked.

"Well," the owner replied, "because you gave me so much money, I decided to blow off work. I slept in and watched television. Then I ordered a pizza, watched some more television, and fell asleep again."

The man then asked for his money back.

"But you gave it to me," the owner said.

"Actually what I gave you was the gift of time," the man answered. "In each day you are given 86,400 seconds. If you use that time wisely, then you will have received its full value. But if you waste it, you will never get it back."

Today I will not squander the time I have been given. I will use each second wisely.

When I first open my eyes upon the morning meadows and look out upon the beautiful world, I thank God I am alive.

—*Ralph Waldo Emerson*

Even on those mornings in which you feel you cannot face another day, you can. Even when you feel you cannot get out of bed, you can. Even when you feel you cannot face another challenge in your life, you can. Even when you feel depressed, overwhelmed, unfocused, or crazed, you can overcome those feelings.

How do you do this? By shifting your focus away from yourself and placing it on the natural wonders around you. When was the last time you got up early to watch the sun rise or listen to the songs of some of the morning's early birds? When was the last time you watched a squirrel leaping from branch to branch or scurrying across a telephone wire?

Appreciate what is outside you, and it can be easier to look at what is inside of you with greater understanding, patience, and compassion. Connect with the world at large, and you might be able to see that your problems are really not so big after all. Notice all of the things your Higher Power created, and you will be able to feel gratitude that you are alive.

Today I choose to live with my eyes wide open to the world around me.

Birds sing after a storm; why shouldn't people feel as free to delight in whatever remains to them?
—Rose Kennedy

A Zen parable tells the story of two monks who were washing at a stream. As they were washing, a scorpion fell into the stream. One monk plucked the scorpion from the water, and it stung him. The monks continued washing, and the scorpion again fell into the stream. The same monk rescued the scorpion, which stung him a second time. The other monk asked, "Brother, why do you keep saving the scorpion when you know its nature is to sting?"

"Because," the monk replied, "my nature is to save."

Despite the pain he knew he would receive from the scorpion's sting, one monk persisted in doing what brought him joy and gave him a sense of purpose in his life. So too can you feel joy despite the difficulties or challenges you may face in recovery.

Even when you cannot always see where you are going in recovery, you can feel joy that your journey is underway. Despite your setbacks, failures, and mistakes of the past, you can feel joy that those things are behind you. Whether today takes you where you would like to go or provides you with detours and setbacks, you can still feel joy.

No matter what happens today, I will feel joy.

No one ever told me that grief felt so like fear.
—C.S. Lewis

When you are filled with grief over the loss of someone in your life, you may spend days immersed in incredible sadness. You may feel hopeless and helpless. You may even blame your Higher Power for your loss. You may ask others, "Why did this happen? What am I going to do now?" And yet no amount of words or comfort will provide answers to your questions.

During such times, you may feel a great spiritual disconnect. You may also feel distant and isolated from people. But even though you may feel as if no one understands what you are going through or that your life is harder than others, that is simply not the case. You are not the victim of a vengeful God, nor are you someone who has been chosen to endure more misfortune than others. The death of another is not personally directed at you; it is a natural part of life.

Rather than dwell in hopelessness, loss, and despair, reconnect with life. Pray to your Higher Power and ask for guidance and support to get you through this time. Ask others for help. Go to places where there will be others who can support you.

I will rely on the support of my Higher Power and loved ones as I grieve.

Every time that I think I'm getting old, and gradually going to the grave, something else happens.
—Lillian Carter

How do you view getting older? Do you feel pride and accomplishment when you think of all that you have done or deep regret at all the things you have not been able to do? Do you break out in a cold sweat at the unknown that lies ahead?

Moving into middle age or beyond can sometimes cause you to feel fear and anxiety. You may be overwhelmed with thoughts of retirement and financial security, diseases and infirmities, an increasing dependency upon others, and making end-of-life plans. When you feel this way, try to remember how you felt on your first day in recovery. You were most likely afraid at what was yet to come and full of doubt. Every minute of that first day may have felt as if it were your last.

The same trust and faith you have developed in the program can be applied in ways to help you handle the process of growing older. You can either look forward to the cycles of life you have yet to enjoy and make the most of them, or fear and resist them. It is your choice.

I will resolve not to take the progress of my years too seriously. After all, as it has been said, "You'll never get out of it alive!"

Faith is not a series of gilt-edged propositions that you sit down to figure out, and if you follow all the logic and accept all the conclusions, then you have it.
—Mary Jean Irion

Years ago administrators at a high school in California told some of their teachers at the beginning of the school term that their students would most likely experience an intellectual growth spurt by the end of the academic year. At the end of the term, students of these teachers had, indeed, dramatically improved their academic performance.

Administrators revealed that the teachers had been selected at random; there was no particular reason why they or their students had been selected. But because the teachers had expected more from their respective classes, they had subtly communicated this expectation to their students. The teachers showed that they believed in their capabilities, and the students responded to this support. Yet, if the teachers had shown doubt in the students' success, the outcome would most likely have been different.

When you believe you are incapable of achieving great things, then these are the beliefs with which you will meet any challenge that comes your way. The higher the regard that you have for yourself and your capabilities, the greater the level of your success will be in anything you do.

Today I will create self-fulfilling prophecies that focus on positive achievement and success.

One doesn't discover new lands without consenting to lose sight of the shore for a very long time.

—*André Gide*

Imagine the stress Christopher Columbus and his crew felt as they set sail. At that time, the world was largely a place of unknowns. Columbus and his crew knew they were risking death and might never see their homeland and loved ones again. But that did not stop them from beginning their radical adventure.

Risk taking means attempting something new, different, or unknown, without the comfort of knowing what the outcome will be. Being ready to take a risk does not mean you will not feel nervous or afraid; fear is a natural reaction to the unknown. But fearing and *still taking the risk* is what risk taking is all about. The most successful risk takers are those who ask two important questions: "What's the worst possible thing that could happen?" and "What do I have to lose?"

Today, think of a risk you would like to take. First write down what you think you might lose by taking the risk. Then write down what you think you might gain. Keep the gain in mind, and take the risk!

I resolve today to shift my attitude from can't to can. I will put my fears and doubts aside and take a risk.

I have always known that at last I would take this road,
but yesterday I did not know it would be today.

—Narihira

It is not always easy to set goals in your life. Sometimes you may know exactly what you want to do and how to achieve it. Other times you may know what you would like, but have no idea how to get it. And there may be times when you simply do not know what it is that you want.

The best way to approach setting goals is to begin by writing down the things you would like to achieve. Perhaps you would like to speak at a meeting or develop a new circle of friends. Next consider the steps you need to take for each of these things. To speak at a meeting, first create an outline for what you would like to say and rehearse your talk. To make new friends in the program, attend different meetings, volunteer at a meeting, or arrive at a meeting early so you have time to mingle with others.

When you do this, you create an action plan for achievement. It is one that provides you with direction as well as manageable activities that will lead you in the right direction.

I will consider what I need to do to achieve a goal, rather than focus on a goal.

Prayer should be short, without giving God Almighty reasons why he should grant this, or that; he knows best what is good for us.

—John Selden

A Native American belief holds that everyone is a house made up of four rooms—a physical room (the body), a mental room (the mind), an emotional room (feelings), and a spiritual room (connection with a Higher Power). The ideal is to "live" in each room equally, so that "occupancy" of one room is not in an imbalance with the others.

But how often do you live in only one or two rooms? Perhaps the room you visit the least is the spiritual room. This may be based on a spiritual disconnect that has gone on for a long time in your life, or may simply be because you are uncertain of how to develop a connection with your Higher Power.

Any spiritual connection begins with prayer. You can use familiar prayers from your youth or repeat a positive affirmation or a favorite slogan from the program. You can ask your Higher Power to watch over those people in your life who matter most to you. But what is most important is that you begin to spend more time in your spiritual room. Dust it off, tidy it up, and make it a comfortable space that you enjoy visiting.

I will set aside time each day for prayer.

A child's attitude toward everything is an artist's attitude.
—*Willa Cather*

Imagine that you have set aside a few hours to take your children to the park. To provide entertainment, you pack a bag with things to keep them occupied—some balls, a game, and art supplies. When you arrive at the park, the children want to run around in circles chasing each other, roll and tumble on the ground, and look up at the clouds. They do not need a planned activity; all they want to do is play.

When you look at the world through a child's eyes, you will see a world of freedom and creativity, where there is no concept of time or reality. It is a world in which anything can happen, if you only wish it or imagine it.

Play is an important part of life—both for children as well as for adults. If all you are doing in your life is working at your job, your relationship, and your recovery, then all you are doing is working. There needs to be some time in your life in which you offset the seriousness of work with spontaneity. There is wonder, marvel, and magic in life. Take time to engage in playfulness, and you can rediscover the fun in life.

What can I do today to help me feel as happy and carefree as a child?

I can only wait for the final amnesia, the one that can erase an entire life.

—Luis Buñuel

It is rare that a person in recovery has wonderful childhood memories. More often than not, your memories of the past are so painful that you feel it is best to not think about them at all. But until you fully come to terms with these memories, they can influence your behaviors in the present and prevent you from engaging more fully with your life.

One way to release the past from its influence in the present is to create a memory journal. In this journal, record each of your memories from the past. Take one memory at a time, striving to remember everything you can, even if it is difficult. Then write what this memory taught you. This is the lesson you have brought with you into the present. Ask, "Is this memory serving me well now?" If it is not, then write down ways in which you can reframe this lesson in a way that will have a positive influence. Rather than think, "I learned people will hurt me," you can reframe this to "People in the past hurt me, but that does not mean everyone will."

I will reframe my memories so I can take positive action.

The Man, the Boy, and the Donkey

A man and his son headed to market with their donkey. A man on a horse passed them and asked, "Why aren't you riding your donkey?"

The man placed his son on the donkey, and they continued on their way. They passed by a family working in their fields. A young girl said, "Look at that lazy boy riding while his father is walking."

The man told his son to get off the donkey, and he climbed on. They passed a group of women and one said, "What a selfish man, making his son walk while he rides."

The man asked his son to climb up on the donkey with him. They passed a traveler on the road, who said, "That poor donkey is carrying too much weight."

Not knowing what to do, the man and his son began to carry the donkey. But the donkey kicked so violently they released their hold and the donkey ran away.

The moral of the story: *In striving to please everyone, you end up pleasing no one.*

Striving to be a people-pleaser can make you feel as if what you are doing is never right, and you lose your ability to make your own decisions.

I will choose to do what is right for me.

We are made kind by being kind.

—*Eric Hoffer*

There are two components of kindness: being kind to yourself and being kind to others. If you find it difficult to care for yourself, forgive yourself, or consider yourself worthy of love and understanding, then you may find it difficult to be kind to yourself. Most people in recovery are their own worst enemies. They may treat others well, but hold themselves up to intense criticism and scrutiny. By the same token, you may consider it far easier to be kind to others.

One way to develop self-kindness is to think of yourself as a child. How would you treat this child? What lessons would you teach? How long would you hold your child hostage to a misbehavior or mistake? Would you use mistakes as opportunities for developing greater understanding, or inflict punishment?

Another way to develop self-kindness is to think of someone you treat well. What are the types of things you do for this person? How do you treat this person when a mistake is made? Are you able to forgive transgressions because the good qualities are much more important to you? Being able to extend kindness to others is wonderful. But so too is being able to show kindness to the person you are.

Today I will treat myself with kindness.

Jealousy is all the fun you think they had. . . .
—*Erica Jong*

There is a difference between admiring another or wanting to emulate someone you consider to be a role model and being jealous of other people. When you are jealous, you are not just focused on what others have, but on what others have that you do not.

Jealousy can arise from a sense of entitlement. You may feel that you are deserving of something you are not getting or that others have. Jealousy can also be an outcome of comparing yourself to others. You may consider that you have worked just as hard as others have. So you may think, "Why can't I have what they have?" Insecurity can also lead to jealous feelings. You may think that what others have is something you will never achieve because you are not good enough.

Just as jealous feelings can arise and strengthen, so too can they arise and be minimized. Rather than berate yourself for what you feel you do not have, look closely at your life and the positive things in it. Breaking free from jealousy begins with how you think and then extends into taking action.

Rather than focus on what others have or are doing, I will focus on what I have and what I need to do.

Just as despair can come to one only from other human beings, hope, too, can be given to one only by other human beings.

—Elie Wiesel

Hope is an essential part of healing and recovery. Without hope, you would not be able to envision a better future. Without hope, you would not be able to feel a connection and unity within the fellowship of recovery. And without hope, you would have no assurance that you can escape from the imprisonment of your addiction.

Hope thrives within a community of like-minded individuals. Hope is conveyed through the stories addicts tell. These stories all share a common theme: things got bad and things grew worse, leading to hopelessness and despair; but then things got better through the program. These are stories of hope and redemption that convey the power of belief in a better future.

Hope can be developed by giving to others. You convey hope by showing them they are not alone and that their suffering and pain can be alleviated. Hope is also developed through choosing to be around positive people. Their ability to view life from an uplifting perspective can help you see that your problems are not insurmountable.

Today I will breathe in hope from those around me and exhale any feelings of despair.

There is no doubt that running away on a fresh, blue morning can be exhilarating.

—Jean Rhys

Think of how a cat or dog awakens from sleep. It will rise up, perhaps give its body a good shake, and then lower its front and engage in a full stretch to its body. Sometimes you may even hear it emit a little grunt of pleasure. While not everyone can leap out of bed at the first sound of the alarm, there are ways you can transform your first moments of awakening so that they benefit you for the rest of the day.

Begin with a full-body stretch. Do more than just reach for the ceiling or bend over and touch your toes. Wiggle and shake every part of your body to loosen up your muscles. As you do this, take in deep breaths and slowly release them. Bring in oxygen to your brain and muscles to restore your energy.

And then offer a simple prayer. Thank your Higher Power for the gift of a new day. Convey your openness to whatever the day holds in store for you. Ask that you be given the strength to meet all of its challenges. By this time you will be more awake and alert, ready to take on the day!

I will begin my day with a morning routine that will energize me.

I've been so lonely for long periods of my life that if a rat walked in I would have welcomed it.

—Louise Nevelson

There is a story about an old donkey that fell into an abandoned well. Many heard the donkey's cries and raced to the well. The donkey's owner assessed the situation and realized it could not be rescued. The animal was old and had lived a long life, and the well no longer produced water, so the man decided to bury the donkey in the well.

He asked the others to help him. They grabbed shovels and began tossing dirt into the well. At first the donkey brayed loudly, but after a short while, the braying ceased. Its owner peered in and saw that as the dirt piled onto the donkey, the donkey shook off the dirt and stepped up on the dirt below it. The well began to fill with dirt and, as the donkey stepped on the ever-growing pile, came closer to the top of the well.

Energized by this turn of events, the people began to shovel dirt furiously into the well, bringing the donkey closer to the top and to its safe escape.

Today I will use my own strengths as well as the strength of the fellowship to succeed.

Shall I give you my recipe for happiness? I find everything useful and nothing indispensable. I find everything wonderful and nothing miraculous.

—Norman Douglas

Too often you may think that your happiness comes from people, places, or things. You may think that if you won the heart of someone you love, moved to a different location, or had everything you wanted, you would truly be happy. But what happens if you do not get who, what, or where you want? Does this mean you must be resigned to a lifetime of unhappiness because the conditions of your happiness have not been met?

Happiness does not come from an object, a person, or place. Nor does it come from endless striving or attempting to capture it like a pot of gold at the end of a rainbow.

Rather, happiness comes from following your true purpose and passion. It is being committed to staying on the path you have chosen. It is enjoying the journey and not caring whether or when the path will end. Just being on the path that is right for you is enough to bring happiness.

Happiness comes from the path I have chosen and the progress I make.

You can't wring your hands and roll up your sleeves at the same time.

—Pat Schroeder

At times you may worry about how well you are doing in recovery. Even if you have not used or abused, you may have thought about drinking or drugging or even awakened from dreams in which you were using. Do such things mean you are not working the program in the right way? If you have not yet started to work on your inventory, made a list of those you have harmed, or made amends to anyone, does that mean you are not doing well in your recovery?

Or maybe you have not accepted the reality of your addiction. Or maybe you do not know why you drank so much and so often or why you did the things you did when you were drunk. Does this mean you do not belong in the program or that you need to figure out the answers to your questions first?

Edith Armstrong once wrote that she conquered worry by thinking of her mind as if it were a telephone. She kept her mind busy with "peace, harmony, health, love and abundance." Whenever doubt, anxiety, or fear tried to "call" her, "they kept getting a busy signal."

Rather than worry about attaining perfection in the program, I will concentrate on making progress. I will keep busy so there is no time to worry.

The real art of conversation is not only to say the right thing in the right place but to leave unsaid the wrong thing at the tempting moment.

—*Dorothy Nevill*

When you are having an intense argument with a friend or a loved one, you may find yourself thinking, "This is not the way I wanted this conversation to go." When it is finally over, you may blame yourself and think that if you had only kept your mouth shut, the argument would have never happened.

Recovery provides you with a greater understanding about communication so you can improve upon the way in which you deliver information to others. One of the most important things you learn is to focus on how you feel. Rather than say to someone, "You make me so mad," you learn to own your feelings by saying, "I am so mad right now." "You" statements deliver blame; "I" statements deliver messages. Keeping "you" out of the dialogue defuses defensiveness and accusation while raising awareness of what made you feel anger.

Starting today, become more aware of changing "you" statements to "I" messages. Even if the other person uses "you" statements, refrain from responding in kind.

I will begin my conversations with "I want . . ." or "I need . . ." or "I feel . . ."

Privacy is something I'm not merely entitled to, it's an absolute prerequisite.

—*Marlon Brando*

Nowadays private lives seem to have become irrelevant. It is not just rich and powerful people or those in the spotlight whose lives have been made into open books. Videos of truly private moments are broadcast on websites. Diaries people once kept under lock and key have been transformed into blogs, made available to the entire world. Personal messages e-mailed to one person can be intercepted and sent to multiple recipients. And even innocent surfing on the Internet can capture enough personal information to wreak havoc on bank accounts and credit cards. Because of this, it may seem as if privacy has become a luxury item.

One place in which privacy is of utmost importance is in recovery. Without respect for the confidentiality of all members, considerable personal and professional damage could be done. When you share with someone else the names of those who attend meetings or some of the things they admit to doing while they were using, it is not just a violation of one of the tenets of the program. It is an invasion of privacy.

I will respect the privacy and private thoughts of others.

Promises are like crying babies in a theater. They should be carried out at once.

—*Norman Vincent Peale*

By putting down the drink or the drug, you have started the process of becoming a promise-keeper. To help you with your promise, there are a number of tools in recovery, including the Promises of Alcoholics Anonymous. These are not guarantees but commitments that the program makes in support of your desire to stop using.

To be a promise-keeper, you can adopt the following promises as the ones you make to yourself:

- I will know a new freedom and a new happiness by staying clean and sober.
- I will learn to treat others with kindness and respect.
- I will be forgiving of myself.
- I will help others in the fellowship and I will give to others.
- I will devote time to meditation and personal reflection.
- I will understand the word *serenity* and begin to find peace.
- I will turn my life over to the care of a Higher Power.
- I will see the world with new eyes.

Today I promise to keep my promises.

Experiences are savings which a miser puts aside. Wisdom is an inheritance. . . .

—*Karl Kraus*

One day a teacher placed a jar on his desk and a pile of rocks. He asked his students to fill the jar. When they were done, the teacher asked if the jar was filled. "Yes," the students replied.

Then the teacher placed on his desk a bucket of small pebbles. "Please fill the jar with these," he told them, and the students did so. "Now," he asked, "is the jar full?" "Yes," the students answered, but with hesitation.

The teacher then placed a bucket of sand on his desk. "Please fill the jar with the sand," he told them. The students placed a scoop of sand into the jar, which settled in between the rocks and pebbles. "Is the jar full?" the teacher asked. The students remained silent. So the teacher placed a bucket of water on his desk, and the students watched the teacher fill the jar with water.

Your experiences can be seen as the rocks, pebbles, sand, and water. You use each at some point in your life to make decisions and expand your knowledge. But it is wisdom that enables you to see that all of your experiences, when placed together in unity, bring about the greatest understanding.

Today I will draw from all of my experiences for greater wisdom.

Self-pity is easily the most destructive of the non-pharmaceutical narcotics; it gives momentary pleasure and separates the victim from reality.

—*John W. Gardner*

You may think that your problems are much greater than those of others. You may believe your feelings, wants, and needs are of greater importance. You insist on being heard at every meeting. You expect your sponsor to be readily available to you.

When your sponsor does not meet your needs or when others at the meeting cut you off, you are convinced such treatment is par for the course. You are tired of others treating you that way. So you cut ties with your sponsor and that fellowship.

One day your new sponsor tells you that you are self-ish and self-centered, and adds, "Believe it or not, the world does not revolve around you." But before you can reply your sponsor says, "You can ask someone else to be your sponsor. I'm cool with that. But I guarantee you, unless you get off your pity pot and realize there are other people besides you in this world, things will end up the same way. Do you want to spend your time in recovery hiring and firing sponsors? Or would you like to learn how to give and receive help, support, comfort, and understanding? It's your choice."

Today I will remember that I share the world with others.

To be a leader, you have to make people want to follow you, and nobody wants to follow someone who doesn't know where he is going.

—Joe Namath

There are two components to sponsorship: finding a sponsor and being one. It is recommended that newcomers get a sponsor during the first month of sobriety. If you are unsure who to ask, ask others if they would recommend someone for you.

To be a good sponsor, you need to be able to provide insight about the Steps and the philosophy and purpose of the program. If you have worked through the Steps with your own sponsor, then you will be familiar with the process and serve as a good guide when the person you are sponsoring begins Step work.

It is important for you to be available to attend some meetings with the person you are sponsoring. Also, understand that you may receive late-night phone calls. By the same token, set boundaries so you are able to pay attention to your own sobriety and so the person you are sponsoring does not become overly dependent upon you. Provide encouragement so the person you are sponsoring speaks at meetings, shares with others, and develops a relationship with a Higher Power.

One of the greatest tools of the program is having a sponsor or being one.

God, grant me the serenity to accept the things I cannot change, courage to change the things I can, and wisdom to know the difference.
      —Reinhold Niebuhr, from "The Serenity Prayer"

The Serenity Prayer has become both a staple and one of the most powerful tools of the recovery program. The first phrase lets you understand that God, a Higher Power, or your personal concept of a greater presence is available to you. It applies the word *serenity* to the process of accepting the things you cannot change in your life. The second phrase uses the word *courage* as it advises you to think about what you can change in your life. The third phrase provides the word *wisdom* in reference to the knowledge you gain by learning how to differentiate between what you are capable of changing and those things you cannot change.

The Serenity Prayer can provide guidance and support in other areas of life. If you are having a difficult time in your job, with your family, or in any other area in which you feel helpless or stuck, say the Serenity Prayer. Listen to the meaning contained within each phrase so you can learn how to let go of the people, places, and things you cannot change and focus instead on the actions you can take to effect positive change in yourself.

I will use the Serenity Prayer whenever I need guidance.

Nothing sets a person up more than having something turn out just the way it's supposed to be. . . .
—Claud Cockburn

Perhaps you know the story of the old man who saw hundreds of starfish littering a shoreline, exposed to sunshine by the low tide, and a child who was gently tossing the starfish—one by one—back into the water. "How can you possibly make a difference to these starfish?" asked the man. "There are too many."

The child looked at the starfish she was holding and said, "It makes a difference to this one."

Another story, passed down from the Aztecs, provides a similar illustration of how one small effort can make a difference. A great fire raged in the forests that covered the earth. Terrified, people and animals began to flee. As an owl was winging out of harm's way, it saw a tiny bird dart to a river, dip its beak into the water, and rush back toward the flames. There the bird opened its beak, released a few drops of water on the fire, and rushed back to the river.

"What are you doing?" cried the owl. The bird replied, "I am doing the best I can with what I have." The owl then summoned all of the people and animals to the river. Together, they put out the fire.

Small favors and simple actions can bring about great change.

Know thyself.
    —*Inscription on the Oracle of Apollo at Delphi*

Step Ten is, in essence, a follow-up Step for your work on Step Four, when you conducted a searching and fearless moral inventory of yourself. Step Ten provides you with a reminder that your inventory work needs to be ongoing so you do not fall back into inappropriate or destructive behavior, that you continue to treat others with kindness and respect, and that you work the program with dedication and commitment.

While it is a good idea to work on Step Four each year in your recovery, Step Ten encourages you to check in with yourself on a regular basis. You can do this each day, such as first thing in the morning or right before you go to bed at night. Or you can set aside a regular time each week in which you engage in self-examination.

Ask yourself, "How am I doing?" and be honest in your response. This can help prevent you from suppressing your feelings or ignoring warning signs of something that could turn into a bigger problem if it is not dealt with immediately. If you realize a situation needs your attention, promptly attend to it and make amends if necessary.

I will continue to take a personal inventory and correct those things that need to be set right.

NOVEMBER

Sought through prayer and meditation to improve our conscious contact with God as we understood Him, *praying only for knowledge of His will for us and the power to carry that out.*

—*Step Eleven*

A prayer is a humble and heartfelt communication with a power greater than yourself. A prayer can admit a weakness, communicate a need, or convey praise and gratitude. Prayers can unburden your heart, give you strength and courage, and deepen your faith and trust in a Higher Power. Use the following prayer as you work on your understanding and acceptance of Step Eleven.

Step Eleven Prayer

Higher Power, I humbly ask that you make me an ambassador of your peace. Help me to understand your will for me so that I may carry out acts of kindness, respect, and love for myself and for others. I pray to you for continual guidance. I resolve to connect with you every day and in every way, so I may grow stronger and more sure of myself in recovery. Through such daily prayer, I trust in your assurance that I will follow the right path.

I promise to keep my connection with you for all of my days and nights. You will show me the way to live, free from addiction and fully engaged with my life. Higher Power, thank you for listening to my prayer.

Everything gives birth to something . . . I water the peach, peaches feed me. . . .

—Mike Garofalo

November is often viewed as the beginning of the season in which nature becomes dormant and many cycles of growth cease. And yet within such dormancy lies growth. Bulbs and seeds are entering a cycle in which they are preparing for future growth in the spring. Animals ensure their survival for the warmer months by growing thicker coats that will protect them from harsh temperatures and weather.

So too do you need to engage in continual growth as you go through similar cycles of activity and inactivity. Each day offers the opportunity to renew your energy and commitment to recovery. Each person you meet offers companionship and support so you are reassured that you are not facing your challenges alone. And each time you engage in daily prayer and meditation, you develop and strengthen your spiritual connection.

When you view each day as a time for a new beginning, you are building a stronger future and enhancing your quality of life. Consider that everything you do, everything you see, and everything you hear is enhancing your growth now, and in the future.

Today I will continue to grow in positive ways.

When everything seems like an uphill struggle, just think of the view from the top.
—*Author unknown*

One slogan you may often hear in recovery is "Easy does it." You may even say it to yourself or to others, but what does it really mean?

At those times when you are feeling stressed or depressed, you may wonder, "How is it even possible to take things easy?" When you are going through a difficult time, feel angry, or are hurt by what someone has said, the last thing you may want to do is think "Easy does it." Instead, you may want to scream, cry, or crawl into a dark hole.

But "Easy does it" reminds you to think before you respond. It provides you with the opportunity to sit back, catch your breath, and reflect on what is really going on. You may find that the way in which you want to respond is an overreaction. You may discover you are taking things too personally or seriously. Or you may learn that you are striving to be overly responsible and have overbooked your day. "Easy does it" reminds you that you are only one person. You cannot do everything or be everything to everyone, but you are someone and you can do something.

I will use "Easy does it" to set limits that are right for me.

We are members of a vast cosmic orchestra in which each living instrument is essential to the complementary and harmonious playing of the whole.

—J. Allen Boone

Migrating geese fly in a magnificent V pattern in the sky. As beautiful as this pattern is, it also serves a meaningful and useful purpose. When a bird flies slightly behind the bird in front, it experiences a reduction in wind resistance. With less resistance, the tailing geese have an easier flight and can endure longer before they tire. Because the birds must fly great distances to reach their new homes, they will often shift positions in flight; as one grows tired, it will fall back and enjoy an easier flight behind the goose that has conserved its energy.

The V formation also serves another useful purpose, which has been replicated by military pilots. With each goose in clear sight, it is easier to monitor all members of the group and to communicate important information.

Your recovery can be seen in a similar way. When you are weak, others can strengthen you. When you are strong, you can empower others. Share your journey with others, and the path to your recovery will be that much easier to follow.

I am connected to everyone in recovery. I share in their journey and need to be united with them so everyone can stay strong.

Determine that the thing can and shall be done, and then we shall find the way.

—*Abraham Lincoln*

It can be a common experience for those in recovery to experience times of dark thoughts, despair, hopelessness, or even suicidal feelings. If you have been depressed for a while or if such feelings have caused disruption in your life, it would be a good idea to consult a therapist. Some forms of depression benefit from prescribed anti-depressant medication and regular sessions with a therapist.

But if you find that you experience bouts of depression from time to time, it is important to be aware of this occurrence and to stay as active and engaged as you can. Even when you do not feel like going to a meeting, go. Even if you feel that you have nothing to give to anyone or anything else, volunteer. Even if you feel like you do not want to leave your house, get outside.

Partner such efforts with a reward system. Go to a meeting when you least feel like it, and then reward yourself with the opportunity to stay at home the following evening. By giving yourself an incentive, you may be more inclined to engage in an activity that will help ease your feelings of depression.

Today I will create a reward system to use whenever I feel depressed.

The doors we open and close each day decide the lives we live.

—Flora Whittemore

Imagine you have broken your arm. You can go to the hospital, get your arm x-rayed and casted, and, when it is healed, do the rehabilitation work necessary to restore function and strength. Or you can ignore your broken arm and try to function as best as you can using only one arm. The choice is yours.

Your life was broken before you came into recovery. Perhaps you ignored taking care of this breakage for a long time, working around it and all of the damage it was causing you and others. But eventually you came to the realization that being broken was no longer working. You chose to enter a program of recovery.

By choosing recovery, you are also choosing to put forth the effort to live with abstinence and to engage in different ways of acting, thinking, and behaving than you did in the past. Simply put, you cannot recover unless and until you have made both the decision to recover and the commitment to this decision. Recovery is a choice that needs to be nurtured on a daily basis. You do this by continually exercising your power to choose and your free will to make decisions that are right for you.

I want to recover. I choose to recover. I will recover.

Excuses are the nails used to build a house of failure.
　　　　　　　　　—*Don Wilder and Bill Rechin*

Not everyone is blessed with artistic creativity, an athletic ability, or savvy business sense. But when you tell people that you cannot draw, sing, throw a discus, or cook, such things are simply not true.

You can draw something, even if the image is scribbling. You can sing, even if it is off-key. You can try to throw a discus, even if it does not go very far. And you can cook something, even if it is as simple as boiling water for pasta. Saying "I cannot do this" whenever you face a task or opportunity that comes your way releases you from taking responsibility.

Today resolve to make no excuses. Whenever you face something hard or seemingly insurmountable, say, "I will try." Whenever you think you cannot make it through the day without a drink, say, "I will not drink at this moment." Whenever you need to make amends to someone you have harmed, do not give excuses for why you did something. Simply say you are sorry. The life you create for yourself is one that will either be dictated by your excuses, or freed from the constraints excuses provide.

Today I will create a way of life in which I make no excuses.

For it is mutual trust, even more than mutual interest, that holds human associations together.
—H.L. Mencken

When you are in recovery, it is important to not only build new relationships with those in the program, but also to rebuild past relationships that have suffered from your addiction. Rebuilding trust in those you have harmed can be challenging. Your addiction may have resulted in poor judgment that hurt others, lies that portrayed you as a dishonest person, and even criminal actions against those closest to you.

While you may be ready to reestablish relationships with those you have harmed, keep in mind they may not be. Just because you are clean and sober does not erase the past nor wave a magic wand that makes everything right.

The first step in rebuilding trust is to make amends for the harm you have caused. This apology needs to be heartfelt and meaningful, not defensive or filled with justifications. You can ask for another chance, but with the understanding your request may be refused. It may take days, months, or even years. But by remaining true to the program and to your word, your actions and behaviors may pay off in the long run.

Trust is earned when those I love can see my dedication to recovery.

Mirth is like a flash of lightning that breaks through a gloom of clouds, and glitters for a moment; cheerfulness keeps up a kind of daylight in the mind, and fills it with a steady and perpetual serenity.

—Joseph Addison

You may recall the first few meetings you attended, when you were filled with misery and in deep despair, and heard laughter and joking by others at the meeting. You may have felt put off by such behavior and thought, "How can people laugh at a time like this? How can getting sober be even remotely funny?"

While alcoholism is truly a serious disease that, if left untreated, can have critical or even deadly outcomes, sobriety shows you a way of life that includes creating a balance between work and play. Recovery enables you to see the full spectrum of emotions—one that includes smiles as well as tears. Sobriety shows you that it is possible to have a good time without drugs or alcohol.

Once you work the program, it may not be long before you can join into the laughter, joke around with others, and learn how to play and have good, clean fun. By entering the program, you have earned the right to laugh.

Humor is an essential part of life that helps me stay sane and sober.

Try out your ideas by visualizing them in action.
                                                    —David Seabury

Meditation can calm and relax you during times of stress, and can help you face some of the most difficult tasks in your life. Whether these are things you need to do as part of your daily routine or as part of your work in recovery, spending quiet time in reflection before you take action can help redirect your efforts and improve your outlook so you can be assured of a successful outcome.

To do so, get into a comfortable space—one that is quiet and free from stress or outside interruptions. Lie down or sit in a comfortable position. You can use soothing music or silence to help you relax as you take slow, deep breaths. When you feel yourself relaxed and in a calm state of mind, consider the task that lies before you. Ask, "What do I hope to accomplish by taking this action?" Focus your mind and visualize having achieved your goal. Feel all of your feelings: a great sense of accomplishment, relief, happiness, or pride.

You may now be ready and eager to forge ahead. Meditation has helped you develop a positive mind-set so you can take the necessary actions to bring about the results you desire.

I will use meditation to help me take positive action.

I remind myself every morning: Nothing I say this day will teach me anything. So if I'm going to learn, I must do it by listening.

—Larry King

Think about those times when you are listening to talk radio or a television talk show and the dialogue gets heated between guests. Two or more people may be speaking or even shouting at the same time, and you realize you cannot hear what anyone is saying.

When you first came into the program, your mind may have been filled with so much self-talk that you could not take in what others were saying. Or you may have been so intent at conveying your own problems that you did all of the talking. But when you can still your mind and stop talking, you can experience the value of give and take in conversations. You can also gather information and guidance that will be useful for your recovery and growth.

Today make it a goal to be a good listener. Make eye contact with someone who is speaking. Try to not multitask at the same time. Overcome your need to respond before the speaker has finished talking. If you are not clear with what is being said, ask for clarification. And fight the urge to give advice unless the person asks, "What would you do in this situation?"

Today I will listen and learn from others.

What you become is more important than what you accomplish.

—*Author unknown*

While there are twelve Steps in recovery and your work on them is made by moving through each, completion of Step Twelve does not mean you have reached the end. So how, then, can you measure your progress?

Your anniversary date of when you stopped using is a way to measure the time in which you have been clean and sober. But the progress you have made in your growth, in the shifts and changes in your actions and behaviors, and in the quality of your life cannot be measured by a yardstick.

One way to measure progress is to ask your sponsor how you are doing. Hearing reassurance can help you understand you have made changes for the better. Another way is to reflect upon where you once were, how you once lived, the relationships you once had, and the addiction that once dominated your life. When you reflect upon your past and see it in the rear-view mirror, you can see the meaningful distance you have achieved from your former destructive way of living. When you are doing all you need to do in recovery, you are invested in the process and in the progress you can make.

Today I measure my progress by seeing the distance between my past life and my present way of living.

Do not think that what your thoughts dwell on does not matter. Your thoughts are making you.

—*Bishop Steere*

A group of tree-climbing frogs decided to hold a contest to determine the best climber. The frogs decided that the one who was able to climb to the top of the tower on the king's castle would be the winner. The contest began, creating such a sight that a crowd gathered. People began calling out, "They will never make it!" As some of the weaker frogs pulled out of the competition, the people's cries became louder. "The tower is too tall!" Even some of the strongest frogs started to tire out and returned to the ground.

One frog, however, made slow and steady progress upward. The cries of the people grew more vocal the higher it climbed. "You will never make it!" But the frog climbed higher and eventually reached the top. After the frog had descended from the tower and joined the other frogs, the people ran toward it, shouting in triumph. The other frogs scattered, but the frog remained rooted to the ground.

It turned out that the best tree-climbing frog of them all was deaf. It was not able to hear the pessimism in the voices of the crowd. Instead, it believed in its ability to reach the top.

I will believe in myself and in what I can achieve.

Move out of your comfort zone. You can only grow if you are willing to feel awkward and uncomfortable when you try something new.

—Brian Tracy

If you wanted to add an addition to your home, you would need to extend your home's foundation and frame the room. You would need to match the roofline of your home to that of the addition. You would need to extend your electrical system and add heating and cooling elements. And you would need to paint or wallpaper the walls and add furniture and other decorations.

Similarly, your recovery is filled with abundant challenges. This addition to your life requires you to make many changes from how you once lived. You need to build a foundation of abstinence so you can reframe a new way of living. You need to create new goals so you can continue to take care of your needs and responsibilities. You need to cope with the pain of withdrawal and grieve the loss of your habit. You need to distance yourself from those who might lead you into temptation.

As you recover from your addiction, you will have more room in which to grow. You have also added a greater value to your life and enhanced the quality of day-to-day living.

I will challenge myself in my recovery so my life has greater value and meaning.

The Lion and the Mouse

A lion was taking a nap in the forest when a mouse began to run up and down the lion's body. This awakened the lion, which caught the mouse and was going to eat it. But the little creature spoke. "I beg your pardon, great king of the forest," it squeaked. "Please forgive me for waking you. If you would spare my life I promise to return the favor one day."

The lion let out a snicker. "How could you possibly save a creature as powerful as I? I find that hard to believe, but I am feeling gracious today." So the lion freed the mouse.

Sometime later the lion was caught in a trap. The hunters wanted to impress the king with a live lion, so they tied the lion to a tree and set off to obtain a wagon. After the hunters had left, the mouse came upon the lion. It began to gnaw at the rope. When the lion was freed the mouse asked, "Did I not live up to my promise?"

The moral of the story: Little friends may prove to be great friends.

There are new friends you can make in recovery who can provide you with comfort and support and help you stay clean and sober.

I will appreciate the friends I make in the program.

Successful drug or alcohol recovery involves changing attitudes, acquiring knowledge, and developing skills to meet the many challenges of sobriety.

—Dennis Daley

Twelve Step groups and self-help meetings are your greatest source of safety, security, strength, and support. Without such fellowships, understanding addiction and striving for abstinence would need to be done on your own. Even if you are new to recovery or to a particular meeting group, you will always feel welcome at a recovery meeting. The fellowship shares a common purpose and provides each member with a sense of belonging. By going to meetings and listening to the stories of others, you can hear a wide range of experiences that can be inspirational and beneficial in your own recovery.

Meetings are places to recognize and celebrate those who have conquered addiction for one day, one year, or decades. Seeing others who have overcome their addiction can inspire you and provide proof that sobriety is possible.

Listening to the stories of addicts offers the chance to reflect on the hardships of addiction and the ways in which your life was once spiraling out of control. Those who have relapsed and come back to the program provide valuable reminders about the downside of relapse.

I will keep in mind that a day without a meeting is like a day without sunshine.

If you are aware of your weaknesses and are constantly learning, your potential is virtually limitless.

—Jay Sidhu

Thanksgiving, Christmas, and other end-of-the-year family gatherings can cause you stress and concern, particularly if your family includes those who have drinking or drug problems. Just thinking about being around them can make you wish the holidays would go away.

Family history can play a large role in addiction, but oftentimes recovery is not a shared family experience. Despite having knowledge of the genetic predisposition for alcoholism in your family, many family members may be in denial about their own drinking or the drinking of others. They may ignore such behavior or simply accept it as part of the "family experience." Even if they are aware of your recovery, some relatives may encourage you to drink or disparage the program and the people in it.

While you may dread the upcoming holidays because you will be around alcohol and family members who will be drinking, keep in mind that the good habit you have acquired—recovery—may not be going unnoticed. Your commitment to abstinence and the changes you are making may be a powerful example to others, especially your children and young family members.

I will remember that others can see the positive impact recovery has had on my life.

No man or woman is uniformly successful . . . we must all expect a rather high percentage of failure in the things we attempt.

—*Barnaby Keeney*

Everyone in life experiences setbacks and failures. But when you focus solely on those times in which you have not succeeded, you may find it hard to build and strengthen your self-confidence.

Self-confidence can certainly be buoyed by great success, but it is not solely reliant upon your being a successful person. It is a feeling that, no matter what the outcome of any situation, you can survive and thrive. Without this feeling of trust in yourself, respect for your capabilities, and surety in who you are as a person, you may find it difficult to face even the smallest of challenges.

Before you tackle any challenge, find out everything you can about what it is you need to do. Just as studying before an exam can benefit your final score, empowering yourself with knowledge before you take action can help you feel better prepared. Rather than try to take on a huge task all at once, identify small, attainable goals that will decrease the size of the task and bring you closer to its achievement.

I will work on small things first so I can build the confidence I need to take on the big things in life.

Simplicity is the ultimate sophistication.
—*Leonardo da Vinci*

Just as you need to remember to "Keep it simple" in your recovery, so too is it important to keep your life simple. Having too many things to do or striving to effect too many changes at once can have a negative impact upon your focus and energy level.

Today you can resolve to simplify your life. Take a look at all of the things you want to accomplish and ask, "What is it that I really need to do right now?" By focusing on a few things rather than a long list of tasks, you will be better able to concentrate your time and energy on those things that are most important.

In your professional life, strive to limit the number of meetings or tasks scheduled in your day. If you feel overburdened, ask your supervisor for guidance on how to prioritize your work load. In your personal life, take note of those who ask or expect too much from you and set limits with them, including the organizations and committees in which you are involved. Above all, strive to set aside time each day for yourself to experience peace, quiet, and relaxation.

By simplifying my life I will have more time, greater focus, and less stress.

Integrity is telling myself the truth. And honesty is telling the truth to other people.

—*Spencer Johnson*

Those who use and abuse are adept at all forms of lying—from the art of deception to the ability to create convincing stories filled with misdirection and misinformation. Addiction is, quite simply, full of lying. The greater and longer your immersion was in using, the easier lying may have become for you. Just as you convinced others to believe your lies, so too may you have convinced yourself that all of the falsehoods you told were realities. After a while, it may have become as hard for you to distinguish the truth from mistruth as it was for others.

Recovery helps to strip away the falsehoods from your life and the need to lie. As you learn to be honest with others, you also learn to be totally honest with yourself. This means you cannot cut corners in your work in recovery, cannot offer excuses for relapse or poor behavior, and cannot embellish stories to bring you greater attention.

While honesty may not always be easy, particularly when it presents you with truths that are hard to face, the more you tell the truth the greater the respect will be that you have for yourself.

I will be honest with myself and others at all times.

*Though no one can go back and make a brand new start,
anyone can start from now and make a brand new ending.*
—*Carl Bard*

The upcoming holidays offer times in which you can connect with friends and family members. This can also be a time when you can think about reconnecting with one or two people in your life with whom you have had a falling out or hurt through your addiction.

On your list of those to whom you usually send out seasonal greetings, add the name of at least one person with whom you would like to make a fresh start. Then convey your feelings to that person with heartfelt honesty in a forgiveness card. A simple greeting might be: "I am so sorry we have not been able to reconnect. I would like to take care of whatever water has gone under the bridge between us and begin anew. If this is not what you would like, then please accept my blessings for good wishes, health, and happiness this season. If this is what you would like, I want you to know how much I look forward to hearing from you."

Sometimes when you share forgiveness and extend a hand, someone else will be open to your overture and offer a hand in turn.

I will send a forgiveness card to someone I would like back in my life.

Inside myself is a place where I live all alone, and that's where I renew my springs that never dry up.
—*Pearl Buck*

In this time of year in which busy schedules are the norm, and in the program of recovery where there is a vital need to communicate and be around others, you may find it hard to set aside time for quiet reflection. But there are many benefits to be gained by setting aside quiet time. Solitude is one of the healthiest ways to de-stress as well as to add balance to your life.

Solitude can lead to greater self-awareness and understanding. By truly listening to yourself, you can discover what lies deep within you. By uncovering your fears, doubts, and insecurities, you can become less reluctant to deal with those feelings so you can take action that honors your comfort zone and your capabilities. Solitude also gives you the opportunity to more fully converse with your Higher Power and to listen to the guidance you are receiving.

Finally, solitude helps you appreciate the little things in life. Whether it is watching your children as they sleep, relaxing in a soothing bath, or taking a leisurely stroll with your pet, such things can help you notice and appreciate life in a different and more meaningful way.

I will set aside at least twenty minutes each day for peaceful solitude.

It's not denial. I'm just selective about the reality I accept.
—Bill Watterson

It can be hard to spend time around active alcoholic family members during the holidays. Not only does their drinking bother you, but their denial about having a problem can be infuriating.

So how should you handle being around the raging alcoholics in your family? Chances are they know about your recovery or, if they do not, will notice you are not drinking. You will need to ignore any comments they may make about this. Too, you must ignore denial-based comments they may make about their drinking. Confronting an active alcoholic is often not a wise choice. Not only do you run the risk of causing an argument, you also may end up being verbally attacked.

The best way to handle family gatherings in which there will be alcohol and nonrecovering alcoholics is to enlist the help of others. Talk to your sponsor ahead of time, and keep your sponsor's phone number close at hand. Arrange to attend a meeting or get together with others in the program so you have an excuse to leave early. And remember that the inappropriate behaviors you witness are reflections of a past life from which you are now free.

I will ask my sponsor and others in the program for help so I can handle holiday gatherings.

. . . for the abundance of the sea and the treasures hid in the sand.

—William Brewster

Those brave souls who journeyed to America centuries ago had to deal with hardships that few of us today could ever imagine. First they had to survive a torturous ocean crossing. Then they had to find a place in which to settle and carve out the very basics of necessity to ensure their safety and sustenance.

During their first long winter at Plymouth Colony, seven times as many graves were dug for those who had died as homes were built for those who were living. A ship that was supposed to bring much-needed supplies instead delivered more people and more mouths to feed. One of the settlers, William Brewster, reminded the colonists to thank God "for the abundance of the sea and the treasures hid in the sand."

Even though the Pilgrims had little, they possessed a depth of gratitude for their escape from oppression and the opportunity to experience freedom and a new way of life. One of their customs was to put five kernels of corn on an empty plate before eating a meal. Each person would then pick up a kernel at a time and express thanks for something.

Today I will think of five things for which I am thankful. I will express my gratitude for these things to my Higher Power.

Wisdom is not a product of schooling but of the lifelong attempt to acquire it.

—*Albert Einstein*

There will be times in your recovery when you need to protect yourself from the demands or bad influences of others. To do this, you need to develop the wisdom in knowing when and how to set boundaries.

You first need to become aware of what you will and will not accept from others. Pay close attention to those who make you feel uncomfortable in any way. Also, become more aware of those who make demands upon your time and energy, or who seem to be taking advantage of your giving nature. You will need to set boundaries and learn how to say no to their requests.

If you choose to communicate with these people, keep your voice calm. If you feel having a conversation might escalate the situation, try to distance yourself from this person. If this is someone in your fellowship, attend different meetings for a while. If this is someone with whom you regularly interact, practice meditation techniques so you can be as calm as possible whenever you are together. And if this is someone with whom you share property or the care of children, enlist the help of a mediator or lawyer.

I will set boundaries with others so I can maintain focus and commitment to my recovery.

Desire, ask, believe, receive.

—Stella Terrill Mann

Belief in something greater than yourself can make you feel more at peace. But how can you have this belief if you do not believe in God?

Many in recovery start out without faith. They may doubt the existence of a spiritual presence after years of misery and failed relationships. Too, they may feel they are not worthy of God's attention or consider that God must have abandoned them and their bad ways long ago.

No matter your religious beliefs, the program is not a religion. Utilizing prayer and developing a conscious contact with something greater than yourself are components that help your spiritual development. If you are uncomfortable considering a Higher Power, instead consider developing faith. This faith is based upon hope for a better way of life, hope for staying clean and sober, hope for learning how to accept and feel love. Faith that is founded on hope can help you overcome fears and doubts, provide you with the strength and will to make the necessary changes to improve your life, and enable you to develop greater awareness of who you are. The more hopeful you can become, the more faith-filled you can be. Hopelessness will not help you to recover, but hopefulness can.

I have faith in my potential for something more and something better in my life.

He who is greedy is always in want.

—*Horace*

In your former days of using, you would do whatever you could to use and would take whatever you could to satisfy your cravings and desires. Your focus was solely on you and your needs. Being able to admit now that you have been selfish and greedy in the past signifies a great achievement. But just because you have stopped using does not mean all of your selfish desires have been stilled.

It is not uncommon for those in recovery to think that what they are going through should be the most important thing in everyone else's lives. You may still find yourself focusing solely on your own needs in ways that minimize or neglect the needs of others.

There are people in the world who are selfish, and there are those who are selfless. There are those who are greedy, and those who are givers. Between these two extremes is a midpoint that presents a compromise between the polar opposites. This is what you need to strive for in your recovery. When you can give to others as well as to yourself, you are able to experience the best of both worlds.

I will find time to give to others, time to give to myself, and time to celebrate my ability to balance giving and receiving.

To travel hopefully is a better thing than to arrive, and the true success is to labour.

—Robert Louis Stevenson

Very rarely do things work out in the way you want them to. Each day has imperfections, glitches, and snafus. Some days work out better than others, but one thing is for certain: there is no perfect day.

The same holds true in your recovery. If you set your expectations too high or expect everything to flow smoothly, then you are setting yourself up for disappointment. Just as there is no perfect day, there is no perfect way in which to work through your recovery. You can expect to make mistakes, to fall short of your desires, and to face challenges.

Life is made up of chaos, but if you cannot accept chaos in your recovery, then you may find yourself constantly disappointed. Set the bar too high, and you may fall short. Set it too low, and you may find the slow pace of change frustrating. Rather than expect your recovery to go a certain way, let go of your need to control people, places, and things and simply let your recovery—and your life—unfold.

I will start my day with no expectations for how things will turn out. Instead, I will go with the flow and adapt as much as I need to.

You must pay the price if you wish to secure the blessings.
—Andrew Jackson

Although the program teaches to live and recover "One day at a time," that does not mean you cannot dream about who you would like to become or what you would like to be doing at a future time in your life. Being able to live and recover in the present as well as being able to look ahead and envision a future path can give you something to look forward to, something to work toward, and something to help keep your present feelings focused on the path ahead.

Too, dreaming about things you would like to come true can add a positive perspective to your present life. Rather than wallow in despair or self-pity, having something to look forward to can minimize negative feelings. Those things you are facing in the present will eventually pass, and at some future time you will have moved on to a better way of living.

When you have hopes and visions for the future, you can still the demons of the present. You can feel less troubled and more energized for your future. Dreams give you the promise of another day, another way, and a better life.

I will create dreams for the future that will infuse energy into my recovery today.

Prayer is not an old woman's idle amusement. Properly understood and applied, it is the most potent instrument of action.

—Mohandas "Mahatma" Gandhi

Prayer is not a time in which you ask for what you do not have, but when you ask for guidance to understand what you need. It is not demanding fulfillment, but remembering to look around you and give of yourself so others are fulfilled. It is not begging for happiness, but understanding that a positive attitude will help you in life.

Prayer is not asking for your problems to be solved, but learning how to figure things out for yourself. It is not asking for forgiveness, but understanding your mistakes and errors and learning how to forgive yourself. It is not a time in which you make lists of demands, but when you sit in stillness and listen. It is not a time for making promises, but an opportunity to think of the promises you can fulfill.

Prayer is not a time in which you ask your Higher Power to think of you, but a time in which you think of your Higher Power. Prayer is the closest you can come to a spiritual presence, and when you can become closer to yourself.

Today I will use prayer and meditation to connect with my Higher Power so I may more fully understand my purpose in life.

DECEMBER

Having had a spiritual awakening as the result of these steps, we tried to carry this message to alcoholics, and to practice these principles in all our affairs.

—*Step Twelve*

A prayer is a humble and heartfelt communication with a power greater than yourself. A prayer can admit a weakness, communicate a need, or convey praise and gratitude. Prayers can unburden your heart, give you strength and courage, and deepen your faith and trust in a Higher Power. Use the following prayer as you work on your understanding and acceptance of Step Twelve.

Step Twelve Prayer

Higher Power, you are always there for me. Your guidance has helped me undergo a profound spiritual awakening. Because of you, I am more confident in my recovery. The comfort and understanding you have given me is something I will pass on to others. I will extend my heart and my hand to those in need. I will be kind and respectful to those in the program and to others in my life.

Higher Power, I will pray to you each day so you can continue to guide me on the road to spiritual progress. I pray you will grant me the strength and wisdom to practice the principles of recovery in all that I do and say. Higher Power, thank you for listening to my prayer.

If you were going to die soon and had only one phone call you could make, who would you call and what would you say? And why are you waiting?

—Stephen Levine

Making amends is a crucial part of your recovery. But it also requires you to think before taking any action to repair damaged relationships. This thinking process enables you to distinguish between those relationships you wish to have in your life and those with whom you no longer want interaction.

Even if you do not want to maintain relationships with some—an ex-partner in business or love or former drinking buddies—you need to resolve the harm you have done, whether it is by squaring up financial debts or saying, "I'm sorry for what I have done to you."

For those people you wish to have in your life—a partner with whom you share child care, friends, family members, and others—you need to dedicate time and patience to show your apology is meaningful. You need to back up your promised actions with trustworthy behaviors and show you are committed to making things right and better. Remember that it is not what you want or need from others that is most critical, but being able to compromise so you can honor the wants and needs of others.

I will be patient as I make amends and rebuild relationships.

God gave us memory so that we might have roses in December.

—*J.M. Barrie*

A popular event in the winter is a flower show. When snow has covered the ground and howling winds are raging outside, it is sheer pleasure to see the beauty of colorful flowers in bloom and smell their fragrant scents. Attending such an event awakens your senses and gives you hope that spring will arrive.

Similarly, recovery is like an investment you make for your future—one that gives you hope and promise of good things to come. Even during times of darkness and despair, recovery offers many positives to overcome the negatives. When you are in recovery, you can feel:

- Forgiveness instead of resentment
- Healing instead of hurt
- Courage and love instead of fear
- Optimism instead of negativity
- Respect instead of contempt
- Acceptance instead of rejection
- Balance instead of obsession
- Serenity instead of tension
- Clarity instead of confusion

Recovery is an investment I make for a better future.

In a real dark night of the soul it is always three o'clock in the morning, day after day.

—F. Scott Fitzgerald

Even the most positive people may be prone to sadness during winter. Seasonal affective disorder (SAD) is a clinical mood disorder that affects many people when there is less exposure to sunlight. This can disrupt the normal rhythms of life as well as decrease levels of melatonin and serotonin in the body, which are natural mood enhancers.

Symptoms of SAD include difficulty awakening in the morning, an overall fatigue or lack of energy, a lack of desire for social interaction, disinterest in things that typically bring pleasure, and a sense of hopelessness. If you suffer from SAD, you typically have good mental health throughout most of the year and only experience periods of depression in the winter.

You can use preventative measures to alleviate some of these symptoms. Alter your home environment to allow more sunlight by opening blinds and curtains or trimming trees and bushes around your home. Spend time outdoors, particularly when the sun is shining. Or plan a vacation to a sunny climate. If your finances preclude travel, post a tropical island screen saver on your computer and imagine yourself in this warm, sunny location.

I can take a tropical vacation in my mind and imagine how good the sunshine and warmth will feel.

Check your road and the nature of your battle. The world you desire can be won. It exists, it is real, it is possible, it is yours.

—*Ayn Rand*

Long ago, a king placed a large boulder on a narrow road, then he hid to watch what the people would do. Some people skirted the boulder by walking through brush on the sides of the road. Others saw the obstacle and simply turned around.

A peasant came along and leaned his shoulder into the rock, pushing it with all of his might. Several minutes passed as he slowly inched the boulder off to the side of the road. When he had cleared the road, he noticed a purse lying in the road where the boulder had been. Inside the purse were gold coins and a note from the king: "Whosoever moves the boulder has earned this reward."

What this story illustrates is that every obstacle placed along the paths you travel in life presents you with an opportunity. The travelers who came upon the boulder before the peasant avoided the opportunity or ignored it. Great riches can come from your willingness to take action whenever you confront an obstacle. The effort you make can enrich your understanding of your capabilities.

My actions will show there is no obstacle that cannot be overcome.

Do not wait for your ship to come in. Swim out to it.
                                                    —*Author unknown*

Have you ever noticed that those people who are most optimistic seem to experience great fortune? It is as if they attract people and opportunities and seem to have things turn out for them in beneficial ways. At the opposite end of the spectrum are those people who are pessimists. They seem to live under a dark cloud that follows them everywhere. They rarely have anything good to say. They seem to never catch a break and always have something catastrophic or dramatic happening to them.

The law of attraction can be applied to the attitude you bring to life. If you are a negative person, you have a good chance of attracting negative energy and outcomes. But when you are a positive person, you have a good chance of attracting positive energy and having things turn out well.

Today think about the image you usually present to the world. Imagine this image is translated into the energy that courses through your body and your mind. It is the energy that emanates from you and surrounds you, and it is what you attract in kind. Consider how you can transform a negative image and outlook into one of confidence and a positive attitude.

I will greet the day with a smile on my face and lightness in my heart.

It is not the situation . . . it is your reaction to the situation.
—*Bob Conklin*

Sometimes the pain you feel can linger for too long, particularly when you are unable to let go of the past. This can cause great unhappiness, strain your relationships, and distract you from work and responsibilities.

Letting go of the past enables you to move forward so you can change your life. This does not mean you must erase your past from your memory. Nor does it mean you can undo what has been done or change how others have treated you.

But unless and until you let go of the influence the past has upon your present, you may continue to hold onto hurt, sadness, anger, and resentment. Once you commit to letting go, you can put your past to rest and move on to a better and more comfortable place. Remember to be patient. You are not going to be able to let go of your past in a few hours or even a few days. Remember also that every conflict, hurt, or misunderstanding has two sides. You may have been partially responsible for a past hurt, such as a bad ending to a relationship. Recognizing your part can help you let go.

I will identify something from my past that is weighing me down, and release it from my life.

You won't develop courage by being happy in your relationships every day. You develop it by surviving difficult times and challenging adversity.

—*Epicurus*

You may feel there is so much that is unknown in your recovery, so much that needs to be done, and so many feelings you have suppressed that you do not know where to begin or how to start to make things better. Even if you have spent years in recovery and are confident in your ability and commitment to being clean and sober, there may be things you have put off doing that need to be done. Or you may be experiencing a dramatic life change that may challenge your courage to stay on the right path.

Mastering your fear of facing such things and learning to work through them takes courage. Everyone has the ability to be courageous, but you must work hard to develop and strengthen it.

Each time you take steps toward those things that frighten or overwhelm you, you develop greater confidence and strength. And each time you stand up for yourself in the face of disagreement or controversy, you are moving closer to building a foundation of courage deep within you. Build your courage, and it will be something you can depend upon for the days that lie ahead.

If there are demons to slay today, I will do so. I have courage.

It is very difficult to be wholly joyous or wholly sad on this earth. The comic, when it is human, soon takes upon itself a face of pain . . . .

—Joseph Conrad

Recovery encourages you to recognize and manage your feelings so you can reduce your chance of relapse, develop open and honest relationships with others, and improve your overall health and wellness. Feelings are sometimes referred to as positive or negative. Positive emotions include love, joy, happiness, pride, and excitement. Negative emotions include hatred, anger, jealousy, fear, and guilt.

But such labels can be limiting. Take, for instance, the emotion of pride. When you feel proud of something, it can infuse you with positive energy. But if you feel too much pride, you run the risk of displaying an overblown ego. On the other hand, anger is often considered to be a negative emotion. However, anger can also be seen as positive, especially when it provides you with a valuable warning that your boundaries have been encroached, when you have been mistreated, or when you are feeling tired or vulnerable.

Consider the positive and negative aspects offered by any emotion you feel. They are your most honest expressions of what is going on, so pay attention to them.

I will pay attention to my feelings so I can better understand myself.

Treat your friends as you do your pictures, and place them in their best light.
—Jennie Jerome Churchill

Long ago, a ship was wrecked during a storm at sea. Two crew members swam to a small island and decided to pray for their survival. They fashioned a challenge to find out whose prayers were more powerful and they agreed to stay on opposite sides of the island as they prayed.

The first man prayed for food. The next morning he had a fruit-bearing tree on his side. The other man's land was barren.

The first man prayed for companionship. It so happened that another ship was wrecked, and he welcomed a woman. The other man had no tree and no woman.

Finally, the first man prayed for rescue. The next day he saw a ship anchored close to his side of the island. He boarded the ship and decided to leave his friend behind. As the ship was about to depart, a voice from the heavens called out, "Why are you leaving your friend?" The man answered, "My blessings are mine because of the power of my prayers. His prayers went unanswered. So, he is not deserving."

The voice replied, "Your friend had only one prayer, which I answered. He prayed that all your prayers be answered."

I will treat my friends with kindness and wish them to receive everything they need.

Happy or unhappy, families are all mysterious.
—*Gloria Steinem*

Children often adopt roles to help them cope within a dysfunctional family. You may identify with these roles.

- *Hero.* Your role was making everyone in the family look good. Your struggles today are with your need for perfection and learning how to face conflict.
- *Mascot.* Your role was to make light of the bad situation in your home. Your struggles today are dealing with anger and resentment, and understanding the difference between humor and sarcasm.
- *Lost Child.* Your role was maintaining silence and staying out of everyone's way. This timidity is something you need to learn how to overcome today so you can find your voice, express your feelings, and take risks.
- *Scapegoat.* Your role was to act out in ways that created distraction from the addict and family problems. More often than not your actions resulted in punishment and abuse. You need to come to terms with childhood abuse and the consequences of rebellious actions.
- *Caretaker.* Your role was to try to make everyone happy. Your struggles today are learning how to balance taking care of others with developing the ability to focus on yourself.

I will shed my childhood role so I can become who I need and want to be.

We are what we think.

—*Buddha*

When you learn there are members of your fellowship who are using again, you may wonder what they were thinking about before they made the decision to drink. "Why did they choose to throw away all the work they have done and all the progress they have made?" Those who relapse often do so because they have been overwhelmed by the slick talk of the Demon of Denial. Like the sirens of lore who, with their beautiful singing, lured ships to crash into treacherous rocks, the Demon provides seductive enticement.

At this time of year, the Demon uses the upcoming holidays as a good excuse to resume drinking. But the Demon also entices with other excuses: stress, family dynamics, finances, an illness in the family, or the anniversary of the death of a parent or loved one. The Demon is skilled at convincing recovering alcoholics that because their life is better now, it was not their drinking but something or someone else that created past problems.

Beware of the Demon! It can show up at the most unexpected times to push, prod, and influence. Resist the Demon whenever you feel its presence by enlisting help from your sponsor.

I will beware and be aware of the Demon of Denial.

No individual raindrop considers itself responsible for the flood.

—*Author unknown*

A story has been told about a young girl who loved to play the piano. Her mother bought tickets to see a famous pianist perform. On the night of the concert, the mother took her daughter into the grand venue. They found their seats, and the girl sat spellbound as she stared at the piano onstage. When the mother spotted a friend in the audience, she left her daughter alone for a few moments. Then the lights flickered to signal the concert was about to begin. The mother returned to her seat and found her daughter missing. As she was about to alert an usher, she heard a familiar song being played on the piano.

A hush fell over the crowd and everyone looked to the stage. The girl sat hunched over the piano keys, slowly tapping out her practice piece. Before anyone could escort the girl offstage, the pianist walked over to her. He observed her, then joined her at the piano and whispered something in her ear. The girl stopped playing.

Then, together, the great pianist and the novice played her simple piece together. A few times the grand master placed his hands over hers and guided her movements. When the song was concluded, the audience erupted in wild applause.

I am ready to give newcomers a helping hand.

Realize you are licked, admit it, and get willing to turn your life over to God.

—*Ebby Thacher*

On December 14, 1934, Bill Wilson was at Towns Hospital, a detox center located in Manhattan. He had been there three times before. Each time, he resumed drinking once he was released.

While he was at the clinic, Ebby Thacher, one of his old drinking pals, paid him a visit. Thacher had given up liquor and replaced it with religion. As he spoke with his friend, Thacher advised him to give up drinking for good. "Realize you are licked," he advised him. "Admit it, and get willing to turn your life over to God."

The story of Wilson's recovery from addiction recounts that later that evening, while suffering through intense withdrawal, Wilson cried out that he was willing to try anything. He asked God to show himself. At that, Wilson reportedly saw a vision and felt he was released from the hold of addiction. Upon his discharge from the clinic, he began attending Oxford Group meetings, a Christian fellowship. There he met surgeon Robert Smith, who was a heavy drinker. Smith, who later became known as Dr. Bob, gave up drinking on June 10, 1935, and, with Wilson, founded Alcoholics Anonymous.

Today I celebrate the founders of Alcoholics Anonymous and the help they have given to me.

The Belly and the Members

One day it occurred to many members of the body that they were doing all the work and the belly was having all the food. So the members decided to go on strike until the belly agreed to share in the work.

But after a week had passed, the other members began to feel strange. They discovered they could not perform any of the work they had previously done. The hands could hardly move. The mouth was parched and dry. The eyelids began to droop. The mind felt jumbled. And the legs found themselves unable to support the rest of the members.

What they discovered is that the belly had been working all along. Even though its work was done quietly, what it accomplished was of benefit to all of the body's members. Without it, none would be able to function.

The moral of the story: *All must work together.*

If each member in recovery decided to focus solely on individual needs and desires, there would be no unity, no support, and no outreach. The fellowship is one based on unity, made whole by its many members.

I honor and support the work of others, as they honor and support the work that I do.

Rest is not a matter of doing absolutely nothing. Rest is repair.

—Daniel W. Josselyn

The phrase "positive addiction" refers to those activities that have positive benefits to their pursuit: a hobby, following the game schedule of a favorite sports team, exercise, and volunteer work. But as you know from your own addiction, too much of anything can be harmful.

Whenever your focus and energy are committed to things in ways that cause you to neglect the people and responsibilities in your life, everyone suffers. Even being obsessive about the number of meetings you attend in a week or being overly committed to serving the fellowship can put the people in your life and your personal and professional responsibilities on a back burner.

Today think about how much time you spend in activities and pursuits you enjoy, and how much time you spend taking care of your responsibilities. Are they in balance?

Too, develop greater awareness of all of your physical, emotional, and spiritual needs. For example, pay attention to how your body feels. There will be days in which you feel energized and vigorously engage in exercise or activity. There will also be days in which you need to still your body so your muscles and your mind can be rested.

I will pay attention to my mind, body, and spirit. Each day I will seek to create a healthy balance between activity and rest.

One should eat to live, not live to eat.

—*Molière*

The stress of the holidays, combined with holiday gatherings offering delicious treats, can tempt you to overindulge. When you consume too many sweets or junk food, your overall health can be affected.

You can satisfy your nutritional needs and boost your energy by planning meals that include a bright array of colorful fruits and vegetables. Depending on their color, fruits and vegetables offer a range of beneficial effects.

Green foods such as green beans, grapes, and dark leafy lettuces have antioxidants, promote vision, and reduce the risk of cancer. Orange and deep yellow produce such as carrots, peppers, and butternut squash strengthen the immune system and promote vision. Purple and blue foods such as eggplant, blackberries, and blueberries contain antioxidants, improve memory, and enhance urinary tract health. Red foods such as cranberries, strawberries, and red peppers offer heart-healthy benefits and may reduce some cancer risks.

If you cannot find fresh fruits, substitute frozen fruits and use as a topping for oatmeal or in a smoothie. Eat a balanced meal before you go to a gathering and then limit your intake of sweets and empty calories as you socialize.

I will pay attention to my nutritional needs to enhance my health and wellness.

Those who follow the crowd are quickly lost in it.
—*Author unknown*

Children will often defend something they want to have or do by using the argument "But everyone else has it" or "All of my friends' parents said they could do it." As you well know, such arguments often fall on deaf ears, and parents make decisions and choices based on what they feel is right for the child and right for the family in general.

While it is important for you to follow the process of recovery, the tools of the program, and the guidance of your sponsor and others, it is equally important for you to develop your own voice, identify your own needs, and make choices and decisions that are right for you.

Sometimes it will be appropriate for you to "follow the crowd" as you recover. Other times it will be vital for you to create your own path and "go it alone" as you set goals and guidelines that address your particular set of circumstances. How you make reparations with your family members, partner, or children; how you rebuild your life in the community; and how you renew or revitalize your career will be unique for you. You can certainly embrace the similarities you have with others in the fellowship, but you also need to honor your differences.

I will develop independence in recovery.

If you value the pursuit of knowledge, we must be free to follow wherever that search may lead us.
—Adlai E. Stevenson, Jr.

Highway signs provide valuable information about what lies ahead. They designate the route on which you are traveling, the posted speed limit, exits, and mile markers. Without signs to guide your travels, it would be easy to get lost.

The road to recovery is similarly filled with multiple "signs" that provide you with information so you can more fully develop your knowledge about addiction and the effects it has had upon your life. The Twelve Steps, for example, comprise valuable "mile markers" that enable you to see the progress you are making and, as well, the focus and work that lies ahead. The Big Book can be viewed as an inspirational atlas that conveys the journeys others have taken and the obstacles they have overcome to gain a new way of life.

Each day in sobriety represents a time in which you can increase your mileage in the program. Every meeting you attend enriches your knowledge and understanding about recovery as others share their experiences. Each time you pray brings you closer to your Higher Power and a spiritual awakening.

I welcome the signposts in my recovery and the knowledge they bring me.

Sharing is sometimes more demanding than giving.
                    —*Mary Catherine Bateson*

Not letting others see or know who you really are—
your thoughts, feelings, dreams, past experiences, hob-
bies, and your wants and needs—is like spending hours
climbing up a mountain and then stopping just short of
the summit. Being outdoors, feeling the physical exertion
of the climb, and ascending higher with each step are
all enjoyable activities, but not bringing your journey to
its intended destination shuts you off from being able to
fully appreciate and understand the experience.

Similarly, spending time with others but keeping conversations limited to general topics is not sharing. Listening to the thoughts and feelings of others but being
guarded with your own can deprive you of the full experience of emotional intimacy. Even though sharing with
others can make you uncomfortable and is similar to
taking a risk because you are entrusting them with your
innermost thoughts and feelings, it is vital to building
meaningful relationships.

Intimacy is a gift that can be as glorious and life-
changing as reaching the top of a majestic summit. It can
help you discover ways in which you are like others, foster
greater trust and honesty in your relationships, help you
to develop faith, and nurture healthy personal growth.

I risk intimacy so I can experience life in more meaningful ways.

There seems to be so much more winter than we need this year.

—*Kathleen Norris*

The shortest day and longest night of the year is known as winter solstice. It signals the gradual lengthening of light in the days to come and the approach of spring. But when you are stuck in the midst of winter, you may find it hard to believe the renewal of spring lies ahead. You may have the tendency to shut yourself off from people. You may have less interest in attending meetings. You may feel overwhelmed by the pressure and stress of the holidays. Or you may just generally feel out of sorts.

The winter offers you opportunities to strengthen your resiliency. You have faced tough times in the past and survived them. Use this knowledge to survive any dark periods in the present.

Strive to maintain a positive attitude. Understand that you have the strength and commitment to face any challenge. Nurture yourself. Pay attention to your needs. Set aside time each day to engage in enjoyable activities. And utilize prayer and meditation to strengthen your spiritual connection. By doing these things now, you will be that much stronger in the days that lie ahead.

Winter is a time in which I can grow toward renewal.

To fear is one thing. To let fear grab you by the tail and swing you around is another.
                                        —*Katherine Paterson*

Everyone feels afraid at times. Do you allow your anger to limit you, or do you release the hold it has upon you?

The best way to handle your fear is to welcome it into your life. First identify your fear. What is it you are afraid of at this particular moment? Then, feel this fear. Close your eyes and let it course through your body. As it does so, focus your attention on the energy it is exerting. It may be causing your muscles to tighten or your body to shiver. Your palms may feel cold and clammy. Or you may be sweating. Then identify all of the emotions your fear is bringing up for you, such as worry, doubt, or pain.

Once you have done these things, you have welcomed fear into your life. You have named it and become more familiar with how it makes you feel. You can then strive to minimize your fear. Think about actions you can take that will help ease the tension your fear is causing so you can put your fear into better perspective. Call your sponsor, write your feelings in a journal, or put your energy into a constructive activity.

I welcome my fears so I can release them from my life.

[Christmas] . . . seemed to be a trip across a mine field seeded with resurrected family feuds, exacerbated loneliness, emotional excess, and the inevitable disappointments that arise when expectations fall far short of reality.
—Joyce Rebeta-Burditt

Celebration of the holidays can present gatherings where it is hard to avoid alcohol and the temptation to indulge. Use these tips to stay safe and sober.

Be sure to prepare yourself. Ask, "Am I in the right frame of mind to overcome any desire to drink?" If you are fraught with emotions or feeling stressed, avoid the party.

Stay away from the bar area so you will be less tempted by the sight of bottles and mixers. If alcoholic and non-alcoholic beverages are being served at the same location, ask a friend to get you a soda.

When you are offered a drink, simply say no. You do not need to give an explanation. If someone persists or hands you a drink, do not make a big deal about it. Give the drink to someone else or set it aside.

Have an exit strategy in place. Drive yourself or go with your sponsor or a trusted friend so you can leave whenever you feel nervous or uncomfortable.

Before I attend a party, I will come up with a plan to stay safe and sober.

When a man meets an obstacle he can't destroy, he destroys himself.

—Ryszard Kapuściński

Stress can have damaging effects on your health, your relationships, and your outlook on life. Knowing how to identify and handle stress can alleviate its effects and help you better manage it. External stress happens around you and can be difficult to avoid because it is often out of your control. You cannot make your work environment less busy, escape a traffic jam or crowded mall, or avoid those in your life who are emotional time bombs.

The other kind of stress happens inside you in how you respond to your work environment, traffic jams, crowds, or difficult people. You can also create stress whenever you obsess about memories of the past, focus on your fears, are overly worried and anxious, or try to control things that are out of your control.

Whenever you are feeling stressed, first take a moment and just breathe. Then think about what you can do to alleviate the stress you are feeling. You can walk away from the situation, shift your focus onto something else, or accept that what is happening is temporary and will pass.

I will change the way I respond to stress so I can approach things in a more relaxed frame of mind.

Christmas is for children. But it is for grown-ups too. Even if it is a headache, a chore, and nightmare, it is a period of necessary defrosting of chill and hide-bound hearts.
        —Lenora Mattingly Weber

Spending time with family over the holidays can make you realize how powerful the messages and memories of your childhood are. Indeed, you may discover that how you define yourself today has a lot to do with your past—and not always in the best of ways.

Rather than stay entrenched in the negative influences from your childhood, you can let go of your attachment to the past by changing your outlook today. Even if you choose to obsess about your past, punish yourself for it, or feel extreme guilt or remorse over it, there is nothing you can do about it now. It is over. Tell yourself this repeatedly.

Rather than hold onto regrets about the past—what you did or did not do, what was right or wrong, or what could have been or might have been better—forgive yourself and focus on what you can do now. Most people cling to people, places, or things not because such things are good for them, but because they are most familiar. You can become comfortable with new people, places, and things when you give them a chance.

Today I will release the hold the past has upon my present.

We have no right to ask when sorrow comes, "Why did this happen to me?" unless we ask the same question for every moment of happiness that comes our way.
                                                    —*Author unknown*

A millionaire wanted his son to understand that the world was made up of those who had great happiness in the world because they never wanted for anything, and those who lived in unhappiness because their struggles were never-ending. He asked one of his lowest-paid workers if his son could stay for a weekend, and the employee agreed.

When the weekend was over, the millionaire picked up his son. On the way home he asked his son, "What did you learn about how others live?"

"A lot," the boy replied as he sat with his shoulders slumped. "We have a dog, but they have three dogs and a couple of cats. They even have chickens and ducks and a donkey. We have a swimming pool, but they have this great big lake. We have a deck, but they have a back yard that stretches for miles and miles. And at dinner, they all sit around a table and laugh and talk together."

The millionaire sat in silence, listening to his son.

"I guess the lesson I learned, Dad, is how poor we really are."

Rather than rue what I do not have, I will be happy for all that I have been given.

Morning is when the wick is lit. A flame is ignited, the day delighted with heat and light, we start to fight for something more than before.

—*Jeb Dickerson*

Most addicts consider themselves to be night owls rather than early birds. Even if you were an early riser when you used, you most likely woke up hungover or spent the morning working at half-speed as you tried to clear the fog in your brain.

As your body frees itself from the restraints imposed by addiction, you may find that you greet the morning in a whole different way. If you are not naturally an early riser, you can become one. Train yourself to awaken earlier in the morning by going to bed a few minutes earlier each night. Use the increased amount of time you have in the morning to exercise, meditate, prepare a healthy breakfast, or spend time with your children. You can also use this extra time in the morning to go into work and catch up with e-mails, prepare for meetings, or even take on extra responsibilities.

In the evening, set aside some time to prepare for the next day so you will be able to arise and start your day with direction and purpose. Over time, you may discover that what once was your least favorite time of day becomes your favorite time.

I will greet the day with energy and enthusiasm.

I've never not taken a risk in my career, and it's been pretty grueling. . . . You just don't stop, no matter what anyone says.

—Steven Tyler

There are addicts who think that their life as a user was one of great risk. But were they really taking a risk, or were they making choices that were fundamentally a roll of the dice?

There is a world of difference between behaving in dangerous ways and taking a life-enhancing risk. Quitting your job without any possibility of employment and limited finances, and then hoping you will land on your feet and find something you like to do is risky. But investigating other interests and then quitting your job with a clear career path in mind is taking a risk. One involves leaping into uncharted territory with no idea of where you are heading; the other is making the leap, but doing so with more planning and a greater understanding of your desired outcome.

Similarly, attempting to quit drinking on your own is risky. But using a program of recovery, where there is support and like-minded individuals, is taking a risk. Even though risk taking is scary, and outcomes are not always certain, you will never know what you can be, what you can do, and how your life can change until you take a risk.

I will not put everything at risk—but I will risk something.

Don't be fooled by the calendar. There are only as many days in the year as you make use of.

—Charles Richards

Do you remember playing the childhood game "Mother May I?" In this game one person faces a group and assumes the role of "mother," directing the progress of players as they attempt to advance forward until one person overtakes the "mother" position.

In much the same way, recovery is a journey that involves a step-by-step process of growth and achievement, with the ultimate goal of placing distance between your former life in which you used to a life of abstinence. Some days you may find the steps you make to be large, and it may seem as if you are making great progress. Other days your recovery may feel like the steps you make are small and your progress is painstakingly slow. And there may also be days in which you find yourself moving backward rather than forward.

But there is no timetable or calendar in recovery. It is not a race, a game of winners and losers, or a timed event. Recovery takes as long as it needs to take. Rather than be cheered when you make great progress and disappointed when your progress seems small, be equally satisfied with whatever you accomplish.

I will celebrate each day of abstinence.

*In trying to make something new, half the undertaking
lies in discovering whether it can be done.*
                                    —Helen Gahagan Douglas

New Year's Eve marks a time in which you can put the
past year behind you and celebrate the beginning of a
fresh, new year. You can celebrate this New Year's Eve
sober while still enjoying a variety of activities.

- Sober dances and gatherings planned by your meeting or other AA groups provide opportunities to be
  in alcohol- and drug-free environments.
- Host an alcohol-free dinner with your friends in the
  program.
- Use the end of the year as a time in which to reflect
  upon the past year. Think about the good things that
  have happened, what you have accomplished, and
  the new friends you have.
- If you like to make resolutions, think about some
  of the things you would like to accomplish in recovery. Strive to keep these resolutions simple and easy
  to achieve so you begin your new year with success.

I will welcome the new year clean and sober.

If every day is an awakening, you will never grow old.
You will just keep growing.

—*Gail Sheehy*

How do you know when you have had a spiritual awakening?

- You will be less confused and have greater understanding and clarity.
- You will know what it feels like to be at peace.
- You will understand that forgiveness begins when you are capable of forgiving yourself.
- You will be gentle and kind with yourself and with others.
- You will be more willing to surrender to God's guidance.
- You will be able to see and appreciate the beauty and wonder in life.
- You will discover that your life has purpose.

Having had a spiritual awakening in recovery as the result of your work on the Steps, Step Twelve asks that you engage in outreach and giving to others by sharing what you have learned. By serving as a role model to other addicts, you talk the talk and walk the walk in all that you do and say.

I will practice the principles of recovery with myself and with others.

INDEX

Acceptance .... Jan. 18, Feb. 8, Mar. 13, Apr. 17,
July 16, Sept. 10, Dec. 25

Action .... Jan. 30, Feb. 23, Mar. 8, June 12,
Aug. 15, Oct. 2, Dec. 5

Age .... Feb. 27, Apr. 6, July 20, Oct. 8

Anger .... Jan. 5, Mar. 16, May 11, Aug. 5,
Sept. 18

Attitude .... Jan. 3, Feb. 12, June 4, Sept. 3

Awareness .... June 29, Aug. 3, Sept. 24

Beginning .... Feb. 25, Apr. 8, Aug. 10, Oct. 3

Blame .... May 8, July 18, Sept. 27

Challenge .... Jan. 7, Apr. 9, June 13, Nov. 14

Change .... Jan. 29, Feb. 4, Mar. 28, Apr. 13,
May 4, June 17, Aug. 30, Oct. 30

Choices .... Jan. 16, Mar. 27, Apr. 16, July 15,
Aug. 14, Nov. 6

Communication .... Feb. 21, May 17, July 21, Oct. 23

Confidence .... Mar. 3, Apr. 24, July 25, Sept. 14,
Nov. 18

Confidentiality .... June 10, Oct. 24

Connection .... Feb. 9, Mar. 22, May 26, June 26,
Aug. 9, Sept. 6, Nov. 4

Cooperation .... Mar. 10, Aug. 19

Courage .... June 9, Aug. 26, Dec. 8

Denial........................... Nov. 23
Depression .... July 13, Nov. 5, Dec. 4
Dreams.......................... Apr. 11, July 14, Nov. 29

Easy Does It .... June 19, Nov. 3
Excuses .... June 27, Sept. 22, Nov. 7
Exercise .... Jan. 17, Mar. 23, Aug. 4, Dec. 27
Expectations .... May 29, Nov. 28

Fable............................ Jan. 15, Feb. 15, Mar. 15,
                              Apr. 15, May 15, June 15,
                              July 15, Aug. 15, Sept. 15,
                              Oct. 15, Nov. 15, Dec. 15
Faith .... Mar. 14, Apr. 23, Aug. 7, Sept. 4,
                              Oct. 9, Nov. 26
Family .... Jan. 13, Jan. 28, May 10, June 16,
                              Dec. 11
Fear .... Jan. 24, Apr. 19, June 11, Dec. 22
Feelings .... Mar. 5, Apr. 22, Aug. 25, Dec. 9
Fellowship................... Jan. 25, Mar. 4, June 18, July 9,
                              Oct. 20, Dec. 15, Dec. 18
Forgiveness .... Nov. 21
Freedom....................... June 20, July 4, Dec. 19
Friendship................... Jan. 10, July 19, Nov. 15, Dec. 10
Fulfillment .... Feb. 17, May 2, Dec. 29

Giving.......................... Jan. 9, Feb. 19, Apr. 26, June 24,
                              Sept. 29
Goals .... July 8, Oct. 11
Gratitude .... Jan. 26, Mar. 20, Aug. 6, Oct. 5

Greed .... Sept. 26, Nov. 27
Growth .... Feb. 7, Apr. 3, May 6, Aug. 13,
                                Nov. 2

Habits .... Feb. 22, Mar. 25, May 30,
                                July 10, Aug. 18, Nov. 17
Happiness .... Jan. 19, Mar. 24, Aug. 27,
                                Oct. 21, Dec. 26
Healing .... Mar. 17, May 22
Health .... Jan. 8, Feb. 16, Aug. 12, Sept. 21,
                                Dec. 17
Higher Power .... Feb. 13, May 12, June 5, Sept. 8,
                                Dec. 14
Holidays .... Nov. 23, Dec. 23, Dec. 30
Honesty .... Jan. 4, Apr. 5, Apr. 15, Aug. 8,
                                Nov. 20
Hope .... May 27, June 28, Oct. 18, Dec. 3
Humor .... Feb. 10, Mar. 26, Aug. 20, Nov. 9

Jealousy .... July 23, Oct. 17
Joy .... Apr. 18, May 13, Oct. 6
Just for Today .... Mar. 6, May 7, Sept. 16

Keep It Simple .... Feb. 3, May 14, Sept. 25
Kindness .... June 21, Oct. 16
Knowledge .... May 28, Sept. 2, Dec. 19

Letting Go .... Feb. 11, May 3, Sept. 17
Life .... Sept. 13
Listening .... May 9, Aug. 16, Nov. 11

Living in the moment ... Jan. 6, Apr. 21, Sept. 12
Loss .... Mar. 2, Apr. 2, July 29, Oct. 7
Love............................... Jan. 14, Feb. 14, Apr. 27, May 25,
Sept. 5

Making amends .... Feb. 15
Meditation..................... Apr. 20, July 6, Nov. 10
Meetings........................ June 6, July 11, Sept. 19, Nov. 16
Memory.......................... July 5, Oct. 14
Morning .... July 24, Aug. 21, Oct. 19, Dec. 27

Newcomer...................... June 8, Dec. 13

One Day at a Time .... Jan. 20, Mar. 6, May 21, Sept. 9
Optimism....................... Feb. 5, Mar. 19, Apr. 28, June 25,
Nov. 13, Dec. 6

Pain .... Feb. 2
Past................................ June 14, Sept. 28, Dec. 7
Patience .... Jan. 27, Mar. 12, Apr. 12, June 3
Perfection .... Jan. 22, Apr. 25, Aug. 29
Perspective .... Feb. 18, Mar. 11, July 2, Sept. 11
Play................................ July 3, Oct. 13
Powerless....................... Sept. 20
Prayer .... Feb. 20, May 20, Oct. 12
Progress......................... June 15, July 30, Nov. 12
Promises........................ Mar. 7, Aug. 17, Oct. 25

Relapse .... Feb. 6, May 24, Dec. 12
Relationships................. July 12, Dec. 2

Resentment .... Mar. 15
Responsibility .... Mar. 21, July 27, Aug. 28,
                            Sept. 23
Rest............................... May 19, Dec. 16
Risk .... Mar. 9, July 17, Oct. 10

Self-acceptance.............. Jan. 15
Self-image..................... Jan. 11, Mar. 18, Apr. 7, May 18,
                            Aug. 11
Self-pity .... Feb. 24, May 15, Oct. 27
Serenity .... Jan. 21, July 26
Serenity Prayer............. June 7, Oct. 29
Sharing........................... Dec. 20
Simplicity .... July 7, Nov. 19
Solitude .... Apr. 10, July 28, Nov. 22
Spirituality .... Mar. 30
Sponsor .... Oct. 28
Strength......................... Feb. 26, Apr. 14, Aug. 22
Stress............................. June 2, Dec. 24
Support .... Jan. 2, Apr. 29, Aug. 24

Temptation.................... Mar. 29, Aug. 2
Time .... June 23, Oct. 4, Dec. 21
Trust.............................. Jan. 23, May 23, June 22, Nov. 8
Truth .... Feb. 29, May 5, Sept. 7
Twelve Steps
   Step One.................... Jan. 1, Jan. 31
   Step Two.................... Feb. 1, Feb. 28
   Step Three .... Mar. 1, Mar. 31
   Step Four................... Apr. 1, Apr. 30

Step Five .... May 1, May 31
Step Six .... June 1, June 30
Step Seven .... July 1, July 31
Step Eight .... Aug. 1, Aug. 31
Step Nine .... Sept. 1, Sept. 30
Step Ten .... Oct. 1, Oct. 31
Step Eleven .... Nov. 1, Nov. 30
Step Twelve .... Dec. 1, Dec. 31

Wisdom .... Apr. 4, July 22, Oct. 26, Nov. 25
Worry .... Jan. 12, May 16, Aug. 23, Oct. 22

Hazelden Books by Amy E. Dean

Night Light: A Book of Nighttime Meditations

*Making Changes: How Adult Children Can Have
Healthier, Happier Relationships*

*Once Upon a Time: Stories from Adult Children from
Alcoholic and Other Dysfunctional Families*

Other Books by Amy E. Dean

*Caring for the Family Soul: Enriching the Family Experience
through Love, Respect, Intimacy, and Trust*

*Facing Life's Challenges: Daily Meditations for
Overcoming Depression, Grief, and "The Blues"*

*First Light: Morning Meditations for
Awakening to the Living Planet*

*Growing Older, Growing Better:
Daily Meditations for Celebrating Aging*

*Letters to My Birthmother:
An Adoptee's Diary of Her Search for Her Identity*

*Natural Acts: Reconnecting with Nature to
Recover Community, Spirit & Self*

*Natural Creativity: Using Nature's Raw Materials to
Craft Simple, Functional, and Attractive Objects*

Peace of Mind: Daily Meditations for Easing Stress

Pleasant Dreams: Nighttime Meditations for Peace of Mind

Unmarked Trails: 10 Pathways to Change and Self-Fulfillment